A CURIOUS MIND

The Life and Legacy
of Sidney Jourard

A Curious Mind

The Life and Legacy
of Sidney Jourard

Marty Jourard

A Curious Mind: The Life and Legacy of Sidney Jourard.

First Edition
ISBN 978-0-578-77392-6
www.sidneyjourard.com

Cover by Modern Dog Design Co.
Cover photograph by Antoinette Jourard

Contents

Author Notes

Many quotations from Sidney Jourard in this book are taken from a transcribed audio interview conducted in New Orleans on September 1, 1974 by C. Roger Meyers for the Canadian Psychological Association Archive (CPAA).[1] Unless otherwise credited in text or footnotes, all quotes from Sid are from this interview.

Gender bias in referenced and quoted texts

The English language is always evolving, as new words are added, previous usages become obsolete, and perceived meanings change through time. Readers of older writings encounter word choices that conflict with contemporary meaning and use. Sidney Jourard's use of the abstract noun "man" to describe persons of both sexes is now perceived as non-inclusive, as is his use of the word "mankind" and the related pronouns "he," "himself" and "him." Although to the contemporary reader these words stand out as gender-specific, at the time of their writing such terms were used by authors of both sexes to describe persons in a general sense. Rather than replacing Sidney's use of masculine terminology with contemporary alternatives I chose to present his words as originally written or spoken, along with the explanation that his references to "man" and "mankind" include all persons. This excerpt from Sid's writing provides some context:

> Each person—man or woman, ... —is a center through whom being is extracted; a center of orientation for the entire universe, a point of origin for action. Yet some persons are treated as if their perspective did not exist, ... our society cannot endure in [this] form. The perspectives of everyone whom we have hitherto denigrated as one of Them will have to be heard and respected. .... for the production and continuous development of a pluralistic society....[2]

Foreword

In the nineteen-fifties, it was customary for mainstream psychologists to view psychological health as the capacity to conform or adjust to status quo values and expectations of society. Conforming to what society determined to be "normal" was considered psychologically healthy. A new breed of psychologists, however, began to raise questions about this view, and fashioned a different image of the person as they focused upon the healthy personality and sought to promote the optimal growth of human beings. One of the chief architects of this humanistic, person-centered movement was Abraham Maslow, who labeled it Third Force psychology (distinguishing it from two prior forces in psychology, the psychoanalytic model associated with Sigmund Freud, and the behavioristic model promoted by B.F. Skinner).

In the nineteen-sixties, the University of Florida emerged as a significant center of Third Force psychology. Students from inside and outside the United States journeyed to Gainesville, Florida to be a part of the humanistic revolution in education and psychology. The authors of this Foreword were among them. I (Anne), a graduate of Brandeis University, who had been encouraged by Professor Abraham Maslow to pursue a doctorate at the U of F, drove south through KKK country to study with Sidney Jourard and Arthur W. Combs in 1968. I (Fred), an English teacher, ex-seminarian, and former merchant seaman, arrived in 1969 and began studies after reading books by Art and Sid which Anne loaned to me. We married there in 1969.

At the university, Arthur W. Combs, a student of Carl Rogers, taught in the College of Education. Combs viewed human behavior as an expression of human experience, including one's perceptions of adequacy, and championed an image of the person as whole rather than divided. Ted Landsman, in the U of F Counseling Department, saw the optimal end of human growth as the "beautiful and noble person" or "best self," someone intelligent and kind, productive and open-hearted, courageous and compassionate. Philosopher Tom Hanna, in his *Bodies in Revolt* and elsewhere, described traditional culture as declining or dead and considered the human soma to be in a state of rebellion. Others who went on to make a name for themselves in Humanistic Psychology circles include Don Avila, Bob Blume, Walt Busby, Eleanor Criswell, Franz Epting, Dorothy Neville, William Purkey, and Betty Siegel.

One of the most transparently real and creative individuals among the Gainesville contingent contributing to this humanistic transformation of the image of the person was Sidney M. Jourard, a psychologist, therapist, researcher, educator, family man, author, world traveler, and a cherished friend. Sidney explored vital psychological questions and produced an impressive body of research and publications that are as relevant today as they were during his lifetime. Extraordinarily curious about his own life experiences and the experiences of others, he sought, through his research and therapy, to better understand the existential human condition in order to invite others (including ourselves) to live more authentic, joyful, and productive lives.

He wrote and spoke with a sense of both humor and urgency, warning that the "average" personality is just not good enough. He invited us to be magnificent, to be exemplars of self-disclosure, transparency, and genuine dialogue. Viewing each person as "a center of orientation for the entire universe, a point of origin for action," he protested against persons being treated as if their experience or point of view was non-existent or irrelevant.

Sidney's prophetic voice declared dead the small-minded images of God contained in doctrines and dogmas that excluded a reverence for life in all its forms. He recognized as unhealthy religious organizations conforming to the values of a capitalistic, consumer society and ignoring the suffering of the poor and marginalized. He spoke on behalf of persons of color defying oppression, racism, and social injustice and lauded women who refused to remain silent and who protested against the limits and roles imposed on them by a patriarchal society. He described lethal aspects of traditional male roles. He opposed describing the mentally ill as "mad" or "crazy," believing with Martin Buber that not valuing what they tell us about living in this world can impoverish our understanding of our own humanity. And he supported the right of homosexuals to declare who they are and love whom they choose to love.

Sidney challenged himself and everyone by asking: "Who do you think or believe you are or can become? What do others—parents, bosses, spouses, partners, neighbors, teachers, and preachers—tell us about who we are or who we have to be?" He cautioned all of us—persons of color or not, rich or poor, straight or gay, male or female, young or old—to carefully choose those to whom we listen, in order to discover and affirm who we are and who we want to become.

In his professional writings and work as a therapist, Sid often acknowledged his indebtedness to Martin Buber. Buber's writings on Jewish philosophical thinking and mysticism, his philosophy of dialogue and relation, and his extensive study of Hasidism and the image of the Zaddik or spiritual leader of the Hasidic community resonated with Sidney's image of the secular psychologist, the centrality of dialogue, and his growing interest in exploring his Jewish roots. Buber called upon us to go beyond the thinking that persuaded us to live life alienated from our true self and others. He felt that confirming the truth that rises up between persons in genuine dialogue is at the heart of a true religious life. In Hasidism, one honors human life by living it fully, sensuously, passionately, gratefully. The Zaddik, like Jourard's image of the humanistic psychologist, invited others to be real by being real in their presence and to change by being nonjudgmental and self-disclosing. Ironically, during the years Sid spent searching for a deeper understanding of his Jewish heritage, his personal and professional life can be seen as an embodiment of this heritage.

Marty's account of the life and legacy of his father Sidney Jourard describes the journey of a young Canadian immigrant as he becomes an American citizen, an internationally-known author and psychologist, and one of the major contributors to the emergence of Humanistic Psychology in America. In this publication, readers have a unique opportunity to read pieces of correspondence and excerpts from recordings of Sid's presentations and lectures that clarify what is too often overlooked, even now, in psychological studies and descriptions of the human condition. We encourage you to thoughtfully examine and savor the material you are about to read, believing that it will lift your spirits now as it continues to this day to lift our own.

FRED RICHARDS, PH.D.
Psychotherapist
Carrollton, GA

ANNE C. RICHARDS, ED.D.
Professor Emerita, Department of Psychology,
University of West Georgia, Carrollton, GA

Introduction

This is the story of a psychologist named Sidney Jourard whose work in the field of psychology focuses on one of life's more profound questions: How should one live? This biography was written to bring some of what he discovered to a new generation of readers, and to share insights about being a person that are of particular value in our contemporary culture.

Sidney Jourard was my father. I am his middle son, a professional musician and a member of a pop group that achieved commercial success in the nineteen-eighties and continues to record and perform today. I'm also a writer and author of several music-related books. I grew up in Gainesville, a small college town in north-central Florida, where my father was a professor of psychology at the University of Florida.

This book began as a modest project—I was researching my father's life and academic career for a family history archive. During the process I determined that his life was atypical in both content and style, and that his insights as a psychologist could be of value to present-day readers. I delved deeply into his academic career, and by integrating it with his personal life wrote this biography.

Starting around the mid-fifties, my father became increasingly involved in a new approach to the study of mind and behavior—Humanistic Psychology, a perspective developed by other humanist thinkers such as Abraham Maslow, Rollo May, Erich Fromm, Carl Rogers, Charlotte Bühler, and Virginia Satir. He was the first elected president of the Association for Humanistic Psychology (1963-1964). Among his collected writings is *The Transparent Self*, a primary text in the field of self-disclosure, a process by which one person communicates personal information to another person at varying levels of intimacy, ranging from likes and dislikes to hopes and fears and deeply-held beliefs. Sid examined the beneficial role of self-disclosure in personal and societal interactions. Other areas of his study and research include self-image and body-awareness, physical contact between people and where they touch, the concept of authenticity (a state in which your inner personality is congruent with your outward presentation to others), the psychological need for privacy, perspectives on education, psychotherapy and marriage, and the relationships between body, mind and spirit. As early as 1958 Sid was exploring the subjects of healthy personality and personal growth, and developing insights that helped people become free agents of their own lives. He proposed that most people function well below their capabilities and have the potential to control their lives to a higher degree than they thought possible, and that each has the capacity to continually grow in both self-awareness and ability.

His life and academic career were intertwined in a way that often made the line between them indistinguishable, and his passion for intellectual pursuits was mirrored by a passionate and intense personal life. Sidney was an uncommon blend of cerebral and earthy, a rare mix that wasn't universally understood or accepted by others in academia. His keen intellect was combined with a mischievous personality and a well-developed sense of humor. I have yet to meet anyone who was even remotely like him.

* * *

Evidence of the continued presence of his ideas in popular culture appears without particularly seeking it out, and in unexpected places. During the process of writing this introduction in 2020, two examples presented themselves. My daughter is a massage therapist, and as she watched an online ethics course as part of her continuing education and certification process, the narrator mentioned Sidney's "touch study," a series of casual social observations he made between 1963 and 1966. When the socialite Paris Hilton recently remarked that "I'm so used to playing a character, it's hard for me to be normal…I don't even know who I am sometimes," she describes a problem Sid identified in the late fifties: that the construction and continual reinforcement of a false public self at odds with your private self can eventually lead to self-alienation.

* * *

Perhaps Sid's overarching goal as a psychologist was to guide psychology away from the interests of institutions and esoteric areas of investigation, and toward the service of human beings and the everyday experience of being alive, as revealed in comments he made at a psychology conference in the early seventies. A colleague who was there recalls:

> I have no idea to this day why Sidney Jourard was on this particular panel, except I appreciate the irony of Sid being there. What the panel was about was paranormal phenomena. There must have been six people on that panel. And they talked about seeing ghosts, and moving objects without touching them, and sensing the communication of humans from one person to another without the ordinary methods of communication like talking or writing or those kinds of things; laying on of hands. . . . Sidney Jourard was the last person on the panel, and what he said was, "We've been treated today to one miracle after another, and what I want to say is, that I'm not impressed. I'm having enough trouble just trying to keep my life together. And what I want is a psychology that teaches us how to live. Daily. Just keeping our lives together. And then, if we've got that kind of psychology, perhaps we'll have time for miracles."[1]

Sidney developed valuable insights for anyone striving to better recognize and understand the controlling forces that drive their lives and who seek to recognize those that are counter-productive to their personal growth. His ideas, insights and persona will be found herein, along with my belief that among his views you may find some that bring insight into the workings of your own life.

Simeon Zurar (1831-1910)

Antecedents   1

SIDNEY ALWAYS DESCRIBED the Jourard family line as "sturdy peasant stock" and it is traceable to Pre-Revolutionary Czarist Russia where Sidney's paternal grandfather Simeon Zurar was born in 1831 in Maišiagala, Vilnius District, Lithuania, a town founded in the 13ᵗʰ century. Simeon lived his entire life in this area, peddling clothing and other goods by horse-drawn wagon. Periods of violent anti-Semitic riots called pogroms destroyed many such shtetls, the small Eastern European Jewish villages. Often included in this destruction were synagogues, where documents of birth, marriage and death were stored. The lack of earlier documentation places Simeon as the Jourard patriarch by default.

The spelling of Jourard as a family surname is problematic as there are no existing documents revealing how it was written in Cyrillic or Hebrew script. This spelling seemed to vary by the language in which it was originally recorded, based on the spoken sound of the name. Jourard is one of several spellings; others seen in material passed down in the family include Gerrard, Jourar, Zhurar, Zurar and Djurar.

Simeon married twice; his second marriage to Sarah Kehz produced five children. Michael Zurar became a Warsaw high school teacher; Riva Zurar, the mother of two children with Eliezer Gittel. Third-born Henri Jourar left for Paris some time before 1900; his one son Leon was born in 1898 and killed in action in World War I at age nineteen. Henri also saw war service and was gassed and wounded. He lived on a small pension and suffered deprivation during the second World War. Photos of Henri show a thin, malnourished man leaning on a cane.

Simeon's fourth child, Maurice Gerrard, emigrated to Canada sometime before 1905 and the spelling of his surname may be the referencing of an immigration official to Samuel Gerrard, a successful Canadian fur trader and politician.

Maurice, a peddler of jewelry, was tall and slender with blue eyes. His three children were also blue-eyed: Ben Gerrard, a professional violinist; Saida Gerrard, a dancer married to pianist Aube Tzerko (who became head of the piano department at UCLA), and Helen Gerrard, secretary.

Simeon Zurar's fifth and final child was Albert Louis Jourard, Sidney's father, born around Dec 24th in 1880.[1]

Rubinoffs

Sid's maternal ancestry was similar in nature and geography, as both sides of his family were from areas a few hundred miles apart. His maternal grandfather Rachmæl Rubinoff was a devout Orthodox Jew born 1865 in Hwaniecki, Minsk near the Latvian border. Rachmael left Russia for Toronto sometime before 1905 where he founded a wholesale grocery business. His second wife, Sarah Usprech bore him four children; a son Israel, who became Rachmael's business partner, and three daughters: Annie Rubinoff, Sidney's mother, and her two sisters, Fannie and Bertha.

An Immigrant's Tale

Under the reign of Czar Nicholas II (1894-1917) Russia was not a celebratory environment for Jews living there during the latter part of the 19th century. Recurring anti-Jewish pogroms took place during 1881-1884 when Louis was a young child. There was an upsurge in these riots during 1905-1906 coinciding with a period when Louis had been drafted into the Czar's army and was being transported east to participate in the Russo-Japanese War. Much later, Louis's daughter Sadie recounted his early life before he emigrated to Canada.

> He [Louis] learned woodworking, and worked in the Ukraine in Zhytomyr until, at twenty-one, he was called up for military service. He served three years in the Czarist army in Saratov on the Volga until 1904 or 1905, when the Russo-Japanese War broke out. His regiment was ordered to go east, but Louis, who had no personal quarrel with the Japanese, decided to go west and deserted the army. He was helped by local Jews who provided civilian clothes and false papers, and he made his way back to Vilnius.

Albert Louis Jourard, Russia, circa 1903

His older brother, Henri, who had been in Paris since the turn of the century, wired him money so Louis was able to join him there, after various adventures riding in boxcars and having his food and belongings stolen. He [Louis] loved Paris and the French, but stayed only six months and came on to Canada, where his next older brother, Maurice, had been for some time.[2]

Army desertion was a crime punishable by death, but fear of being killed in action was stronger than his fear of possible capture so Louis deserted, a significant example of existential freedom of choice and exercise of the will.

Louis left Paris, where he had added the 'd' to the end of Jourar to create the Jourard surname, and ended up in Toronto around 1906 and worked as a wood turner in Berlin, Ontario until a large piece of wood fell on his head and he quit. He then became a peddler of watches and jewelry on Manitoulin Island in Ontario.[3]

Louis and his brother Maurice purchased their merchandise inventory in Toronto and routinely attended the annual Toronto Industrial Exhibition, a large event where they hoped to meet girls. Photos of Louis and Maurice at this time show them both as dandies, with neatly curled hair. Louis met his future wife Annie at a Toronto labor union picnic

Annie Rubinoff was ten years younger than Louis and born in 1890 in Hwaniecki, Minsk (Belarus). Annie immigrated to Canada from Russia at the age of fifteen via steamer from Liverpool to Nova Scotia, traveling with a group of friends and arriving New Years Day 1906. Eventually Rachmael brought the remainder of his children to Toronto but chose Annie first because she had skill at sewing and was immediately employable. Annie lived with Rachmael and older brother Israel who ran their wholesale grocery business in Toronto, and she was immediately put to work sewing buttons on coats in what would now be described as a sweatshop. Annie had learned these skills while being apprenticed at age twelve to a tailor.

Louis and Annie married October 6, 1910 and moved to Wingham, Ontario, where their first child Harry was born in 1911. The family relocated to Mt. Dennis, at that time a western suburb of Toronto. Louis then bought a storefront on Weston Road and with his wife opened a clothing store. A photograph from 1917 shows Louis attired in a business suit and boater hat, posing alongside his Chevrolet Baby Grand. Behind him in the entryway of the store stands Annie with hands on hips, beneath the signage Mt. Dennis Clothing Store Dry Goods A.L. Jourard Men's Furnishings. By then Louis had been in business five years and in the photograph he radiates a discernible level of self-satisfaction. In the background looms the water

Louis and Annie Jourard, 1133 Weston Road, Toronto, circa 1917

tower of the Kodak camera factory, a large industrial site behind Weston Road.

Mt. Dennis Clothing Store eventually expanded to include an adjacent storefront for woman's clothing. Louis and Annie worked as business partners running the combined stores, Louis on the men's side, Annie on the women's side. As business improved so did Louis' confidence in supporting a larger family, with the birth of Sadie (1914) and Sam (1917). Sadie recalls

> Pa deeply appreciated the opportunities provided in this new country
> still a British colony, and he became a British citizen. I often heard him
> say that the British flag was a blessing. We were the only Jewish family in
> Mt. Dennis, and suffered almost no anti-Semitism. I do remember one
> customer—a little Cockney woman named Mrs. Foster who got into an
> argument with Pa and called him a "dirty Jew!" He took her by the scruff of
> the neck and put her out the door, saying "Don't come back!"[4]

Six years passed before a third wave of Jourards were born: Claire (1923), Sidney (January 21st, 1926), and Leon in 1929. All six of the Jourard children were first-generation Canadians, born of a Lithuanian deserter of the Imperial Russian Army and his younger Belarusian wife.

Differentiation

2

THE JOURARD FAMILY LIFE and business activities occurred under a single roof. Above the store was a combined living space that included five bedrooms, a basement with several rooms, a kitchen and dining area.

The primary and secondary schools Sid attended were close by—Dennis Avenue Public School and York Memorial Collegiate. The newly-opened public library was down the street.

Sid was described by his family as cute, charming, extroverted—and a mischievous brat. His Hebrew given names Schmul Michal (Samuel Michael, in honor of deceased uncles) were quickly converted by his two older sisters. Sadie felt they "had to be fancied up and we decided upon Sidney Marshall."

Sidney's World

According to oldest sister Sadie, Sid was a bit of a show-off from an early age. When Sidney was two, his older brothers taught him a parody of a current popular song, "Ramona," and his mother would put him up on the store counter where he would sing "Ramona, I love you best in your kimona." Sid was generally good-natured until the younger Leon would "…steal his [Sid's] shticks and mimic his best stories." Then Sid would get angry and complain bitterly.[1]

As informal training for a future psychologist, Sidney's home life was a social environment rich with varied behavior. He observed his parents in multiple roles as husband and wife, as a father and mother raising six children, and as business partners. With many siblings living together in a home directly above the family dry-goods store, human interaction, family role-playing and sibling dynamics abounded. Sid experienced psychological manipulation at an early age when, recalls Sadie

> Harry, the great "con-artist" convinced each of his two youngest brothers in turn that he had appointed them his lieutenant, and as such they were privileged to run errands, fetch and carry, shine his shoes, go to the store for cigarettes, etc. They each fell for it and served terms as "go-fers" until they wised up.
>
> An early indication of Sidney's lifelong interest in mental health could have been seen in his discovery at the age of four or so that there was a mental hospital not far from our summer cottage at Long Branch, which his slightly older pal told him about. "Isellum! Isellum! Go crazy!" he told us of his discovery.[2]

The Jourard household was run as a sort of communal social and business entity. It included eight family members, a maid, a cousin "Big Sadie" Usprecht who helped with chores and at the store, and a local woman who assisted Annie and the maid with laundry and general household cleaning. This assemblage generated vast volumes of laundry and the basement contained a commercial-sized washing machine and a Thor ironer of the type used in professional establishments.

Meals around the Jourard dining room table were highly social, spirited functions. The Jourards were the only Jewish family in the neighborhood, yet Louis and Annie were utterly non-religious, describing themselves as "friedenkers," or free thinkers, defined in the Oxford Dictionary as persons who form their own ideas and opinions rather than accepting those of other people, especially in religious teaching. Their orientation was socialist and revolutionary. Both parents were born into Czarist Russia and had emigrated to North America independent of one another in pursuit of new opportunity and to escape pogroms. When the Marxist-inspired Russian Revolution ended the reign of the anti-Semitic Czar Nicholas II and the Romanov family, the appeal of Marxist social views was compelling to the Jourard immigrants. Youngest sibling Leon recalls the home environment as a "progressive, secular, socialist Jewish environment."

Mealtime was an open forum for discussion and opinion, and although Louis was a strong supporter of socialist and communist philosophies he was no autocrat of political belief, and tolerated if not encouraged differing opinions. A non-family member's view of these mealtimes provides further insight. In 1992 journalist and family friend Pete McGarvey wrote in his Orillia, Ontario News-Packet column *Bear with Me* a reminiscence of Leon that includes a description of the Jourard home environment:

It all started in 1932 in the dusty laneways of Mount Dennis, a northwestern suburb of Toronto famous for its doublefront streetcars (The Red Rockets), political activism (Reds and Pinks predominately), and a sky-high rate of unemployment. Mom and Pop Jourard operated a clothing emporium on Weston Road, a new building huge in comparison to the hole-in-the-wall shops elsewhere on the street. Living quarters were behind the store, and seven or eight bedrooms upstairs. The Jourards had four sons and two daughters in their teens and younger in these years, and the family believed in hospitality. Everyone was welcome round the table. It was there, before I was eight years old, I was introduced to the darkly delicious wonders of traditional Jewish fare—spicy soups, knishes, potato latkes, corned beef, garlic dills. I became a lifetime convert.

Dinnertime at the Jourards was a feast for the mind as well as the innards. Political and social observations flew in every direction, in random order. Debate was constant. Voices were raised, but tempers rarely lost. And everyone joined in. Harry, the oldest boy, most sardonic of the crew, boisterous Sam, Sadie of the sad smile, Claire the motherly protector of younger kids in our sometimes violent neighborhood. Sid, destined to become a world-renowned philosophical scholar and author, the good-humored challenger of every idea in sight, and Leon the baby of the family—and the sunniest Jourard of all.

Religion didn't figure too large in the household, but politics did. The senior Jourards were dedicated Marxists—an odd affiliation for the most successful capitalists of our drab neighborhood. Mr. Jourard poured energy and funds into a working-men's clubhouse on Brownville Avenue, and in later years, when we were high-schoolers, would invite Leon and me to join them for Sunday night rallies at Massey Hall. We often went, but it did no good. We thought the pyramid-gymnasts were more entertaining than Tim Buck [General Secretary of the Canadian Communist Party]. Politics bored us. By then we were both caught up in the possibility of post-war careers in the media.[3]

Jourard Family 1930s
Standing L to R: Leon, Harry, Claire, Sidney
Sitting L to R: Sam, Sadie, Annie, Louis

In a 1974 interview Sidney recalls the politics of his father

> ...right up to the time of his death, he was a very devoted fan, you might
> say of Stalin, and I am very grateful he never discovered what a son-of-
> a-bitch and a tyrant, murderer, Stalin was, but he used to receive the
> propaganda from the Russian Embassy in Washington, and naturally—his
> recollection was of Czarist Russia and he followed World War II very
> closely with maps, what was happening to the Russian regime, he was
> always indignant.

Louis was fully engaged in the neighborhood and business communities. As a
Jewish immigrant eager to assimilate he joined local institutions, and was a member
of the Masonic Lodge, with Annie joining the women's equivalent, the Eastern Star.
Louis also joined the provincial Liberal party, the Mt. Dennis Businessmen's Association where he was President one year, and was on the Advisory Board which
resulted in the building of the George Harvey Vocational School (still in existence
as George Harvey Collegiate Institute). Despite lacking any education beyond the

third-grade level Louis Jourard engaged natural social skills with the public on a daily basis in the store and with business and civic leaders.

All six Jourard siblings attended Dennis Avenue Public School and York Memorial Collegiate up through Grade Thirteen, and Sid recalls "The teachers were always making comparisons. This is the dumb one, this is the bright one."

Establishing an individual identity is a gradual and natural growth process, and Sidney had a particularly challenging situation as one of six siblings all sent through the same academic setting as "one of those Jourards." Was it nature or nurture that molded Sidney's interests? It was likely both.

Other People's Lives

It was during his early teenage years that Sid began to observe and become engrossed with human behavior, beginning with the easily observable differences in the personalities of his brothers and sisters and through life in the boisterous Jourard household, a veritable banquet of human behavior. Along with this interest in behavior came a feeling of being both inside and outside the social milieu. Sid's abundant physical energy found expression through sports. He participated in school team sports, but despite his mainstream involvement Sid felt on the periphery:

> As a youngster in Mount Dennis, the working class suburb of Toronto where I lived the first twenty years of my life, I always felt myself to be an outsider; our family was the only Jewish family in the area. Within the family, I felt myself to be rather "freaky," because—I don't really know why. I masturbated a great deal as a child, and felt vaguely guilty about that, until my cousin told me he discovered it some five years after I had. I used to rifle through all the bureau drawers in the house, and engage in petty theft from my brother and sisters and parents, and wonder why, what perverse streak in me led me to be so ungrateful and criminal.[4]

Sid was a poor dissembler. In later years his wife recalls a story she had heard from the Jourard family:

> As a young boy Sid had removed some coins from Harry's bedroom dresser. At the dinner table Harry announced to the family that someone had taken some money from his dresser without specifying the amount. Sid immediately piped up, "I didn't take your fifty cents Harry!"

This interest in others continued, as Sid resumes his remembrances:

I had an insatiable curiosity to learn what went on in other people's heads, and so I both talked and listened a lot with chums. By the time I was in my teens, I was already thinking of myself as a writer, after the fashion of Thomas Wolfe. I used to prowl the streets and back alleys of Mt. Dennis after midnight, on a caffeine "high," unable to sleep, unable to become tired. I would imagine the lives going on behind the shaded windows that I would pass in the night; and in bursts of energy, I would often run three or five miles, and still not be able to drain off the explosions of vitality I felt within myself. All this between the ages, say, of twelve to sixteen. Of course, too, I felt lonely most of my life now as well as then. Except for one chum, there was no one to whom I could fully confide, and even with that special chum, much was taboo. We were living in Canada, and the Canadian culture did not encourage open self-disclosure between people any more than New England reputedly, does, or doesn't.[5]

This interest in varieties of human personality, behavior and motivation began with what appears to be a natural curiosity that was gradually nurtured by life at home, at school and in his neighborhood. With the family business literally underfoot, Sid was routinely exposed to a steady stream of social interaction, of new and familiar faces walking into the store daily. At mealtimes Louis and Annie would likely discuss their encounters with various customers. The freight railroad tracks were directly behind the house, and during the Depression years Annie was known as a soft touch for a handout among the drifters and hobos who rode the rails.

Although Sidney eventually became an accomplished and effective psychotherapist, he later admitted he was not born with a desire to help others; he simply found human beings to be varied, fascinating and opaque. He was also intrigued at an early age with himself; his feeling of otherness and of not fitting in, despite being part of a large and loving family. Sid wondered about his own personality. His career was guided by what he wanted to learn about himself or about others, the beginnings of "self-disclosure," the differences between persons.

I suppose it is fair for me to say, then, that there was not any especial desire to heal the sick, or to relieve suffering that characterized me as a child and adolescent. I was fascinated with human differences and of course, I had a robust interest in myself, in trying to understand my likes and dislikes, failures of moral resolve, the wildness of my imagination, and wonderment over my chronic feeling of being different, an outsider. The peculiar thing is that, from an external point of view, I was a not an uncommon Canadian youngster. I was active at all sports: hockey, swimming, football, soccer, baseball, track and field, water polo, etc. But I read anything and everything in orgies. And I alternated between wild enthusiasms which obliterated any interest in myself, and long periods of ferocious self-absorption.[6]

Enlist or Go to College?

Sidney was class valedictorian at high school graduation in 1943 and spent his second consecutive summer working on a farm for the war effort. As the fall academic season approached he had to decide whether

> I was going to go to war, or was I going to go on to college, and I had great agonies of indecision because I was drafted, and I went for my examination at age eighteen and they rejected me because I was too myopic, but anyway the draft was ignominious, and if you were drafted, you enlisted anyway, but both my older brothers were in the army—Sam was in action[7], he trained in North Africa, and then started on that campaign from Sicily all the way through Italy and [had] a tank shot out from under him, and my other brother [Harry] was in the war, and we had long correspondence and debate should I go, because I wanted to go, it was a legitimate war, and I was talked [to], almost a family decision—look, we've got two brothers [in action], there's going to need to be people around, educated and trained, after the war—go to school, so I went to school.

The University of Toronto campus was a direct streetcar ride away.

Adventurous Ways   3

EIGHTEEN YEARS OLD and living at home, Sidney enrolled at University of Toronto where three of his siblings had already graduated and where his first concern
was choosing an area of study, based more on what didn't interest him rather than
what did:

> I knew I didn't want to go into medicine. I didn't want to go into dentistry. I
> didn't want to go into law. None of these things appealed to me particularly,
> so I had the University of Toronto catalogue and the only thing that
> seemed to make any sense, that gave me maximum options, was social
> and psychological studies. So I applied to that without having the faintest
> idea what it was about, and the way the schedules worked, you had to take
> one from each of several categories, and I remember I took psychology,
> sociology, anthropology, and economics, geography, and then French and
> English and philosophy—they really threw it at us.

His choice of psychology as a major (named Honours subject in Canada) appears to be based on the appeal of a particular professor, Dr. Mary Northway. "Tall,
thin, sort of buck-toothed, bespectacled, and I thought she was magnificent…I
liked the other things too. I couldn't make up my mind, so I made it up on the basis
I liked Mary Northway so the hell with it, so it was all her fault."

In addition to Mary Louise Northway (1909 -1987) who studied the sociometry of children at the Institute of Child Study, Sid was enthralled with two
other undergraduate professors: Magda B. Arnold (1903–2002), who focused on

emotion and the brain, and William Emet Blatz (1895-1964) a developmental psychologist who directed the Institute of Child Study for thirty-five years and developed *security theory*, a precursor to *attachment theory*. Blatz presented the idea that a child who feels secure will grow up as a secure adult.

Blatz's personality had a formative and lasting impression on Sid as much as his teaching did.

> We took lectures from Blatz, his course in mental hygiene. He was magnificent. What a man! He was so full of himself, utterly self-confident, he could handle the rough-and-tumble students. He was the powerfullest teacher because he seemed so sure of himself. Some of us, Honour Psychology students, we would go right into the library to see if we could find something to trick him up; we never could.

Sid's natural interest in personalities and human behavior was further stimulated by these and other teachers, as he recalls over thirty years later in his book review of *Dominance, Self-Esteem, Self-Actualization: Germinal Papers of A.H. Maslow*:

> I took a course on motivation from Magda B. Arnold when I was a student at the University of Toronto. One of the readings was "A Theory of Human Motivation" by A.H. Maslow, newly published in *Psychological Review*. The year was 1944 or 1945. Maslow spoke to me in a way that none of the other authors I was reading ever did. I think I became a "humanistic" psychologist at the time, although my other professors—Blatz, Northway, Line, Ketchum and Myers—all were concerned with man as a human person rather than with his depersonalized behavior or experience alone.
>
> I went to the University of Buffalo in 1948 to work on my doctorate, retaining my interest in Maslow's work, and by this time had read nearly everything he had published. The late Marvin Feldman, then my doctoral chairman, commented, "Sidney, I have been reading Maslow, and I find him very much like a cactus, he has many points but when you get past them, you come to pure mush." This was Feldman's way of saying he thought many of Maslow's terms were loose, and his methods less than rigorous. I always thought that Maslow's methods of study, and his concepts were precise, in the sense that they did justice to the phenomena he was studying—not so focused that they missed the essence he was exploring, nor so sloppy that nobody knew what he was talking about.
>
> His writings, and his person, continued to influence me; indeed, my first

book, *Personal Adjustment*, was inspired by his emphasis on psychological health. I dedicated the third edition of that book, now called *Healthy Personality*, to his memory.[1]

Another of Sid's professors, C. Roger Myers, taught clinical psychology and assigned his students Carl Rogers's *Counseling and Psychotherapy: Newer Concepts in Practice*. Along with Maslow and Rollo May, Carl Rogers was on the forefront of the development of the Humanistic Psychology orientation, named the Third Force in psychology as contrasted with the psychoanalytic approach of Freud and the behaviorist orientations of Watson and Skinner. This early exposure to Maslow and Rogers was to have a deep influence on Sid's interest in a humanistic approach to the study of human behavior.

Adventures of a Canadian Youth

As was the case in primary and secondary school, Sidney thrived in an academic setting. A review of several editions of the college yearbook *Torontonensis* documents his involvement with college academics and social culture. Sid lettered as a member of the Varsity water polo team, winner of the Eckhardt Cup in 1946. He wrote for the school newspaper *Varsity* before joining a group that published a rebel newspaper called *The Campus*. He was in the Literary Club, the Historical Club, on the student Athletic Board, and a member of Beta Sigma Rho.

Although this all occurred in Canada, Sid's college life is indistinguishable from that of a typical All-American college student. Whatever loneliness or feelings of being the "outsider always looking in" Sid may have nurtured—and he surely had read Camus' *The Stranger*— this alienation was not evident in his outward activities. He was highly social, involved in both intellectual and physical activities in the college setting. His radical approach to psychotherapy and his investigation of previously unexplored topics of social research were yet to come. Sid fit in.

One Special Summer

When school was out of session and to contrast with his intellectual life, Sid consciously chose travel and physical labor. One such summer job was demolishing trolley tracks in Vancouver as part of the city's rails-to-rubber project.

Stimulated by the novels of Thomas Wolfe and by his own imaginative energy,

Sidney (center) with unidentified friends, mid-1940s

Sid was ready for the self-romanticized adventures he craved:

> By the time I was through my senior year in Honour Psychology, I had been involved in debating, running a rebel newspaper, presenting papers at the Historical Society, playing soccer, water polo, participating in long-distance running, competitive swimming; I had spent one summer on a travelling carnival, traversing Canada [he was Bingo Sid], another summer hitch-hiking down to California and up to British Columbia, with a one-month sojourn in California, first in Sacramento County Prison for ten days, then for three weeks in a detention camp for aliens; I had spent another summer at a children's camp, where I met the woman I married three years later; and during these four years I had gratefully yielded my virginity at age eighteen to a fourteen-year-old overdeveloped girl I met on the carnival.[2]

Sid's adventures during the summer of 1945 were inspired by the appeal of Thomas Wolfe's fiction and of Somerset Maugham's claim that a writer needs to experience life; Sid took this to heart and rambled from Toronto to Vancouver to Sacramento and eventually back to Toronto in the fall. After working in Vancouver he hitchhiked south to California where he encountered immigration officials who determined he had no permit to work in the United States. After ten days in Sacramento County Prison he was transferred to the Sharp Park Internment Camp in Pacifica, just south of San Francisco, built for the detaining of aliens during World War II.

Sid passed the time through observing his surroundings and writing short stories. The following example is pure juvenilia, and if Sid had not become a psychologist the story would be of no interest. Viewed from the present, however, the story reveals his ability to observe human behavior and to craft fiction from what seemed to be a genuine encounter.

MR. CANADIAN CUPID
Sid Jourard – July 2/45
[19 years old]
-Sharp Park, Calif.

They came out of the mess-hall discussing the merits of the meal, of the camp, and of the various inmates of it.

Ted Marshall, Canadian, university student, age 22, was held at the Mountain View Detention Camp, for injudiciously seeking employment in the States without the necessary papers. He was the lone Canadian amongst some seventy Mexicans, ten Germans and a smattering of Italian, Hindu and Yugoslav seamen.

It was with one of the Hindus, a lad named, for sake of pronunciation, K. Ali, that Ted was talking.

"Ted, will you come wid me to barracks," asked Ali. "I have problem which you can help, if you will."

Though his knowledge of English was far from complete, those words which he spoke had polished Oxonian intonation, evidence of the excellent English teacher he had had in his school days in Calcutta.

"O.K." Ted said when they had reached the barracks, and were settled on the bed. "What's the problem?"

"Roll yourself a cigarette first, and I tell you a-bout it" Ali said, proffering his sack of Bull Durham, and some brown-straw paper.

When they had lit their cigarettes, Ali began. "You know, Ted, I merchant seaman. I leave Calcutta seven years, been sailing much. Been all over world. Well, last mont, we dock in Frisco, and I go ashore. I go to some Hindu friends there, have good time, get drunk. Later, I go down to water front saloon and drink some more. But there I see sight so beautiful, that I sober up quick. It was a girl. She was with drunken sailor who try to kiss her. She look at me as if want help, so I go over and bop sailor."

"And you're the guy to do it, Ali," Ted said, looking admiringly at the biceps swelling on the long, coffee-colored arms of his friend.

"I took the girl out, and she say thanks and ask me to take her home. This I do, and she kiss me. She is so beautiful that I think I'm in heaven. I ask for date tomorrow and she say yes. I very happy."

"What's she look like, Ali?" Ted asked.

Ali took a picture from his wallet, and after gazing at it lovingly for a brief moment, passed it to Ted. He looked, to see a very dark-skinned girl, with long, straight black hair caught in a roll at the back. It was divided evenly on top of her head on either side of a straight part. She had even, white teeth, a large mouth turned up at the corners into a perpetual, shy smile. Her dark eyes seemed to glow with promise, and her small, straight nose projected no further than the tip of her chin. In short, by Ted's standards, she was "O.K.", and he emitted a long low whistle.

"You like her?" Ali asked. When Ted nodded, Ali said in a serious voice, "She is my heart, my whole life. But she cause me trouble."

"Oh, oh. Cherchez la femme. There's always a babe back of all trouble. Tell all to Teddie," he said in a father-like voice.

"Remember that drunk sailor? He was engaged to her. I spend all my shore leave with my heart, buy her many things, have excellent happy time. When ship leave, I stay. I take job just to stay near my heart. We both very happy, going to be married. Mildred, her name, live with girlfriend, no got much money, so I buy clothes, pay rent, give her money. To me, money nothing, for Mildred is all.

"But this sailor jealous. He write letter to immigration officers; they pick me up, send me here. Next week I be deported back to India.

"Since I come in, I get letter every day Mildred," and he showed Ted a thick bundle of air mail, and Special Delivery letters, all from Frisco, about 20 miles away.

"She really wanted to make sure those letters got to you, didn't she," Ted said, looking at the stamps.

"Oh, she write, she telegraph, she telephone every day. She see lawyers, she see consul, every thing to get me out. But is no good, for I go to India next week. But I want you to write letters for me to Mildred, and her girl friend. I no write so good. I tell you what I want say, and you write good English, O.K.?"

"Sure thing, Ali. What do you want to say?" Ted said, getting out pen and paper.

When the letter was completed, it read like this:

My own, my dear heart.

I am being deported back to India next week, and face a hazardous journey across the Pacific. It is possible that I may be killed, but if I am, I do not want you to languish away your life in loneliness. Seek another man in my stead.

But should I reach Calcutta safely, ignore what I said above, for I shall then prepare to come to your side again. Before I go the 400 miles to my village, I shall cross half the globe to see you, dear heart.

I am sending you all of my money before I go, my love, that you may want for nothing.

Keep a tender memory of me in your heart, as I keep all my heart for yours, until I return to you in six months. God permitting, I shall be no longer in coming to your side.

Your own love, Ali.

Another letter went to her girl friend, begging her to care for his beloved Mildred, to see that no harm would befall her, to ensure that she enjoy herself while he, Ali, her life and love, was gone. He generously stated that he would in no wise be jealous if Mildred went out with other men, for such was his love for her that he wanted only her happiness.

The week following, Ali left, on his way to India. He had left his two letters with Ted, for him to deliver personally when he was released. If Ali had mailed them, they would have been censored, and his intentions of returning would be filed.

The day after Ali left, Ted was sitting smoking in the sun, outside the barracks, talking to Gavotti, an Italo-American who, in the 20 of his 25 years in America, had neglected, for various reasons, to draw citizenship papers, and hence was in the process of being deported to Italy.

"I was sorry to see Ali go," Ted said. "In the three weeks that I knew him I learned to like him a helluva lot. He was so different from American, or Canadian kids. Nothing flippy, or casual about him. He was sincere in everything he did. And whatta love affair he was carrying on. None of this 'Hi babe, make with the lips' stuff for him. I wrote letters for him that would make Don Juan blush. And while I felt like a damn fool writing such slush, yet he meant every word he said. Gawd, I can see my friend Liz reading a letter from me like some that I wrote for Ali. She'd call the doctor!"

"Well, you can't tell much about these Orientals," Gavotti said. And that's all he said. When he was with Ted he rarely got an opportunity even to say that much.

"I get released for voluntary departure on Monday, Gavotti old sock. But before I leave, I'm going to paint up Frisco in good red hues. It's been so long since I've seen a girl, or had a drink. I wonder if you should put blinders on me?"

That Monday afternoon, a very eager Ted Marshall stepped off the bus from Mountain View Detention Camp, bade his adieux to his favorite guard, and said "I hope I never see you again. Come up to Canada, some time, and I'll sic the dogs on you."

"Oh, g'wan, Marshall! You know you loved your little holiday with us. Good luck, and be careful."

Ted found himself, at 9 o'clock that night, singing "Oh Canada," and the "Maple Leaf Forever" at the top of his lungs in a bar on the water front. After being screamingly funny for half an hour, he began to extol the praises of Canadian beer, compared to the dishwater he had been drinking all afternoon. But after several non-alcoholic months, that dishwater had quite staggered him.

"C'mon everybody, have a drink on me!" Ted shouted, to the four patrons of the Ancient Mariner Bar & Grill, having placed a ten-dollar bill on the counter. The thundering herd was settled at the bar, thirstily imbibing the most expensive mixtures, as speedily as possible, when Ted saw a sight that sobered him, enraged him. At the end of the bar, a rough-looking, unshaven sailor was wrestling with a very deeply-tanned girl, saying loudly "C'mon, give us a kiss, baby."

"Leave me alone, you rotten pig" she muttered, in a voice meant for no one but her amorous companion. But Ted, chivalrous and righteous after 2 womanless months at internment camp, and four hours of beer-drinking, heard. He ran up to the couple, grasped the sailor by the lapels, and smashed him heavily to the floor.

Five minutes later, when Ted came to, he saw a pair of dark eyes gazing anxiously into his face, and felt his head cradled by two soft cool hands, which occasionally caressed his bruised chin. He said "I'm in heaven, am I not? And aren't you an angel? What happened?"

This dusky-skinned vision, this angel, answered in a lilting voice, with words that somehow seemed incongruous.

"That sonavabitch knocked you out. But I stuck with ya, big boy. But now that yer awake, I gotta be going. So long, bub."

"Just a minute, sister, and I'll see you home. What if that bruiser comes around again. Won't you need protection?"

"Cripes, if what happened before is protection, I'll take a gun. But tell you what, call me a taxi and you can drive me home."

Ted was remarkably pleased with himself. His train left the following morning at 11:00, and his one day in Frisco had been quite full. And the rest of the evening looked promising.

Seated in the taxi, he wasted no time in clutching this tan beauty to his chest. In his huskiest, most fervent voice, he said thickly, "I'm nuts about you baby. I go for bathing beauties. How much time do you spend at the beach?"

Skillfully breaking his hold, his companion said "I'm a life-guard, brother, and let loose, or I'll bust you one."

The taxi pulled to a stop, and the driver said "287 Wilmot, bub! That'll be a buck and a half."

"O.K. driver," Marshall said. "Just a sec 'til I get my wallet." He fumbled futilely in his pockets only to realize that the sailor in the bar had removed his wallet. He could barely make $1.50 in change, leaving him just enough for coffee and a street-car fare to the railway station. Luckily his ticket was in his pocket.

"Well sister, we're home. Can I come in?"

"Sorry, bub, my girl friend's entertaining, and I gotta get up early," the girl said.

A window slid up on the second story, and a head, mindful of a mop because of curling ribbons, projected beyond the ledge and shouted, "Hey Mildred! Get rid of that wolf, and c'mon in. We gotta get some sleep."

"Mildred? Is that your name? Mildred Johnson, of 287 Wilmot Street?" Ted asked her.

"Sure it is. How did you know my last name?"

"Never mind that. Did you know an Indian boy from Calcutta named K. Ali?"

"Sure I did. A real cute kid, and generous to boot. But corny as they come. He was in Detention camp, wasn't he? My girl friend used to write letters for me to him. She went to school once. Real doozers they were too. But we haven't heard from him for a couple weeks.

"He's been deported to India" Ted said, suddenly serious.

"I'm sorry to hear that. I kinda liked the kid. He thought I was an Indian girl, cause I'm so tan, so I told him a line about how my mother was a Hindu girl who married my old man and became a citizen. It was a shame to string him a line, but, what the hell, he didn't mind."

"Mildred, here's a present for you from K. Ali" Ted said, giving her the letter containing all the money that K. Ali had left in America, some 85 dollars. "And here's a letter for your girl-friend. And here, my dear sweet girl is the best of all, a present from me to you personally. Call it good-will policy between nations, or Lend Lease!"

Mildred resigned herself to a kiss, her facial expression indicating much experience in saying goodnight—she knew she would get to bed quicker by kissing a wolf goodnite than by arguing or wrestling with him. Besides, a kiss, meaningless as it was to her, often brought excellent returns in the way of further dates, or gifts. So she reached up her pretty mouth, and closed her eyes alluringly.

"From me to you, Mildred," Ted said in the most romantic of tones, and enfolded her in his arms.

"Stop!, ouch! cut it out! What the hell do you think you're doing?" Mildred shouted, in her no longer lilting voice.

Ted released her from across his knee where he had been applying an old fashioned spanking, got up without a word and walked off into the night.

"Now why on earth did that big lug do that?" Mildred asked her girl-friend as they lay in bed together. "D'ya think he suspects I split 50-50 with Luigi on his roll?"

"Naw, he looked too dumb to me. I read in a book once that uncivilized men make love by beating up their women," said that sleepy sage, that savant who was Mildred's girl friend.

With nothing else to do, Sid then wrote *A Party To Be Remembered*. His pedestrian writing style is offset somewhat by an array of character studies. Margaret Bessborough—-a self-professed bohemian who is "free of her parental jurisdiction" at college—plans a final party for all her friends before graduation. She had "collected plenty; but with one stipulation—they had to possess one particular characteristic, by means of which Margaret might easily stereotype them." Her platonic friend Al Cohen was "chosen among her friends for several reasons. Being a Jew, he served as an advertisement of Margaret's broadmindedness. That, added to the fact that he had been in the Merchant Marine and could be called 'the Wandering Jew' by Bess and her circle, served as his card of admission." There is Battersby, who as a medical student can discuss "such sacred cows as unmentionable anatomy;" Bill Johnson is the wag, the teller of jokes; Peter Rawliegh produces campus plays, Donald Kendricks is assistant editor of the campus paper. And there is Joanne Smithers, a tall girl who wore a "black party dress sprinkled with sequins....Joanne Smithers was wealth opulence and quiet intelligence personified. Or so she led one to believe. Being more radical than most social science students, she broke the mores—of the very students who scoffed middle class ways—and appeared dressed in conventional manner."

Sid describes a dozen characters through their various self-identities and social roles. Later that summer Al Cohen encounters Margaret, who responds to Cohen's comment that the party was a "lulu," "Well, I told you it would be. That party was the culmination of conditioning. All the spontaneity we had actually was unconsciously rehearsed, because of all of the other parties we had."

The following summer Sid worked as a camp counselor at Balfour Manour Camp where he met Antoinette Hertz, who had attended the camp for years before becoming a counselor herself.

Antoinette Hertz

Antoinette, born in New York City in 1926, was one of two daughters of Sylvia Morris, also of New York, and of Joseph Hertz, born in Budapest. The parents separated and divorced around 1930 and Antoinette and her sister were brought to Toronto where they were raised at the home of Sylvia's father, Maurice Morris. Photographs of Toni as a teen reveal an attractive statuesque brunette in the Betty Grable style. Sid was entranced and pursued her immediately, as Toni recalls:

> I met Sid in 1946. He was twenty, so was I. We met at a summer camp in
> Muskoka, Ontario, Canada. We were both counselors. I had been going
> to the camp for quite some time starting as a camper. This was the first
> year Sid had been there; he was a friend of the camp owner's son. We went

together that summer and then continued seeing each other in Toronto during the year where I had moved to, from St. Catharine's and took courses at the Institute of Child Study. Sid had begun working on his master's thesis at University of Toronto. He was involved in many activities and I found them and him fun and exciting. He was one of the editors of a semi-radical off-campus student newspaper. He was interested in music and introduced me to the music of Burl Ives, Josh White, the Carter Family, Lead Belly and many others....

The year before I met Sid he ran for some office, I think it was student president. I can't recall if he got it or not but I do remember a campaign poster he had in his room which amused me and still does:

"You'll Find It Hard
To Beat Jourard!"[3]

Sidney and Antoinette Hertz, Balfour Manor Camp, late 1940s

Sid married Toni in June of 1948 when he received his M.A. in Psychology from the University of Toronto.

During his undergraduate years Sid had studied experimental methodology in psychology, a science that had in the last few decades emerged from philosophy as a new social science. This separation was a new development in academics and the emphasis was, naturally enough, on empirical data, measurable results.

University of Toronto yearbook photo 1947

The basic approach to a research study in psychology was that of any other science. An experiment begins with an idea or hypothesis. In social psychology this could be a correlation in a subject between social acceptance and academic achievement, or religious background and judgement of character. To determine if such a correlation exists, an independent variable is shown empirically to correlate with the dependent variable by controlling the independent variable. Sample randomness, statistics, control groups, avoiding bias, error percentages, factor analysis; these practices were all part of his training and he used these measurement methods throughout his career.

One of the controversies of psychology in general, and Humanistic Psychology in particular, is the validity of attempting to measure—and therefore quantify— such non-tangible data as feelings, emotions, will power, etc., using the methods associated with the natural sciences. Measuring the response of a frog's leg to various applied voltages is one thing; measuring how hopeful someone feels after the loss of a loved one is another.

Sid's 1948 master's thesis was written utilizing the standard approach to research in social psychology. For his sample group he chose the members of a men's dormitory:

> I went in and made my acquaintance, and got myself trusted by all the people there; and I had them fill out a whole batch of tests: sociometric tests and how long had they known everybody, and then I gave them the Bell Adjustment Inventory, and [the old] Allport-Vernon Scale [of values], and then I picked out the most accepted and the least accepted, and I did T-tests, and got virtually nothing. Actually, there were some hints, as a matter of fact, of differences. It wasn't a bad study when you get right down to it, and then I wrote it up, I learned on that primitive equipment—they had these hideous Burroughs hand-cranked calculators. I had to learn how to punch them, and I did correlations, T-tests and so on, and finally wrote it up. It was given a grade of B+, and when I finished my Masters, Bott wrote everybody a letter, and I can remember his letter; Dear Jourard: We do not think you should consider going on for further advance studies in psychology because you did not seem to excel in any of your seminars or your thesis. Yours sincerely, E.A. Bott, B.A. O.B.E.[4]
>
> I had a lovely new wife, no job, no prospects, no place to go, no money, and we had a job at this children's camp where we met. I was program director, Toni was the director of the children's camp. And while I was there and getting used to being married we didn't know what we were up to; trying to run a camp; trying to do research, trying to be married; and wondering how in the hell am I going to make a living? And what am I good for anyway? The only jobs in Canada at that time for someone with an

M.A. from the University of Toronto were some kind of a psychometrician or something at a hospital for $1200 a year, and my fellow [camp] program director was from the University of Buffalo, a law student, and he said just casually, "The University of Buffalo is hiring a lot of people with M.A.'s as instructors because they have an influx of G.I.s. Why don't you write?" So I wrote a letter. He gave me the name of the Department Chairman. I wrote a letter and I got a letter back while I was still at camp: We are interested in considering you. I knew that I wanted to continue studies, and I wanted to work, and here I did this masters thesis[5]—and I didn't know my ass from my elbow about research, and neither did anybody else.

So I went on to Buffalo where they had started a brand new Ph.D. program. They took me on as a new instructor with about ten other people to teach Psych I, and then since I was in clinical, I taught three-quarters of the time in the psychological clinic there.

It was just like a breath of fresh air. They had some Ph.D.s who had been trained with psychoanalytic orientation, Rogerian orientation, and Sullivanian orientation, and this was just heady to me. I started out right away doing diagnostic things, and started out being a psychotherapist one way or another, and taking graduate courses and teaching, at the princely rate of $2350 an academic year, and since I was Canadian I thought, my God, I'm rich, I think we can live on a thousand and save the rest. With my new bride I loved it, those three years were just magnificent.

Sid's voracious appetite for reading was augmented by the British-influenced classical style of education he had received in Canada. He was now living and working in the United States and he noticed a difference in his educational background and that of his associates:

> In many ways the experience I had at Toronto, I was better educated, the Ontario high school, and then four years at the University of Toronto, than many of my fellow graduate students, and certainly the students at the University of Buffalo, I thought they were semi-literate, and I suppose in a sense they were, and yet Buffalo was a fine private university at the time.

Through serendipity he gained an opportunity to learn public speaking skills. Tom Kennelly, the chairman of the Clinical program whom Sid admired, was going through a divorce and an analysis at the time.

And he was a Rotarian. He gave hundreds of talks all over the place, and for some reason or other he took a shine to me, so when he was that depressed and confused and anxious he couldn't give a hundred talks: one to the Rotary, one to the church, one to the Y., he said, "Sid, do it," and I would go, and I learned how to talk, how to lecture. I am grateful to him.

Marriage, America, Fatherhood

Sid and Toni lived in a series of rented rooms before moving into their own house at 164 Hinman Avenue in Buffalo, where a son Jeffrey was born in 1951. The following month Sid applied for a Research Fellowship grant. This application provides much information about his work history, current situation and his future plans. Listed jobs held in the last five years include Track Laborer (Summer '45), Mental Health Consultant (Batavia, NY 1950), Vocational Counselor (Summer 1949, Buffalo) and Program Director (summer employment 1947-'50 Camp Balfour Manor, York Mills, Ontario). He was a member of the Canadian Psychology Association, the American Psychological Association, the Eastern Psychology Association and Sigma Xi, a scientific fraternity. He was twenty-five and still a Canadian citizen. In the application Sid describes his research topic, which became his doctoral dissertation.

What are your plans for a future career? How would this Fellowship if awarded, fit in with these plans?

Plans consist in proceeding with a career which will include research, clinical work, and teaching in the field of psychology. Fellowship would materially assist continuation of my research project which is at present in the "pilot study" stage.

Give details of the most important research problem on which you have obtained definitive results.

I conducted a study (Summer 1948) to test the hypothesis that social acceptance among children is related to the "degree and direction of their outgoing energy." When the activities of a summer camp programme were used as an index of the aforementioned, the hypothesis was upheld by the data. (A report of this study will be published in SOCIOMETRY following the customary lag between time article is submitted and its publication).

Give a brief description of the research you plan to conduct in relation to your Fellowship.

"An experimental analysis of the theory of ego-strength"

<u>GENERAL PROBLEM</u>: To test certain hypotheses derived from the psychoanalytic theory of "ego-strength." The strong ego is generally regarded by psychoanalysts as possessing certain attributes, viz: 1.) a high degree of resistance to stress. 2.) Minimal distortion in the perception of "reality." 3.) Considerable plasticity, or flexibility in behavior. 4.) Reduced tendency to make use of pathological defense-mechanisms, such as repression.

<u>SPECIFIC HYPOTHESES</u>: It is predicted that variations in <u>ego-strength</u> will be accompanied by variations in:

1. Discrepancies between aspiration scores and achievement scores in a Level of Aspiration test-situation. (our index of reality-contact).

2. Scores on a series of tasks and tests designed to measure rigidity-flexibility.

3. The recall of Interrupted as opposed to Completed tasks in a Zeigarnik-type test situation. (our index of self-defensive forgetting)

Our independent estimate of ego-strength will be based on <u>Form-Level scores</u> on the Rorschach test. <u>(F-plus %)</u>. Another psychologist, M. Williams, used this variable with promising results to predict decrements in performance under stress. (<u>J. Consult. Psychol. 1947</u>)

<u>SUBJECTS</u>: Fifty subjects who have been equated for age, sex, I.Q., will be selected from a college, or non-hospitalized population.

<u>PROCEDURE</u>: The subjects, individually, will be administered the battery of test-situations. The order of the tests will be varied randomly, to partial out the effects on performance of the serial position of each test.

It is proposed that the data will be treated as follows:

The subjects will be divided into a number of groups, the division being based upon their <u>Form-Level scores</u> on the Rorschach test. Comparisons will be made between these groups on their performance on the various measures used, by means of the analysis of variance, Chi-square, t-tests, etc. Intercorrelations will be undertaken between the various variables as well.

GENERAL IMPLICATIONS: This study will attempt to demonstrate that the theory of ego-strength can be a fruitful one for integrating variables which are commonly regarded, outside the realm of psychoanalytic personality theory, as unrelated. The research will also test the validity of some aspects of the Rorschach test as a predictor of certain types of response in an experimental situation.

April 20, 1951 Sidney M. Jourard
University of Buffalo, Buffalo, New York.

The following announcement ran in the *New York Times* on September 11, 1951:

———

RESEARCH AWARDS MADE
Public Health Service Grants $445,000 in Fellowships
September 10. The Public Health Service awarded research
fellowships totaling $445,300 to 171 science students today.

———

Among the thirty grants listed was Sidney M. Jourard, $2000, University of Buffalo.

Digging In

4

In 1952 Sidney completed his doctoral dissertation *A Study of Ego Strength by Means of the Rorschach Test and the Interruption of Tasks Experiment.* His three-year contract as an instructor at the University of Buffalo had ended, and after applying to several universities Sid accepted an offer to teach clinical psychology at Emory University for $3850 an academic year. In the fall he drove from Buffalo to Atlanta, arriving at Faculty Row in a battered Frazier automobile towing a trailer, accompanied by his wife, son, and a collie named Laddie.

Man At His Most Adjusted

Sid took stock of his teaching situation immediately: "They gave me—I don't see any reason not to say it—the 'shit' course, the adjustment course."

The term "adjustment" was in common usage by psychologists during the early nineteen-fifties, as an indicator of a healthy personality, with the focus on how well persons fit into their social environment. The concept of health as measured by conformity to the status quo was the starting point for much of Sid's future writing and research, but his immediate task was teaching three courses: a class in abnormal psychology, a graduate seminar and a class in Mental Hygiene—the aforementioned "shit" adjustment course. He learned that nobody took the course seriously as taught by his predecessors:

They would get a book, D.B. Klein, *Mental Hygiene* or Carroll, *Mental Hygiene: The Dynamics of Adjustment*. They were Mickey Mouse books, they were written for cretins, so when I started the course, I threw away the books. I said, we are not going to have a text book, and I started fiddling around and asking the students what they thought a course like this should do, and they were interested in what does it mean to be mentally healthy.

I started re-reading Freud, and Jung, and Adler, and philosophers, and anybody else for what they said about man at his best. Very gradually I built up my lectures so that the students were just keenly interested in them and I was quite proud of them.

Sid was fully confident in his intellect and academic training, and his ego was strong. As the word "ego" is often used as a pejorative term, as in "egotistical," what precisely was a strong ego? Freud viewed the personality as consisting of three conflicting forces, id, ego and the super-ego. The id, present at birth, is primitive, instinctual and driven by the pleasure principle, a drive toward gratifying needs immediately. The ego is the rational, conscious self that deals with the real world and its setting, conflicting with the id through the strategy of delayed gratification; this compromise is negotiated with the help of the super-ego, the aspect of the personality that applies the moral and ethical guidance provided by family and culture. Although this tripartite model of a person's psyche was of interest to clinical psychologists and therapists, in Sid's exploration of healthy personality he found Freud's recognition of repression to be especially significant. To a certain extent Freud felt that the essence of society was repression of each individual, in order to fit in, and the essence of the individual was repression of their true nature. The roles of repression and adjustment as contributors to unhealthy personality seemed a worthy area of investigation.

Rather than viewing his teaching responsibilities as a distraction from research projects, Sid saw teaching as a vital aspect of his career and he modified the syllabus according to the suggestions of his students, and thus began a growing interest in studying the behaviors that determined and embodied mental health. Rather than study illness and how to cure it he focused on health and how to recognize it, a subject not well-represented in psychological research and writings at that time.

Learning to communicate his ideas clearly was of continual interest to Sid and he would revise his writings through many drafts, possibly inspired by his love of literature and having read many books in college whose insights he sought but whose style was stiff and difficult to read. Selections from Bergson, Kierkegaard, Husserl, Nietszche, and Sartre translated from the original language will provide examples. Sid hoped to avoid the contorted syntax and artless prose he had experienced in his academic journey toward a doctorate degree.

These combined traits served him well as an academic author, lecturer and writer of articles in mainstream publications. He read voraciously both within his field and in fiction and sought out stories of people who reached beyond "adjustment" to achieve greatness in their field. According to Sid, the abnormal psychology course he taught had

> an emphasis not on pathology, but on where do you go, having recognized pathology, in the direction of living a liveable life. I always tried to hang on to the English language, as opposed to jargon, and the sense of how then do you live life, and these courses went very well. I started doing research there.

The term "abnormal" was problematic to Sid in light of his growing awareness of unhealthy aspects of what was deemed normal, adjusted behavior. From the word "abnormal" alone he found much to consider and explore.

Sid then became interested in aspects of the body and body-awareness, and during the next several years published five studies with colleague Paul Secord, "The Appraisal of Body-Cathexis: Body-Cathexis and the Self" in the *Journal of Consulting Psychology* (1953); "Body-Size and Body-Cathexis" in the *Journal of Clinical Psychology* (1954), "Body-cathexis and the Ideal Female Figure" in the *Journal of Abnormal and Social Psychology*; "Body-cathexis and Personality" for the *British Journal of Psychology* (both 1955) and "Mother-Concepts and Judgments of Young Women's Faces" in the *Journal of Abnormal and Social Psychology* (1956).

A study from 1954 was named "Moral Indignation: A Correlate of Denied Dislike of Parents' Traits," and was published in the *Journal of Consulting Psychology*.

How did Sid come up with these research topics? He pursued areas of interest triggered by patterns of social behavior he observed: conformity, aggression, denial, indignation, suppressed anger. All human social behavior was fair game for observation, and a continual groping about for an idea would eventually lead to a hypothesis, the core of any scientific study. One example of this process is through a recollection in *The Transparent Self*.

One of the things I found rampant at Emory was what I called moral indignation. The faculty, especially faculty wives, were very ready to gossip and backbite about any kind of behavior that to them seemed deviant. I found this problematic so I did a study on moral indignation. One of the things I noticed was that, though our neighbors on "faculty row" would gossip viciously about offbeat characters, they would never ever criticize their mamas and their papas. So I thought, "Good heavens, is there a correlation between moral indignation and repression of anger and hostility toward one's parents?" I developed a technique for measuring attitude towards one's parents and another technique for measuring moral indignation. I tested a lot of people with these instruments and found a low, but significant correlation. The more morally indignant the people were toward offbeat behavior, the less they criticized their parents and the more they glorified them.[1]

A version of his doctoral dissertation, "Ego Strength and the Recall of Tasks," was published in the *Journal of Abnormal and Social Psychology*,

Southern Living

The present writer was born in the summer of 1954. Sid now had two infant sons, the start of an academic career and a growing number of research papers published in a variety of social science journals. Sid taught at Emory University for the next five years, contributing papers and articles while writing a textbook on healthy personality. An early book draft is dated 1955.

His attempts at commercial mainstream writing—separate from the theoretical papers and research studies submitted to academic journals—were rejected by Esquire and Good Housekeeping. He saved the rejection slips.

Sidney understood the power of the written word, and had been influenced by books about and by the greats—in the social sciences Sigmund Freud, Carl Jung, Martin Buber and Friedrich Nietzsche; in fiction Thomas Wolfe, Nikos Kazantzakis, John Steinbeck, Joseph Conrad, James Joyce. Precision in writing was his goal along with the avoidance of abstruse technical terms. Although Sid's writing topic was psychology, his writing style was crafted to express his ideas clearly to a general reader who, Sid felt, would be naturally interested in any discussion of the human condition. This overarching premise guided his approach to the written word.

Emory University was named for John Emory, a bishop of the Methodist

Episcopal Church. As the years went by Sid grew to experience Emory as highly conservative, not a good fit for a person of spontaneous nature and creativity or for anyone of perceived eccentricity. In Sid's words

> it had to do with going along with the ethos of Emory, just not easily describable, but it helped if you were quiet, if you didn't call too much attention to yourself, if you went to church, that would be very good, and showed a certain noblesse oblige which is another name for a peculiar kind of hypocrisy, especially for people of learning.

Sid had a "pivotal meeting" with Curtis Langhorne, the chairman of the Psychology department. Sid and Langhorne shared a mutual respect for one another, but

> he let me know, "Sid, you can stay here as long as you want, but you shouldn't feel that there was a future here for you at Emory because you are not—well, you are not making a good Emory-spirit citizen," and he couldn't explain more, and I took the hint and I started looking instantly for another job.

This confrontation and the result demonstrates the contrast between Emory University culture and Sid's particular combination of spirit and intellect, a man whose parents were friedenkers, free thinkers who rejected the tenets and traditions of organized religion as being incompatible with reason. At the time, this metaphysical orientation was not what Emory University was seeking in a faculty member.

Sidney took Langhorne's words to heart and a brief job search resulted in an offer from the University of Alabama in Birmingham at the Department of Psychiatry and Neurology. Before accepting the job, and while still at Emory, Sid volunteered for a scientific experiment involving a drug whose hallucinogenic properties had only recently been discovered and explored.

LSD

Sid's open-mindedness was an integral aspect of his intellect and his spirit. Experiences were available in life, and any that might expand or modify consciousness without causing permanent mental or physical harm attracted Sid's curiosity and interest. He had already explored alcohol, hard work, literature and study as modifiers of consciousness. In 1955 his position as an Emory university faculty member led him to experience the effects of LSD, a drug discovered by Swiss scientist Albert Hoffman in 1938 who learned of its hallucinogenic properties in 1943. The drug was used in the study of schizophrenia and other mental disorders long before being co-opted by the counterculture of the sixties.

Sid was working with a pharmacology professor, Carl Curt Pfeiffer, M.D., Ph.D.,[2] whom Sid later described as having

> taken hundreds of trips—he was bombed out of his skull. I didn't know it at that time. We made a film together. I tested him before, during and after, and we filmed it, and he used it as an educational document, and asked me, did I want to try it? Well, one of our graduate students had tried it and it didn't seem to hurt him and it seemed like an interesting experience, so I took it [.40 cc], and I had a colleague give me a Rorschach, a T.A.T [Thematic Apperception Test], a Rosensweig [Picture Frustration Test], and an MMPI [Minnesota Multiphasic Personality Inventory] before, during and after.

The records of this event have survived. Sid views the experience as a scientific experiment involving himself as both Experimenter and Subject, generating the data in the form of his notes written in real time.

> Saturday, Nov. 5, 1955
>
> At 9.00 a.m. I took .40 cc of LSD and by 10.00 I was at home eating breakfast. At about 10.25 I started laughing, but no other obvious indicators of any effects of the drug. As I sit here and write, I feel a wave of tears come to my eyes, and then it passes. I noticed that my legs as I walk felt a bit wooden, but no different than they feel when I have had a bit too much whiskey. I sighed quite often from about an hour after I took the drug, and I am sighing right now as I write (11.28)
>
> In a way, I feel a bit disappointed at having taken the size of dose which I took, although it may be too soon to know really. Perhaps I am fooling myself when I say that it was too little, that it will have no effect on me. I hardly know whether what I feel is genuine, or the by-product of suggestion from having seen Milton and Pfeiffer under the influence of the drug in the past couple of days.
>
> I certainly do not feel warranted in taking psychological tests again, as I do not feel sufficiently different from my usual condition—at least in my judgment. As a matter of fact, the people who observe me alter their

reactions to the knowledge that a person has taken this drug—I would hazard the guess and say that the drug affects the observers—making them much more suggestible, and grinny, than the subject becomes.

Saturday, Nov. 5, 1955 1.30 p.m.,

I had no really pronounced effects from the drug of any dramatic nature. No hallucinations, except for a time, when I closed my eyes, and when I was in the dark-room, I had a vivid flicker-experience. No nausea, or apparent physical by-products, except perhaps a feeling that people, tho they are here, they don't really understand. They don't get the full richness of meaning that you intend when you say anything, or express anything to them. The giggles and laughter which the drug produces— at least with my dosage—are fully experienced as alien, i.e., as drug-produced, and not as provoked by anything that is amusing in the world. What I did see with great clarity is that people need desperately to find logical reasons for their actions, which may be prompted by things of which they are unaware and so they search around for these reasons. The brighter the person, the more plausible the connection between explanation and action, but as with the laughter, the reasons never really does it justice. I noticed also that I tended to be readily easily drawn out in conversation to discuss things I never ordinarily would, such as mentioning a couple of things from Dr. Pfeiffer's Rorschach protocol to Goodling—tho this is really OK, I felt, and also mentioning something about his personality to the boys who were "in charge" of me. Yet even here, it was as it felt to me, within the confines of ethics.

Right now my palms are very sweaty, and I have a feeling which I can only liken to other things in my experience, as for example the results of a gin drunk the morning after—but without the nausea and headaches. If I subtract those phenomena, I approximate this feeling—it's sort of that things are not quite real—tho this is a cliche, and I don't think that's what I mean. Detached—things don't matter so much in the infinite scheme of things—that's more like it. It's rather pleasant. I am enjoying the experience—tho I wish I had taken a larger dosage. I wanted to experience the hallucinatory phenomena.

Saturday: Nov. 5, 1955. 4.45 p.m.

I still have palmar sweating, and a vague feeling of "detachment," if that word can describe the feeling. Yet I must avow that it is to me a familiar feeling, one usually brought on by fatigue, or alcohol hang-over. I notice that I have been extremely short-tempered during the effects of the drug—the slightest deviation will bring an angry comment from me. I recall that when Milt drove me home I was extremely irritable with him. His directional-signal on his car remained clicking after a corner-turn, and this badgered me considerably. Yet all the time I was aware that this was not like me, or the "usual me." When we got home, I drank some coffee, and I found Milt very irritating to me. I resented the implication that I needed someone to monitor me, and I abruptly told him to go home and leave me be. When I phoned Sara, as I had promised, I became unreasonably angry that her phone was busy, and when I finally reached her, I blasted her for tying up her phone with nonsense.

Here are Sidney's responses to an Incomplete Sentences Blank—College Form both before, and four hours *after* the drug was taken:

1. I like—women/*women*

2. The happiest time—I spent was as an undergrad at Toronto/*was in college*

3. I want to know—the secrets of the universe/*what it's all about*

4. Back home—live my parents, of whom I am fond/*the kids are sick, dammit!*

5. I regret—in some ways my refusal to teach the med students this year/ *not many things*

6. At bedtime—I read/*I like to read*

7. Boys—are delightful at age one, and terrors at age four/*will be boys. What an idiotic saying*

8. The best—things in life are free/*things in life are free*

9. What annoys me—is righteous people/*is pompous, stuffy people*

10. People—are a source of endless curiosity to me/*sadden me—we none of us live as richly as we're capable of*

11. A mother—seldom knows her children/*is man's best, etc. Likewise idiotic. Sometimes mothers aren't.*

12. I feel—sometimes self-confident, sometimes full of self-doubts/*rather odd, and yet I know I feel rather odd*

13. My greatest fear—at present is that I'll lose a court case over my dog, and have to pay $100/*is fear of fear—yet when I face fears, they no longer frighten*

14. In high school—I was awkward/*I was pretty awkward, shy*

15. I can't—wait to finish my book/*be all the things I'd like to be. More's the pity.*

16. Sports—have given me some satisfaction/*are fun, in measured doses, for the sportsman*

17. When I was a child—I was something of a brat/*When I was! Who ever stops being one, completely?*

18. My nerves—are quite steady/*are strong*

19. Other people—are important to me/*are nice—at least some of them are*

20. I suffer—from anxieties about my next vocational move/*from insufficiency of money*

21. I failed—to make myself *persona grata* at Emory/*When I get really honest, I can't say I have failed*

22. Reading—gives me much satisfaction/*gives one much satisfaction*

23. My mind—is a fine one/*—Yes, my mind does too*

24. The future—will probably be allright, tho I feel doubts about it/*is uncertain, but isn't that the fundamental property of futures?*

25. I need—a congenial job with a good salary, stimulating colleagues/*more salary so I can forget it, & do productive work, which I love to do*

26. Marriage—is all right for bachelors/*must have been invented by idiots*

27. I am best when—I am relaxed/*I feel loved*

28. Sometimes—I wish that I lived in Canada/*I get bored by the people I meet, work with—they limit themselves*

29. What pains me—is the way I shout at my oldest boy at times/*is to be forced to stay in the company of bores*

30. I hate—myself when I give my child a "blast"/*Bores. When I am a bore, I even hate myself.*

31. This school—is heavily populated with mediocre minds/*has an unrealized potential*

32. I am very—ambitious/*nice*

33. The only trouble—with me is that I am very egocentric/*is that I'm broke.*

34. I wish—I were a wealthy man/*I weren't broke. Money does buy happiness for those who know how & where to shop.*

35. My father –is a wonderful man, tho it took me many years to feel this/*is a fine man. I came to love him relatively late.*

36. I secretly—worry, but not always in secrecy/*—well, not so secretly, is a better word for it*

37. I—am a Jew in the agnostic-intellectual tradition/*am myself— sometimes I think too vigorously*

38. Dancing—I cannot do too well, tho I like it/*is fun—I must practice it more*

39. My greatest worry is—my immediate future ápropos a proper job/*no doubt to meet the bills*

40. Most girls—are lovely. I think women are delightful/*are lovely. Women are, or can be persons who have an additional asset—that of being women for men.*

"So I took acid," Sid recalls,

and nobody knew at that time what it was doing to people. It helped dissolve the structure of your world, it had nothing to do with model psychosis or whatever, and around that time, too, in my marriage I got into terrible conflicts with another young woman—several other young women—I moved out of my house, and I lived apart, trying to unscramble things, and then after about four months I moved back. In the meantime I had gotten a job in Birmingham, and this was my last academic year—I was working on, I had finished the manuscript for my first book, *Personal*

Adjustment. Everything happening at once, my father dying, I had taken acid, I was finishing my first book, and my marriage was going through its first real test. Well, as it happens, I got a job—a terrible job—but it was a job, and I took my family with me to Birmingham, in the psychiatry department in the University of Alabama Medical College in Birmingham, and that was a disaster, the Chairman was a horse's ass, an absolute oaf.

Sid did not suffer fools gladly—at least, those whom he considered fools.

He had been in the Navy for twenty-five years as a Navy surgeon with the rank of Captain and he had gotten Philadelphia Psychoanalytic training, and he ran the department like a ship and he used Navy metaphors. He said, well, welcome aboard, and you had to sign a log if you were going in to town to give a lecture, and he thought that an assistant professor was an assistant to the professor, so he got books to review, and he'd say, "Hey Sid, you're assistant here, review this book and I'll put my name to it," and "Why don't you write an article on this one." He told me once to lecture. He said, "Well Sid, I want you to lecture on psychological testings"—he used the word testings—"to the residents and interns here—I want you to tell them about the I.Q., you know, tell them about the M.A. over the C.A. times a 100, or is it C.A. over M.A. times a 100, but you know what to tell them, tell them that," and so I put up with this shit for about six months. In the meantime I was reading galleys for my new book—they were excellent— and I got the idea of self-disclosure at that time, just excited me no end, but I found him just an ass, truly an ass, and after about nine months it was time to come up for a talk, what about next year and he said, "Sid, you show a certain independence of spirit here that's admirable, but you got to be a member of the team. Now if you see your way clear to doing things the way we think they should be done, why there's no telling how far up you can go. You can become the head of this, and the head of that; on the other hand, if you want to continue in your present way, I don't see how we can get along together." I said, that's splendid, and I resigned.

In 1956 a third son, Leonard, was born. With a wife, three sons and no job, Sid cobbled together a collection of retainer positions at a vocational rehab facility, a Children's Aid, and a social family counseling agency, where he had use of their offices in off-hours to do private practice in diagnostic testing and psychotherapy. By the end of the year he had doubled his salary.

Private Practice and Self-Disclosure

The standard approach of a therapist with Rogerian training in those days was based on the writing and clinical practice of Carl Rogers, who developed a "non-directive therapy" technique of reflecting back to the patient what the patient had just revealed, i.e., Patient: "I feel lonely and scared a lot of the time," Therapist: "You often feel frightened and isolated," with the idea that clarification, acknowledgment and unconditional support for the patient helped the patient find the solutions to the problem from within, without specific directives. This empathetic approach could be emulated but required sincerity rather than rote execution of mere technique.

Sid, now in Alabama, found that the Rogerian approach was often ineffective and downright baffling to the patient. What may have worked for urban, middle class intellectual college students and college graduates seeking counseling did not work with provincial people. Sid learned the limits of practicing the techniques of a school of thought—Freudian, Rogerian, etc.— as opposed to being in the moment and dealing with each patient as who they were—a specific person sitting across from him. This took energy and observation, and such insight may not have happened had he not moved to the South and a culture much different than that of other parts of the country.

> I was made aware of the ways in which my initial training and experience were obstructing my therapeutic work when I encountered impasses in relation to patients I was treating in the Southeastern United States. I received my training in an urban setting, in the North. The stilted, technical way of responding to patients, with carefully thought-out interpretations or polished reflections of feelings—which patients of the Psychological Clinic accepted readily enough and even thrived on—"cut no ice" with patients one generation away from a Georgia dirt farm. As one patient put it to me, "Doc, why do yew keep on a-tellin' me back what I jus' tol' y'all? Cain't yew talk lak folks ought to?" Reactions such as these, from patients I was supposed to be helping, gave me pause. I listened to tape recordings I had made of sessions with patients and to recordings of colleagues' sessions. I compared the way we sounded, the way we spoke when we were with patients, and the ways we were when we were among friends or colleagues. Heard from this vantage point, it indeed seemed as if we were putting on our idioms the way a physician puts on a white coat—in our case, as a badge signifying we were "therapists on duty."[3]

The Craft of Writing

Sid's worries about money led to a new plan of action. There was no money in writing for academic journals, so he began writing and submitting articles to popular periodicals. An article submitted to Esquire magazine in December of 1956 was returned with the standard rejection slip. Originally typed on the back of University of Alabama stationery and entitled "When Are You Manly?" before being renamed "What Is A Man?," the article opens with this teaser: "One of the fastest ways to get punched in the nose is to accuse a man of being a 'sissy,' a 'queer,' a baby, or otherwise let him know you think him unmanly."

Replete With Inadequacies

The textbook Sidney was writing had evolved through several title changes, and drafts and fragments of various versions are in his collected papers. His interest in literature—Somerset Maugham and Thomas Wolfe —revealed to him the power of the word, and he worked on the craft alongside the content.

On a technical level early versions were not promising. Sid was a canny observer of human behavior and a great mimic of speech and mannerisms, but a born writer he was not. A critique of an early draft from 1955 provides a window into Sid's struggle with the craft of writing. The subject of his manuscript was a survey of the traits of a healthy personality, of what was then called an "adjusted" person. In an oddly conflicted summary, this unnamed critical reader for the University of Florida Press has much to say about how Sidney wrote:

Critique of "Healthy Personality in an Age of Conformity"

PLEASE COMMENT ON THE ORIGINALITY AND SCHOLARLY ACCURACY OF THE MANUSCRIPT.

Neither original nor scholarly and not so intended, I believe.

I could not make an accurate estimate of the number of paperbacks in the market interpreting the ways to mental health. There are a very large number of higher grade books on the same subject. Why would any person write another? There are no references given for statements offered as inferential or as fact.

DOES THE MANUSCRIPT MEET THE NEEDS OF THE READERS TO WHOM IT IS DIRECTED?

The early chapters, numbered, 1, 2, 3 and 4 are all jumbled up. Chapter 5 is the first chapter that appears clear and fairly coherent. The advice of the writer is generously but not consistently given on when to conform and when not to conform.

IS THE MANUSCRIPT A WELL-ROUNDED CONTRIBUTION TO ITS FIELD?

It is a very poor contribution to mental health procedure and thinking.

IS THE STYLE PEDESTRIAN, BETTER-THAN-AVERAGE, DISTINGUISHED?

The writing is generally poor.

MANUSCRIPT EVALUATION

Ineffective communication. The disturbed person would not know what to do. The professional person is better trained than the writer of this manuscript in my estimation. The nonprofessional person who counsels could not benefit from this material nearly as much as he could from reading existing literature.

ADDITIONAL REMARKS:

There is not any future for this material

[Attached Letter]

I have read with considerable care the manuscript entitled "Healthy Personality in an Age of Conformity." There is much helpful material in this MS which, if rewritten, rearranged, and reconstructed might well receive my favorable recommendation. However, I cannot recommend this MS in its present form for publication by the

University of Florida Press for the following reasons:

1/ Inadequate English composition.

a) Diction. Intermittently words and phrases appear which are encased in quotation marks. The terms consist of fillips of smart jargon which might be better be expressed with simple dignity. For example, note "to 'dope' it with drugs" (p.10) and "one important 'payoff'"(p.70) to cite two of many.

b) Punctuation. The use of double dashes to mark off clauses occurs frequently and needlessly. Also, phrase and sentences are underlined without uniformity and regularity.

c) Poor sentence structure such as ..."we are dependent on—" (p. 72)

d) Repeated use of contractions such as two "aren'ts" (p.77)

e) Confusions of person. At times the MS proceeds on an impersonal third-person basis. Then it suddenly shifts to second-person statement and the reader is addressed directly as "you" (see pp. 12, 20, 46)

NOTE: I do not believe that the author could afford to publish this MS in its present condition without damage to his status and reputation. Certainly, the University Press would be ill-advised to manufacture it.

Yet, in spite of this, the author's style is vigorous, refreshing and readable. He achieves dignity of style in places (chapter IX for instance) even though the first few chapters are replete with inadequacies.

2/ Unevenness of content and presentation.

Chapter I seems not only badly written but the imperfections of "normal" people are given muddled treatment. Definition of "Healthy Personality" adds little necessary enlightenment of the beginning of topic.

Chapter II starts with a good idea, namely: the difference between repressing feelings and curtailing overt action, but the treatment of anger fizzles out and many points are not illustrated.

Chapter III contains the treatment of sex matters. The presentation is much too flippant. "Sex can be fun," it says, which may be true, but which can be stated with delicacy in more appropriate ways.

The material of this chapter might better be expressed in semi-scientific language or in more restrained popular phrasing; otherwise the permissive statements might be misquoted out of context by publicity-hungry citizens to the embarrassment of the author and the University.

Chapters IV, VI and IX are much better and Chapters V and VIII are valuable.

Let me depart from chapter by chapter comment and offer my constructive suggestion of rearrangement and partial rewriting.

The essence of Chapter I concerning the inadequacies of normal people might well be condensed into a concise Introduction. Then the chapters might be rearranged as follows:

I Be and Become your Real Self   (present Chap. IV)

II Learn Reality   (present Chap. VI)

III Learn to Love   (present Chap. VIII)

IV Be Intimate More Completely   (present Chap. III Enjoy Sex)

V Find a Purpose For Your Life   (present Chap. IX)

VI Change Your Conscience   (present Chap. V)

VII Do Not Run Away From Emotions   (present Chap. II)

VIII Do Not Neglect Your Body   (present Chap. VII)

NOTE The "Real Self" of the above Chap. I replaces the definition of "Healthy Personality" given in the MS Chap. I. The subjects of facing Reality, learning to Love (self, others, mate, friends), Sex Intimacy, Finding a Purpose—all follow in an orderly sequence.

The nature of Conscience and the troublesome Emotions, together with the proper treatment of the Body, emerge as special problems.

If the revision of subject-matter were given the benefits of a more adequate quality of composition, the resulting MS might be worthy of publication. It might then appeal to laymen disturbed by personal problems, counselors, and the more informed clergy who are hungry for sermonic material.

Truly "...the benefits of a more adequate quality of composition" is harsh. Yet the critic admires the author's style as "vigorous, refreshing and readable" and mentions a dignity of style in places.

Meanwhile, Sid's growing interest in a new topic—self-disclosure—produced "Some Factors in Self-Disclosure," a 1958 study co-authored by colleague Paul Lasakow and published in the *Journal of Abnormal Psychology.*

This research was the core of a feature article published in the May 1958 *Scientific American.* Backed by hard empirical data, Sid was a social scientist and this work was accepted as science. The article reveals a clearer writing style and opens with a quote:

> The novelist Thomas Wolfe asked, "Which of us has known his brother?"
> His question is a sharp social comment which goes to the heart of all
> human relations. No man fully knows another, for no human being ever
> fully discloses himself, even to his closest intimates. Most of us live behind a
> wall or smoke-screen which in some degree hides our true thoughts, feeling,
> beliefs, desires, likes and dislikes. If no one really understands us, we are
> ourselves partly to blame. By the same token, if prejudice, fear and conflict
> between man and man stem largely from misunderstanding, we must lay a
> major share of the responsibility upon man's all-too-human reticence."[4]

Published in the same year as Sid's book *Personal Adjustment,* the article left an impression on writer Will Sparks, who was also a director and producer of films for the television series ''Wide Wide World'' in the 1950s and later wrote speeches for President Lyndon B. Johnson, Robert McNamara and the CEOs of major corporations:

146 Henry Street
Brooklyn 1, New York
September 23, 1959

Dr. Sidney M. Jourard
University of Florida
Gainesville, Florida

Dear Dr. Jourard,

There has recently come to my attention your excellent article in the May, 1958 <u>Scientific American</u> "A Study of Self-Disclosure." I was particularly intrigued by your remarks in the closing paragraph raising the question of whether our culture has made it "bad form" to disclose oneself.

As a writer I have been interested for a number of years by the requirement imposed by readers on the protagonist of almost any melodrama to be a strong silent type. From Sherlock Holmes to the Lone Ranger the successful hero communicates very little of himself to others. We are only rarely taken into his confidence as to his plans and more rarely still are we given his reasons for devising such plans as he does reveal. In motion pictures, television and novels of the frank melodrama or adventure category it would be fatal for a writer to attempt a characterization for his hero in which the hero revealed much of his personal ambitions, fears, uncertainties or dislikes. It is true that certain of these exigencies may be necessary to facilitate plot. But I am convinced that we demand many of these characteristics of our heroes for reasons which belong more to the realm of psychology than to literature.

Without wishing to intrude upon your probably busy schedule I should be very interested to know of any systematic inquiry into such matters that may have come to your attention.
Very truly yours,

Will Sparks

Sid's response was immediate.

September 29, 1959

Will Sparks
146 Henry Street
Brooklyn 1, New York

Dear Mr. Sparks,

Your observations about the male protagonist in popular literature are keen and appropriate, I can see how you, as a writer, would feel the pressures to draw a hero in the stereotyped way.

One of the best analyses of the theme of the strong, silent man is given in Leites & Wolfenstein, "The Movies: A Psychological Study" (I think that's the right title). These two people looked at hundreds of American and European movies, and undertook to compare "national character" of Americans, Frenchmen, Englishmen, Italians, etc., on the basis of the plots and characters.

Another book which treats this theme is a book by G. Gorer on American national character, called "The American People."

I think that the "silence" of the strong man is somehow related to what sociologists call role-theory. They point out that in an social system, or group, the man (like father) assumes the "Instrumental role"—handling foreign relations, hunting, winning, fighting, etc. while women are trained to the "Expressive role"—keeping relationships within the family or group harmonious.

However, as we become more "civilized" male-female differences become somewhat blurred, almost out of necessity. But the concepts of "ideal man" and "ideal woman" continue to hang on as instances of "cultural lag." Maybe this is why Mike Hammer, Cheyenne Bodie, Matt Dillon, etc. are so avidly followed; and also why the corresponding women are so womanly. Wolfenstein and Leites are especially good on analyzing these matters; they derive their analyses from the Oedipus situation, which makes them a bit one-sided, but not the less keen and accurate.

Oddly enough, we are beginning to learn that the male role, as it is played in our society—strong, silent, undisclosing—makes men sick. And as women become more manly, they get men's illnesses.

I'm enclosing mimeographed versions of two papers that touch on some of these matters. Also, in my book "Personal Adjustment. An Approach

Through the Study of Healthy Personality" (Macmillan, 1958), I give a brief run-down on the matter of sex-roles that may be pertinent. (pp. 168-172).

Pardon my curiosity—in what fields do you write? Novels, plays, TV? I'd like to read your work.

Sincerely,

Sidney M. Jourard, PhD

SMJ/dw

Sid's employment situation in Birmingham was coming to a close at the same time as his book was accepted by The Macmillan Company, with the final title *Personal Adjustment: An Approach Through the Study of Healthy Personality.*

Abraham Maslow and the Third Force

A primary influence on Sid's psychology and in living his life were the writings of Abraham Maslow (1908-1970), a psychologist whose 1954 book *Motivation and Personality* introduced to a wide audience his theory of human motivation, based on a five-tiered Model of Human Needs, known as Maslow's Hierarchy of Needs. How Maslow arrived at this conceptualization is the story of the Third Force in psychology.

The term Third Force refers to an alternative view of humankind that grew out of interaction between thoughtful psychologists, psychiatrists and others in the social sciences. The two prevailing psychological models at this time were embodied in motivation theories. What motivated human behavior? Freud's theory of motivation viewed humans as being controlled by deep inner drives formed by early experiences that were resilient but could be changed or controlled with psychoanalysis, a lengthy uncovering of these deeply-buried determiners. The Behaviorist view was that the external environment controlled all human and animal behavior, and life was essentially a series of pairings of Stimulus-Response phenomena.

Guided by Charles Darwin's claim of humankind being an accidental advance from the lower animals, behaviorists focused on experiments with animals, easier than humans to shock or starve to get measurable responses. Abraham Maslow comments in his book *Motivation and Personality*:

We must get over the psychology of the *desperate* rat, the rat who is pushed to the point of starvation, or who is pushed by pain or electric shock into an extreme situation, one so extreme that human beings seldom find themselves in it. (Some such work has been done with monkeys and apes).[5]

The father of behaviorism, John Watson, learned of Pavlov's dogs who, while being fed would hear a tuning fork, and would then salivate at the sound of a tuning fork even though they received no food, a physiological response known as conditioned reflex. Focusing on this, Watson studied and promoted stimulus-response learning as a major explanation for human behavior. Watson was dismissive of higher consciousness in general. "Personality is the sum of activities that can be discovered by actual observation of behavior over a long enough time to give reliable information. In other words, personality is but the end product of our habit systems."[6] B.F.Skinner affirmed this view of humans when writing "The only differences I expect to see revealed between the behavior of rats and man (aside from enormous differences in complexity) lie in the field of verbal behavior."[7] To a classic behaviorist, consciousness per se could not be studied scientifically and as a factor in measurable human behavior behaviorists assigned no value to it, wrote it out of existence, and were unwilling to acknowledge consciousness as an influence in behavior; yet consciousness—the fact of awareness by the mind of itself and the world—was a state that anyone you asked would say existed. Behaviorists also tended to present findings referring to the "average person," defined as the result of a statistical analysis.

In the early fifties a group of academics began meeting who were interested in another line of enquiry. Among them was Abraham Maslow, initially a behaviorist who gradually swung in the opposite direction.

> If the motivational life consists essentially of a defensive removal of irritating tensions, and if the only end product of tension–reduction is a state of passive waiting for more unwelcome irritations to arise and in their turn, to be dispelled, then how does change, or development or movement or direction come about? Why do people improve? Get wiser? What does zest in living mean?[8]
>
> When we examine people who are predominantly growth-motivated, the coming-to-rest conception of motivation becomes completely useless. In such people gratification breeds increased rather than decreased motivation, heightened rather than lessened excitement. The appetites become intensified and heightened. They grow upon themselves and

instead of wanting less and less, such a person wants more and more of, for instance, education. The person rather than coming to rest becomes more active. The appetite for growth is whetted rather than allayed by gratification. Growth is, *in itself,* a rewarding and exciting process, e.g., the fulfilling of yearnings and ambitions, like that of being a good doctor; the acquisition of admired skills, like playing the violin or being a good carpenter; the steady increase of understanding about people or about the universe, or about oneself; the development of creativeness in whatever field, or most important, simply the ambition to be a good human being.[9]

Maslow, a key influence in Sid's approach to psychology, was interested in a view of humankind that focused on aspects of health rather than neurosis or conditioned-response. Maslow was in turn influenced by Margaret Mead, Gardner Murphy, Rollo May, Carl Rogers, Kurt Goldstein, and Gordon Allport. Maslow's rather grandiose goal was to create a comprehensive theory of human behavior that would be used to promote peace. "I wanted to prove that human beings are capable of something grander than war and prejudice and hatred. I wanted to make science consider all the problems that non-scientists have been handling—religion, poetry, values, philosophy, art."[10]

Into this orientation ventured Maslow and a group of like-minded social scientists who were on Maslow's mailing list. At the surface it appeared to be unexplored territory in comparison to the Freudian and Behaviorist approaches. Humanist or humanistically-oriented psychology appealed to Sid's sense of adventure. Here was an area of psychological research where he could leave his mark. His strong background in methods of research in psychology meant he could follow up his hypotheses with scientific data generated by a study.

Sidney's Letters to Abraham Maslow

One can well imagine Sid's sense of isolation working in the Deep South under a department chairman whom he found intolerable. Understandably, Sid began a correspondence with Abraham Maslow.

May 29, 1956

A.H. Maslow
Dept. of Psychology
Brandeis University
Waltham, Mass.

Dear Dr. Maslow,

Thank you for the mimeo copies of a lecture that you gave in 10/18/54, and the copy of your essay in the motivation symposium.

I want to comment a bit on the lecture. This is one of the most beautiful expositions that I think I have come across, on the theme of psychological health. I wonder if it wouldn't be a valuable thing to submit the address, as is, perhaps to *Commentary,* or *Harper's,* or some such magazine for the intelligent and interested layman?

I must admit also that your writings about self-actualization have fallen on pretty receptive ground here. I have been teaching the conventional mental hygiene course here at Emory for five years, but after the first crack at teaching it, I found that the usual text was no more than a dilute abnormal psych text, and a review of psych 101—there was no conception of health explicitly defined. So over the past few years, I gradually worked up my course so that it became one that I now call the psychology of healthy personality. In it, I strove to define as explicitly as I could a definition of healthy personality. More recently, I wrote all this up in the form of a book, tentatively called The Psychology of Healthy Personality. Your writings are referred to very often. It should come out in a year or so from Macmillan; you may already have seen the MS, as I listed you as a prospective editor of the MS.

There is a physician in Washington, Dr. Steiglitz, who contributes to the journal Geriatrics, and is an editor of that journal, who is striving to do to physical medicine what we seem to be trying to do in psychology and psychiatry—namely, to develop a conception of optimum physical health, in order to facilitate "constructive medicine"—the concept of medicine as a field which doesn't just cure disease, but rather which regards people as animated deviations from ideal health—therapy consists in striving to narrow down this deviation.

I would greatly appreciate receiving from you any mimeo material or scales which you have found useful in identifying self-actualization. I plan to launch a project in the "measurement" of personality health when I get settled in my new job; since we seem to be moving along similar lines I would greatly enjoy exchanging ideas and suggestions with you. (after June 15, I'll be working in the Department of of Psychiatry, University Medical Center, Birmingham 3, Alabama.)

Looking forward to further contact...

Very sincerely.

Sidney M. Jourard

P.S. enclosed some reprints which you may find interesting

* * *

Dept. of Psychiatry
University Medical Center
Birmingham, Ala
June 14/56

Dear Dr. M

Thank you for your letter. Enclosed is Dr. E Steiglitz's address. He mentioned 2 books dealing with constructive medicine [both written by him:]

1. A future for preventive medicine
Commonwealth fund, 1945
2. The second forty years Lippincott
I am uncertain yet about attending APA, but will make every effort. I really look forward to talking at length with you.

Sincerely,
Sidney M. Jourard

P.S.—Looking forward to seeing your book "The Self"

SJ

* * *

THE UNIVERSITY OF ALABAMA
MEDICAL CENTER
BIRMINGHAM 3, ALABAMA

THE MEDICAL COLLEGE OF ALABAMA
DEPARTMENT OF PSYCHIATRY

August 13, 1956

Dr. A H. Maslow
Dept. Of Psychology
Brandeis University
Waltham, Mass.

Dear Dr. Maslow,

The cat is out of the bag. I am not supposed, as the author of a
manuscript, to know the identity of the critical reader whom the publisher
engages. However, the identity is fairly screamed from the wonderful
intensive and extensive critique which I have just received. Earlier, you wrote
me that you had seen the Introduction, and I had assumed that you read
it, and then returned the MS to Macmillan for someone else to go over. I
am proud and delighted to have been lucky enough to get your editorial
suggestions. Thank you for the interest and care which you gave.

It's too soon for me to know how well I can do justice to the criticisms
and suggestions which you made, but I am eager to get the MS back in order
to get started.

In a slow and roundabout way, I am trying to get a research program
set up in order to devise explicit criteria and outlines for describing and
evaluating persons from a "health" point of view. The whole procedure really
could be facilitated if I had some colleagues, which I don't. What I have to
do, evidently, is apply for a grant large enough to hire some colleagues, or
else piddle along on my own. Another alternative is to try to move to some
place such as Berkeley, or other similar setting, where there is already a
group of personality-researchers who might be willing to tackle the project
in much the same way as the "Authoritarian Personality" project was done. I
have to admit that I got much of the impetus for this line of work from your
writings—although that too was roundabout. The ground was prepared
by my training at Toronto; I read a lot of your material over the years. My
interest in healthy personality felt as if it was born *sui generis* in myself—
which I suppose is the way most ideas clearly seen and felt are experienced.

This is my first time at working in a medical school setting. It's quite different from an academic setting, In time, I may not like it, but at the present, I have no real gripes, except for the bland assumption of my chief that "everyone who comes to the clinic is helped," and the law that I must not conduct therapy, except some time in the future, and then under the supervision of one of the psychiatrists.

I am going to try to get to Chicago and will certainly look you up. I'd like to talk more about the book with you.

Best wishes,
Sidney M. Jourard

* * *

August 28, 1956

Dr. Sidney M. Jourard
The University of Alabama
Medical Center
Department of Psychiatry
Birmingham 3, Alabama

Dear Dr. Jourard:

I think you have an excellent manuscript even though, of course, I think it can be improved as I suggested. I must say that I consider it publishable right now and it is always a question as to which is more worthwhile—to publish now and make improvements for the revised edition or to delay publication for a time in the hope of making the first edition less vulnerable to criticism.

I will be at Chicago and would enjoy very much talking with you both about your book and about your research project. It sounds extremely interesting. We have planned something of the sort ourselves which I can tell you about.

I will be at the Hotel Sherman from September 1-4. Will you look for me there.

Cordially,

A. H. Maslow, Chairman
Department of Psychology

AHM/bg

* * *

Feb 9/57

Dear Dr. Maslow,

I received a batch of materials from a Finnish fellow at Harvard along with a note to the effect that my name was on a list which you provided him of those interested in creativeness, 'self-being,' etc. A long time ago you had mentioned that you would send me such a list, and both of us have evidently forgotten. Do you have an available copy of this list. I would really like to "j'ine up" with the group.

My work is plodding along. After I sent my healthy-personality manuscript off, I tried to get a project under way in the objective assessment of personality-health. This was discouraged effectively, and so I have dropped it for the time being, and will resume it in some other setting. Meanwhile, I have begun a project which is interesting, and which may bring out some good data. I have devised a simple, even simple-minded questionnaire for the assessment of "real-self communication."

The question I am asking is, "What aspects of the real self have you communicated, or made known, to various significant other persons?" Preliminary results show considerable variability both within persons and between groups of persons for aspects of self and for target-persons. There is the possibility that total scores gotten from the questionnaire will prove to be related to other meaningful psychological variables. Right now, I am simply undertaking comparisons between white and colored male and female subjects on aspects of self that have been communicated, and on targets. I have found a collaborator as well—a research-minded sociologist out of Northwestern who found his way to Birmingham. He is interested in the approach for its relevance to role-theory.

The extent to which persons make themselves known to others, in quantitative as well as qualitative terms, ought to be of interest to clinical psychologists, students of interpersonal relations, etc. It seems to have clear personality-health implications. I have cases of persons who readily admit on my questionnaire that they have made themselves known to nobody, including family, friends, spouse, closest friends, etc.

I'm enclosing a copy of the questionnaire and the answer-sheet which I am presently using. You can see that there is lots of room for changing it—e.g., using different aspects of the self, different target-persons, etc. The overall questionnaire has a reliability coefficient of .94 based on a combined male and female sample of 70 cases. Preliminary data show, among other things, that all subjects—white and colored males and females communicated less to their father than their mother, male friend, and female friend; ignoring targets, all subjects communicate about equally about attitudes, tastes and work—to a relatively high degree. Significantly less do they talk to all targets about money, personality, and body.

Best wishes
Sidney M. Jourard

* * *

THE UNIVERSITY OF ALABAMA
MEDICAL CENTER
BIRMINGHAM 3, ALABAMA

THE MEDICAL COLLEGE OF ALABAMA
DEPARTMENT OF PSYCHIATRY

February 18, 1957

Dr. A H. Maslow
Dept. Of Psychology
Brandeis University
Waltham 54, Massachussetts

Dear Abe:

Looking forward to getting a copy of the list of people. If I didn't tell you before, I'll tell you now; I think it's an excellent idea for all these congenial folks to exchange their ideas. At this end it helps to overcome some of the sense of isolation.

Macmillan's tells me that the book will be definitely out for spring 1958, and possibly by January 1958.

Best wishes,
Sid
SIDNEY M. JOURARD, Ph. D.

SMJ/er

* * *

THE UNIVERSITY OF ALABAMA
MEDICAL CENTER
BIRMINGHAM 3, ALABAMA

THE MEDICAL COLLEGE OF ALABAMA
DEPARTMENT OF PSYCHIATRY

May 14/57

Dear Abe,

I was very pleased to receive from you a copy of the APA address. I was present when you read the paper at the meetings, but I got much more from the written version because of all the distractions at the meetings like noise, hang-over from the last-night party, etc.

I am enclosing carbon-drafts of papers based on the self-disclosure studies that I've been doing here, with my sociological colleague Lasakow. I hope you can read them. I hoped to be able to mimeo them and send them to many of the folks on the list, but unfortunately, am not able to right at this time. The research papers have been submitted to J abn soc Psychol., and I sent the essay to Psychiatry. Don't know yet whether they are acceptable for publication.

The self-disclosure variable grows on you. So far, we have just scratched at some of the more obvious group variables. In time, more specific predictions should become possible. The area I would like systematically to explore is "maladjustment" in relation to self-disclosure, and to see what changes in s-d follow from effective psychotherapy.

Took the bull by the horns, and submitted my resignation from this department last month—it becomes effective on June 1st. So far, I am still investigating a number of leads, but have nothing definite lined up yet. Probably it was foolhardy to resign before having another job lined up, but I had to state my intentions about next year, and so I decided to let my chief know them.

If you should chance to know of any openings in an academic setting with a graduate program, I'd appreciate learning of them.

Best wishes
Sid
Sidney M. Jourard

In Sidney's book *Personal Adjustment,* Abraham Maslow's work is referenced thirty-seven times, second only to psychoanalyst Erich Fromm.

Sid recalled how the book came to be published by Macmillan:

> I wanted to call the first edition, back in 1958, *Healthy Personality,* and the publishers prevailed upon me and I yielded—a terrible mistake. They wanted to call it *Personal Adjustment,* but it wasn't a book about adjustment, it's a book about healthy personality. An interesting connection with the first edition, the publishers asked me who did I want to read this first edition manuscript. Well, grandiose, I said I'd like, in rank order—I had no rank order, but I wouldn't mind if Abe Maslow or Robert White from Harvard would read it and a couple others, and they said they would try. About six months later I received a forty-page typescript single-spaced commentary of my book, line by line, and it became apparent from the comments made that this is Maslow, so the book finally came out, and you know, I really benefited from, [Maslow] really made helpful, larger perspective comments, and I incorporated what I could and I wrote him a letter saying, I think you were the critical reader, now own up, were you? He owned up and we stayed in touch. He liked it because I had what he—he didn't use the word at the time but a humanistic orientation, and he confirmed me in the book. I was very grateful to him for that, and that grew one way or another in the Association for Humanistic Psychology, so I dedicated this last [edition of the] book, *Healthy Personality,* to Abe Maslow.

Maslow's ideas were circulated through his "mailing list," and Sid was among those on this list, primarily psychologists frustrated with the negative orientation of the social sciences. A 1960 letter from Maslow at Brandeis University to Sid shows this involvement.

October 12, 1960

Dear Sid,

Do you have any information on whether self-disclosure makes people more likeable. Do you have any information on self-disclosure as a technique for breaking down antagonisms or for creating a better interpersonal relationship with a disliked person or an antagonistic person?

Do you know Sorokin's experiment in which deliberate behavior of friendliness toward a disliked person made both people feel more friendly to each other?

I have been lecturing about your ideas and these questions came up. They suggest simple but important experiments.

See you in January.

Cordially.
A.H. Maslow
Department of Psychology

A New Start in a New Town

In 1957 Sid visited Gainesville, Florida for a job interview as adviser to the nursing staff of the J. Hillis Miller Health Center, a new teaching and hospital facility and part of the School of Medicine at the University of Florida. According to a history of the University of Florida's Department of Psychology:

> A grant program in the newly established College of Nursing in 1958 led to the employment of Sidney M. Jourard as Associate Research Professor in the College of Nursing, with the objectives of determining how the field of psychology might be brought into application to the training of nurses in a medical center setting, and how a psychologist might relate to a nursing college faculty. Although the grant program with which Sid was employed entailed working within the College of Nursing, he readily and rapidly identified himself with the Psychology Department and found the fellow psychologists here to be his primary colleagues. When the grant expired he came over to the Department staff and budget as an "In House" member.[11]

Sixteen years later, Sid recalls this job description in less formal wording:

> In the nursing college I had no teaching responsibilities. I was hired on part of a grant that different colleges of nursing obtained to—this jargon is hideous—"to integrate mental health and psychiatric concepts into the curriculum and practice of nursing"—have you ever heard such bullshit in your life? And nobody knew what it meant, so I thought what it meant was to help nursing teachers—teachers of nursing—become human beings. I tried to discern in what way they departed. You know, some parts of my career have been hilarious, you know. High comedy in a way, and yet a tragedy is in it, it's just I had sort of a wry sense of humor. So my duty, which paid me enough salary so I could devote myself to research, was to

try to help the nursing faculty, to train or educate nurses without robbing them, or threaten them out of their human compassion, so that instead of imitating what they thought doctors were supposed to be like, they could be warm human beings, and to some extent that project worked out. In the meantime I continued doing my self-disclosure research and writing. I also had an appointment with the psychology department without salary, but they encouraged joint appointment and I actually insisted on it, but it was policy anyway, and I taught one course per semester or quarter.

Based on Sid's recollections, there was no dividing line between his intellectual pursuits and his spirit.

I was bursting with ideas at this time. I was so turned on it was just coming out my ears because I knew this whole idea of self-disclosure was related to everything under the sun and I was interested, and still am [1974] in pursuing it, and so I taught a course each semester in the psychology department; I did my work in the nursing college. I always kept a small private practice going which was important to me because psychotherapy is an area of mine where I learn, and sort of I'm growing into, and it helped me feel that I didn't need to be intimidated. I made a vow that I would never be intimidated by my university administration, and I stuck to it, and that helped me make it less economically suicidal to challenge administration, and so I got on with my work in those four years, and they were very productive years.

Potential For Growth   5

SIDNEY'S ACADEMIC PATH had led him from Toronto to Buffalo, then to Atlanta and Birmingham, and finally to Gainesville and the University of Florida, a gradual migration into the Deep South based solely on job offers. Sid was searching for an academic and cultural environment better suited to his research interests and personality, one that had clashed with administrators at both of the previous universities where he had been employed. In the first month of 1958 Sid moved to Gainesville. Aside from two academic sabbaticals, he lived there the rest of his life.

Gainesville was a geographically-isolated southern college town of thirty thousand in a far corner of the country, yet the university was a well-regarded research center and a member of the Association of American Universities, consisting solely of leading research universities. Sid was hired by the College of Nursing to guide the curriculum for the instruction of nurses at the new J. Hillis Miller Health Center. The content of this curriculum was outlined in the vaguest of terms. For Sid, this was a promising situation.

Sid arrived with strong academic credentials. He had ten research studies published in a variety of academic journals.[1] His *Scientific American* article on self-disclosure was published a few months after his arrival; his book *Personal Adjustment: An Approach Through the Study of Healthy Personality* combined a survey of personality theory with Sid's perspective on aspects of healthy personality.

His state university assistant professor salary of five hundred dollars a month was one motivator of his writing, not just for book royalty income but to aid in achieving tenure as a professor as embodied in the phrase "publish or perish." Sid worried about money in a general sense and eventually determined that writing books, teaching, lecturing, and continuing his private practice had the potential to generate a satisfactory income. Sid earned all his income from writing, speaking, and listening.

Symptoms of Healthy Personality

In the Preface of *Personal Adjustment* Sid describes how the book grew from a course he taught at Emory University from 1951 to 1956 on Mental Hygiene, and how the questions from his students inspired an interest in the meaning of healthy personality.

> Many times, the students asked the instructor the very specific questions: "We are getting a good idea of what maladjustment looks like, but what does good adjustment look like? What is mental health? What is healthy personality? " These were embarrassing questions, and they were answered evasively: "We can't really answer; people differ very much from each other; what is good adjustment for one person may be bad adjustment for another."
>
> But then an idea became implanted in the author's mind. Perhaps one could regard healthy personality as an expression of *values*. Unhealthy personality—mental illness—refers to behavior which is negatively valued by society, and usually by the patient. It this were so, then the obverse should also be true: healthy personality should reflect the best values for man which prevail in society. When the problem was stated in this fashion, it became possible to survey relevant literature in which students of personality attempted to spell out their concepts of man's potential for growth. The writings of Freud, Fromm, Horney, Maslow, Reisman, Rank, Mowrer—to name but a few—provided a virtually untapped mine for this purpose.
>
> This book, then is an attempt to describe the "symptoms" of healthy personality. In addition to description, an attempt is made wherever possible to explain how personality health is achieved, by pointing out the independent variables of which it is a function.[2]

Operating from this theme, Sid explored the obverse of unhealthy personality—healthy personality, and beyond that, what he often referred to as "magnificence," human activity difficult to measure using the methods of natural science yet evidently recognizable in behavior and through the humanities, in physical achievement and endurance; a worthy subject for psychological study, one that Sid felt was relatively unexplored.

Fiction and the arts provided examples not available in the academic canon. On the shelf in his home office alongside works of Freud, Jung, Sartre, Kierkegaard, Nietzsche, Buber, Heidegger, Fromm, Rank and other social scientists were narrative accounts by persons who faced and conquered extreme physical and psychological hardships: Ernest Shackleton's *South*; *Alone in the Antarctic* by Admiral Richard E. Byrd, *The Worst Journey in the World* by Appsley Cherry-Garrard; *Gypsy Moth Sails Around the World* by Sir Frances Chichester, *Congo Kitabu* by Jean-Pierre Hallet, a Belgian naturalist and humanitarian; *Annapurna* by mountaineer Maurice Herzog; the tales of Joseph Conrad and Jack London, stories of nautical adventure and hard-fought survival in the Yukon.

What drove these people to push against the outer edges of life, and which traits allowed them to survive? How did Ernest Shackleton and his crew live through the hardships of the Antarctic? Sidney found these stories intriguing. Although a person very much aware of and in his body, Sid was essentially an academic and may have envied the purity of these intense physical struggles with Nature, of survival against the odds, the mythical journey and return of Odysseus told in modern form. Through these stories Sid hoped to locate the source of motivation and strength demonstrated by these adventurers. Some chose their struggles, others faced them unexpectedly, but all survived to tell the tale.

Sid also enjoyed reading the fictional adventures of Mickey Spillane's detective Mike Hammer, Raymond Chandler's Philip Marlowe and Ian Fleming's James Bond. These broad characterizations revealed deeper truths about masculine roles in society, and reading such light fiction served as a welcome break from his academic research and writing. To Sidney both areas of reading revealed various aspects of the human condition.

Personal Adjustment

Much of Sidney's professional life consisted of exploring traits of healthy personality, seeking the answer to the ageless question posed by religion and philosophy alike: "How should one live?" Sid came to believe that healthy personality consisted of more than the absence of neuroses and more than successful assimilation into culture and society. Sid's private psychotherapy practice allowed him to apply his theories of personal growth in a clinical setting and he received immediate feedback from his patients as to the success or ineffectiveness of his methods.

In the first chapter of *Personal Adjustment*, Sid draws a distinction between physical health and mental health: the mind, unlike the body, cannot be examined in terms of visible signs of health. Rather than using the term *mental health*, one that had replaced the earlier *mental hygiene*, Sid proposes the term *healthy personality*, then presents traits of personality health as described in Abraham Maslow's self-actualizing model, Freud's capacity for love and work, Carl Rogers's fully-functioning person, Wilhelm Reich's orgastic potency, William Blatz's independent security, Harry Stack Sullivan's non-parataxic interpersonal relations, Erich Fromm's productive orientation, Karen Horney's self realization, and Otto Rank's creativity.

In Chapter Two Sid describes healthy personality as embodying traits that enable individuals to gratify their needs through behavior that is personally and socially acceptable.

In the following chapters this view of healthy personality is examined in reference to needs, reality-contact, emotions, sexual behavior, interpersonal behavior and relationships, love, self-structure, defenses, conscience and guilt, the body, and therapy. In a final chapter Sid describes how therapy can promote healthy personality, and clarifies the term *healthy adjustment* as referring to "those efforts on the part of a person to effect a rational cure of psychological suffering. In principle, there are two broad modes of adjustment possible to the individual: changing the structure of the self or changing the structure of the environment. The former is referred to as *autoplastic* adjustment, while the latter is *alloplastic* adjustment."

From what we know of Sid's reasons for leaving Birmingham the next passage sounds self-referential:

> ...a person may find himself suffering because of the way in which his work environment is set up. He does not like the physical or the social arrangements in his work situation. He may devote his skills and efforts to altering these arrangements; if these fail, then he might seek another position where work can be accomplished at a lesser sacrifice of ease, productivity, and comfort, and where an unhealthy change in the self is not required.[3]

By leaving Birmingham and moving to the University of Florida Sid had made an alloplastic adjustment. There are healthy and unhealthy adjustments in both categories, and Sid concludes that "adjustment' to societal norms is not necessarily an indication of a healthy personality, and in many cases implies that adjustment can be harmful in that regard. The term *adjustment* is now no longer used in reference to healthy personality.

Working

Conforming to the status quo, either academic or social, was not in Sid's character. His father had left his previous life behind when fleeing the army to find a less threatening environment. Sid's problem fitting in was never a matter of competence but of personal style and conflict with social structures he could not or would not adapt to. At the University of Florida he found his place in a liberal academic and social environment.

When he joined the faculty at the University he became fully engaged in lecturing, writing, speaking engagements, research and communicating research results in published articles. His earlier experience in Buffalo speaking to various social groups improved his verbal communication skills which led to his writing style becoming less academic and more direct in style. Sid understood the power of the written word, and that ideas not clearly communicated had little chance of influencing others. He began to flourish. On November 20, 1958 Sid spoke to the North Florida section of the American Personnel and Guidance Association in a presentation that was later published in *Mental Hygiene* and was the basis for a chapter in his next book *The Transparent Self*.

In January of 1959 he presented "Away With the Bedside Manner!" to the Faculty Training Group at the College of Nursing, followed the next month with "Getting Mental Health Into Nursing," published later in the journal *Canadian Nurse*. In April he presented "Conversations between Psychology and Theology" to the Presbyterian Student Center at the University. Later in the month he presented "I-Thou Relationship versus Manipulation in Counseling and Psychotherapy" in St. Augustine at the Southeast Psychological Association symposium on Behavioristic Approaches to Counseling and Psychotherapy, subsequently published in the *Journal of Individual Psychology*. A mainstream article "Do You Make Yourself Known to Others?" appeared in the May 3rd, 1959 Sunday newspaper supplement *All Florida Magazine*.

Sid's research into aspects of healthy personality even received attention from the Federal government. Sid was hired for a two year period in 1958 by the National Office of Vital Statistics, resulting in "Notes on the Quantification of Wellness."[4] In order to quantify traits of healthy personality Sid created a scale of descriptions; in attempting to quantify marital health, he offered these various levels of health or lack of health in a marital relationship:

1. Feels a complete failure as a spouse. Gets no satisfactions out of being a spouse.

2. Can perform marital role with borderline adequacy, gets no enjoyment out of it.

3. Adequate as a spouse, gets more satisfactions than frustrations out of it.

4. Adequate as a spouse, gets positive satisfaction out of it.

5. Adequate as a spouse, the relationship is growing.

It was through this quantifiable approach to aspects of human relations that research into healthy personality was deemed scientific, generating hard data even a behaviorist could recognize.

By the early sixties Sid and family moved to a larger home close to the university campus and Sid rode to and from classes on an Italian Lambretta motor scooter. He once brought Timothy Leary home on the back of this scooter while Leary was still a Harvard professor.

1960 began with publication of "The Bedside Manner" in the *American Journal of Nursing*. Sidney presented three more academic papers during the year, two in Atlanta for the Southeast Psychological Association and one for the National Student Nurses Association in Miami Beach, "To Whom Can a Nurse Give Personalized Care?," all serving as the basis for chapters in his next book.

The American Association for Humanistic Psychology

Psychology embodies a vast field of enquiry into the human condition. Following the Second World War, Humanistic Psychology began to form in the mid-fifties as a reaction against the two prevailing approaches in psychology—psychoanalysis and behaviorism, the former emphasizing past experiences as guiding current behavior, and the latter focusing on the external control of current behavior. Psychologist Floyd Matson viewed humanistic psychology as a reaction against behaviorism's rejection of psychology's focus on consciousness:

There have been, as I believe, three distinct conceptual revolutions in psychology during the course of the present century. The first, that of behaviorism, struck with the force of a revelation around 1913 and shook the foundations of academic psychology for a generation. Behaviorism arose in reaction to the excessive preoccupation of 19th-century psychology with consciousness, and with introspection as a way of getting at the data of conscious mental activity. The behaviorists reacted with a vengeance. They threw out not only consciousness, but all the resources of the mind. The mind, to them, was the ghost in the machine, and they did not believe in ghosts. The founding father of the movement, John B. Watson, declared in an early proclamation, a kind of behaviorist manifesto, that the behaviorist began "by sweeping aside all medieval conceptions. He dropped from his scientific vocabulary all subjective terms such as sensation, perception, image, desire, purpose, and even thinking and emotion as they were subjectively defined. [5]

The second revolution was that of Freud and psychoanalysis. Whereas behaviorism placed all its stress upon the external environment (that is, upon stimuli from the outer world) as the controlling factor in behavior, psychoanalysis placed its emphasis upon the internal environment (upon stimuli from within, in the form of drives and repressed instincts). Either way, the person was viewed as determined by controlling factors. Humanistic psychology was born as a reaction against both these deterministic views of the human condition.

Sid increasingly identified with this emerging movement through his readings of Carl Rogers, Rollo May and Abraham Maslow, who along with Anthony Sutich in 1961 founded the American Association for Humanistic Psychology, later renamed the Association for Humanistic Psychology (AHP). From the Articles of Association:

> *Humanistic Psychology* may be defined as the third main branch of the general field of Psychology (the two already in existence being the psychoanalytical and the behavioristic) and as such, is primarily concerned with those human capacities and potentialities that have no systematic place, either in positivistic or behavioristic theory or in classical psychoanalytic theory, e.g., creativity, love, self, growth, organism, basic need-gratification, self-actualization, higher values, being, becoming, spontaneity, play, humor, affection, naturalness, warmth, ego-transcendence, objectivity, autonomy, responsibility, psychological

health, and related concepts. This approach can also be characterized by the writings of Goldstein, Fromm, Horney, Rogers, Maslow, Allport, Angyal, Bühler, Moustakas, *etc.,* as well as by certain aspects of the writings of Jung, Adler, and the psychoanalytic ego-psychologists, existential and phenomenological psychologists.

In that same year the *Journal of Humanistic Psychology* began publication. The second issue presented Sid's paper "Sex In Marriage," one of five he wrote in the first nineteen issues.

In April Sid was in Gatlinburg, Tennessee presenting a talk at the Southeastern Psychological Association on "The Phenomenon of Resistance in the Psychotherapist," adapted as a chapter in his next book. In this paper Sid explains how his behavior as a therapist

> has changed slowly, but radically, over the past couple of years. I am as good a listener as I ever was, perhaps better. My capacity for empathy and my over-all judgment are both greater now than they were earlier. I reflect feelings and content as I always did, but only when I want the patient to know what I heard him say. In fact, I agree with [Carl] Rogers that there is no better way to tell a patient you heard him, and this acknowledged listening seems to reinforce further disclosing of *his* being from him. But I find myself sometimes giving advice, lecturing, laughing, becoming angry, interpreting, telling my fantasies, asking questions—in short, doing whatever occurs to me *during* the therapeutic session in response to the other person. This change could mean either that I am growing as a person and as a therapist, or else that, through lack of close supervision, I am losing in "discipline." Yet, I do discuss my work with colleagues, and I am not isolated.[6]

A Different Approach

This unorthodox engagement with the patient was radical in the early '60s and remains so today, requiring an intuitive stance from the therapist that necessitates a balanced combination of skills. In a clinical setting the sum of Sid's spirit and intellect was a subtle balancing act, as he admits:

> My actual disclosures to the patient are still checked by common sense or by my judgment (I sometimes suspect that this is automatic and unconscious checking, though I realize this sounds mystical), but increasingly I find myself being more unpremeditated and spontaneous in

my responses to the patient. It is as if I am coming more to trust myself, as if I trust that what comes out of me in response to a patient will not harm him or create a situation with which I cannot cope. This does not mean I am anti-intellectual, because I am not. Rather, it seems that, just as I can hear with a "third ear," I can sometimes listen to my "second voice"—the voice of my spontaneous response.[7]

With few if any precedents for this therapeutic approach it was heady stuff in 1961. Perhaps his years of clinical experience gave Sid the courage to try it. Maybe it occurred out of boredom. But it began to grow as an idea.

Sid's observation of human behavior was not limited to formal research studies. Here is a handwritten note, dated 7/7/1961:

On Identification

My middle child, Marty, (6 yrs, 10 mos.) has been saying all summer, "Daddy, I wish I was you."

(Why?) "Because you're better, you have better muscles, you're smarter and you just look better."

(What's wrong with you?) "I'm little, I don't have muscles, my face doesn't look good, I'm skinny... everything has gone bad, just the way I didn't want it"

(How did you want it?) "I wanted muscles, to be not skinny, and have everything go right."

(What else don't you like about you?) "That's all, and I need a new bike, mine is so little. Everything has just gone wrong."

When the four-year grant for his teaching role at the School of Nursing expired in 1962 the Dean of the Nursing College offered a choice to Sid, who recalls the dean telling him

"Do you want to stay in nursing, we will make you Assistant Dean, you can do anything you want," and I thought it was time for me to go back among the sharks and wolves, my colleagues. Well, to me it got increasingly unrewarding to be in the medical setting. I had given what I had to give, I thought, received what I wanted to receive in the way of time and opportunity, and my career was in psychology, so I went over to the Psych department, was put on salary there, and there I've been ever since.

Building E

Sid moved from the School of Nursing to the Psychology Department. Located behind the Administration Building, Building E was a rambling single-story wooden building, one of many such structures transported from an army barracks to the campus in 1948 that, although designated as temporary, were in use for thirty-five years.

Sid's office was the setting for his private practice and meetings with students; a room filled with books and academic journals, papers to be read or reviewed, in-and-out trays for correspondence, a manual typewriter, pipe rack and ashtray, a fan. As Florida was hot and humid and the building had no air-conditioning, the windows facing the sidewalk were usually open for ventilation. Sid enjoyed this nominal academic workspace with its connection to the street and daily human activity, as students walked by between classes. When in 1972 the department moved to a modern multistory brick building, he was not happy with his isolated office setting on an upper floor. Sid preferred being connected to the natural environment.

Corresponding

Much of the routine communication during Sid's professional life was through the exchange of letters. Long distance phone rates were expensive at the time, but a first class stamp was four cents, and the postal system permitted domestic exchanges between parties in two or three days. The nature of this medium allowed for thoughtful and often lengthy dialogues, as well as providing a more intimate view of the personalities and ideations of the writers.

One such exchange occurred between Sid and psychologist O. Hobart Mowrer.[8] Sid's initial letter is critical of Mowrer's new book *The Crisis in Psychiatry and Religion*.

September 25, 1962

Dr. O. Hobart Mowrer
Department of Psychology
University of Illinois
Urbana, Illinois

Dear Hobart:

I am still engaged in a careful reading of the Crisis book. To anticipate a more detailed reaction, let me say that I endorse your assertions about the therapeutic power of disclosure or confession plus subsequent restitution and more open, authentic being-with (or being-against) others. More emphasis needs to be placed on the health-engendering or health-undermining effects of a patient's (or sinner's) way of life following his acknowledgment of what he has done, what he thinks, feels, etc.

I disagree vigorously about a couple of things, viz: what I regard as ad hominem arguments with Freud to strengthen the acceptance of your position, viz: Freud as the Devil, observations about his motives for constructing the system of psychoanalysis, etc.

Another point I will make is that you have moved into as monolithic a position or theory of illness as Freud officially upheld. The sin, or conscience-repression theory is, without doubt, valid to explain some (not all) neuroses. There are still neuroses and there is still suffering arising from needless frustration of basic needs, the frustration ensuing from guilt or fear associated with anger or lust.

Your emphasis on openness, and authentic fellowship is salutary, but your views, by omission, seem to be "anti-pleasure." I think Maslow does a better job of tying together the biological basis of behavior and health with the interpersonal and spiritual bases. What is your view of the role of "basic-need" gratification in healthy personality? Once I heard you paraphrase Shaw, I think it was, to the effect that "marriage is a lustful institution"— this you said, I think, to answer some question about how man can find legitimate gratifications without rupturing his sociality.

If we ask the question, "What does man need in order to attain and maintain healthy personality?," we can agree with you (as I do) that wholeness, authenticity in relation to his fellow man is surely one such factor; but so are various "lower-level" satisfactions. Indeed, courage to break out of confining subcultures and dyadic relations also seems to be such a factor. Perhaps this courage is fostered by a sustained dialogue with God, and sometimes it may be fostered through a dialogue with a therapist.

I hope we will have a chance for some good talk when you are here. I'd also like to have you meet my seminar in personal counseling, which meets on Tuesday morning, from 8:40 to about 10:00 a.m. If it's okay with you, I think Bernie will keep the schedule free for you to do this.

Best wishes,

S.M. Jourard
Associate Professor

P.S. Enclosed a reprint which I don't think I sent you, which articulates some of my views on openness and health.

* * *

September 27, 1962

Dr. O. Hobart Mowrer
Department of Psychology
University of Illinois
Urbana, Illinois

Dear Hobart:

I was in a pedantic frame of mind which ill becomes me when I wrote my last note to you. While I believe that the comments I made have some basis for them, I now see them as picayune beside the basic import of the substance of the Crisis book. You have had a tremendous insight into the basis for (neurotic and psychotic) suffering, and you have pursued it with enormous power. And you are following it wherever it takes you with risk and courage—and these are, in this day and age strange places for a man of Division 3 [APA Experimental Psychology category]. By "strange places," I mean serious reading of theology, study of Salvation Army and AA; and you are taking on formidable dragons—the American Psychiatric, literalists in religion. Marvelous! I salute you.

Any disagreements I might have with what you have written, on those matters of which I have some knowledge, are fundamentally minor in comparison with our point of accord. This pleases and encourages me no end, and I hope you hear me muttering, "That's right, he's right, good, yes, etc." in response to such passages as "…it is probably more discerning to say that he has been sick for some time and that what we now perceive as a manifest illness is really an inner revulsion against a duplicitous life style and an attempt…at correction and cure."

And, "…therapy must go beyond mere counseling to self-disclosure…to the significant others in one's life, and then on to active redemption…"

I admit to some little "shocks" at terminology, viz: redemption, Holy Spirit, etc., but I recognize these shocks as hangnails of the authoritarian conscience instilled by the Fausts who trained most of us, and I read you loud and clear.

When you get here, I would like to talk with you about the disintegration and re-attainment of physical health as well as of mental health. We may yet be able to prove something for which I have no rigorous laboratory evidence, but very strong clinical and everyday life observation, to the effect that the victims of various stress ailments, sudden heart attacks, etc. are as much downright liars to the significant others in their lives (and themselves) as neurotics.

There is no question but that the man who has stopped a duplicitous and contrived mode of life with others, and who starts to be authentic, taking all the blows that may come with it, will improve in overall physical health. Official medicine still places its reliance on pills and surgery, and only dispenses placebos to patients who are rather despised for responding to them. How many physicians (except some who happen to be good <u>men</u>) could we find who prescribe to a headache-ridden, ulcerated, low-resistance to flu patient, "Start being authentic."

Pasternak recognized the correlation between the necessity to be false, the necessity of semblance, and physical ills, such as coronary disease, in a passage in Dr. Zhivago. Pasternak himself retained his integrity, and lived to a reasonably ripe age.

Official medicine, as Rene Dubos has pointed out, hasn't licked the problem of preventing disease—though of course it has made strides in making many diseases less fatal. But official <u>medicine</u> spends <u>less</u> research money exploring the health-engendering and health-destroying effects of man's modes of relating to his fellows than it does on tranquilizer-research, a curious instance of brainwashing that is just as effective as Freud's powerful effect on psychologists and psychiatrists, making us overlook the moral or spiritual implications. Let's take on the AMA!

I wish I had been in attendance when you gave your lectures at the various seminaries. In the talks I've given at various religious centers, and to workshops on pastoral counselors, I have expounded, among other things, the observation that there is value in ministers themselves being simply human and authentic, and less seekers after the techniques of manipulation. I offer to instruct all ministers in brainwashing procedures and in mass hypnosis, as well as in the message-packaging techniques of Hidden Persuaders, and they decline, just as many decline the suggestion that they may be most effective by interacting with members of their congregation in a rather transparent, mutually disclosing manner.

I concur with your remarks about Bergman's dire predictions concerning the fate of the open man, and Bakan's "Pandora's Box." In fact, it may well be that the world can <u>only </u>be saved through mutual openness. The risk is tremendous, and the question always is, "Who takes the first step?"

Best wishes,
S.M. Jourard
Associate Professor

P.S. Just received your enclosures, and am looking forward to reading them.

***

October 8, 1962

Dr. Sidney M, Jourard
Department of Psychology
University of Florida
Gainesville, Florida

Dear Sid:

Thank you ever so much for your letters of September 25 and 27. It was particularly gracious of you to write the second letter so close on the heels of the first one.

In response to your first letter what I had intended to say was essentially this. Psychoanalysis preens itself as a science and condemns religion with its dogmas. However, so far as I can observe the analysts are about as big a bunch of dogmatists as ever came down the pike. Neither clinically, socially, nor in terms of specific research findings do I know of any substantial evidence for the doctrine of the overly severe superego, whereas evidence for inadequate conduct is profusely strewn about. With almost monotonous repetition, we find that the women who come into our group at the Galesburg State Research Hospital have guilty secrets of major proportions and that they often make dramatic recoveries when they admit to either deviations and sins and start <u>doing</u> something about them. However, it is not to be supposed that all "sick" people have been guilty of the more flamboyant types of sin: sex violations, brutality to children, thievery and dishonesty, etc. One also occasionally encounters disturbed people who, so far as can be determined, never did anything very actively wrong. However the point is, that neither did they ever do anything that was very actively <u>right</u>. I have in mind right now a young woman who is in our local group, here in Champaign-Urbana, whose principle sin seems to be that of irresponsibility and indolence. She just wants the world to feed and take care of her, as if she were an infant. When I began seeing her in August, she insisted that there was nothing that is seriously guilt-producing in her life and that her principal problem was and is irresponsibility. However this did not fully come home to me until she acted-out in this respect: she enrolled in school (as a graduate student in library science) and got a job as a laboratory technician. However, without telling me about this or even giving any intimation of it, she stopped going to classes and gave up her job, and just took off for the balance of the week to see relatives in various parts of the state. One just can't <u>do</u> this kind of thing and retain any kind of connectedness with society or peace with his own conscience. …With the exception, then, of <u>this</u> kind of "sinner," I don't see any reason to question the "monolithic" kind of theory which seems to me to be the acceptable one.

But both your second letter and the article entitled "Being with Others versus Manipulating Others" indicates that we are in much more fundamental agreement than your first letter perhaps suggested. Your article particularly whets my appetite to get at the other papers you recently sent me, and I hope to be able to do this on a trip to the University of Mississippi Medical School this coming week. Somewhere in this collection of papers I'm sure there is one which I hope to publish soon under the title of MORALITY AND MENTAL HEALTH. In fact, the paper just referred to would do very nicely in this connection if you don't plan to include it with the collection you're negotiating with the Van Nostrand people about.

I shall be only too happy to meet with your seminar on Tuesday morning, November 20. I've got several things I'd like to try out on the members of the group—and you. …

One final comment about your own writing, Sid. You have a precious capacity for vividness and impact in your communication. I'd love to see a whole book written by you in the free and open style of your September-27 letter. Incidentally, I took the liberty of sending a copy of these two letters to Dave Sparks: first, to let him read what I think is an extraordinarily penetrating appraisal of the CRISIS book and, second, to afford him this opportunity to get a little better acquainted with <u>you.</u> I hope you and he can get together on plans for some sort of an Insight book.

Yours most sincerely,
O.H.M

Body and Soul

Sid did correspond with Sparks, and his book *The Transparent Self* was published as part of Van Nostrand's Insight Books imprint, described by the publisher as "devoted to filling a vital need in the efficient study of human behavior."

There was little disparity between Sid's personal areas of interest and his activities as a psychology professor, lecturer, clinical practitioner and researcher. Although Sidney often said he found most people boring, to the point of admitting that he himself could be boring—he was fascinated with *Homo sapiens* as a category of study, as he was part of the study group himself.

As an individual and as a researcher, what was of interest to Sid? The attraction of the sexes, his attraction to women, the authentic identity of a person hidden behind public masks and actions; motives and behaviors driven by past events, the power of belief, the ends to which persons will go to have needs satisfied, or their true nature hidden, the varied ways consciousness could be expanded, chemically or otherwise. The subject was always people and the human condition.

Far from being a reclusive aesthete, Sid was highly social and would speak to anyone he found interesting, and was skilled at a line of enquiry that often led to a revealing response. His talent at mimicking accents and body gestures is an indication of his observational acuity and his interest in a person was genuine and disarming. The continual appeal of this area of scientific research was that anything he learned could be applicable to his own life, since, unlike behaviorists who studied the stimulus-response patterns of rabbits, monkeys and rats, Sid was studying the behavior of his own species. This enthusiasm blurred the boundaries between his professional research and his innate curiosity about other people's lives.

He would talk to anyone he thought could provide more information on the human condition. He would often talk with the African-American husband of our housekeeper (we called them maids back then), who told Sid of his visits to a root doctor in a nearby rural area. Sid found this area of belief deeply engaging. Each person represented a specific viewpoint of the world and each of these encounters enriched Sid's understanding of human motivation and behavior.

Along with this basic interest in other people was his interest in the physical world, of experiencing his body, a balance of mental and physical exertion that made for a fuller life. Sid's basic goal as a person was to integrate his intellectual and physical interests. The university campus and its proximity made this easy. After trying out golf and tennis, Sid found the game of handball the most satisfying, requiring only sneakers, gloves and a handball. After a day of teaching and other academic activities Sid often played handball on the university courts with a friend or in pickup games with students, happily reporting when he beat younger players and confessing when he'd been beaten by superior players he always called "sharks." After playing Sid would move to one of various bars and restaurants for refreshment. Having exercised mind, body and elbow Sid would drive home in his Triumph TR-3 and head directly for the living room sofa, where he would announce to no one in particular that he was "utterly zonked " and lay down for a nap, followed by dinner around eight. Reading, grading of papers, writing letters, socializing with sons and wife depending on availability and interest level from either parties, and then to bed. If he woke up in the night he would read or walk the few steps to his study and type or read.

This was Sid's basic routine as a professor and an individual, with intervals of travel around the country and overseas, lecturing, attending conferences, presenting papers. Sid's writing was steadily published, he was an effective lecturer, his undergraduate classes were popular. After several false starts he had found his academic milieu and was thriving.

Puerto Rico

In May of 1963 Sidney was employed for one month by the Peace Corps as a Field Assessment Officer.[9] Just two years old, the Peace Corps was directed by Sargent Shriver, John F. Kennedy's brother-in-law. Sid flew to Puerto Rico where he spent much of the month at Camp Crozier near Arecibo to study and create psychological profiles of the volunteers and make an assessment as to their suitability and ability to deal with overseas volunteer work. Whether by choice or design he participated in the physical training program, returning home with stories of jungle survival hiking, cliff and dam rappelling, the cooking and eating of insects for survival training, and drown-proofing, a method of surviving for long periods in the water. The final test for the latter included being placed in the water with hands and feet bound and staying afloat for a half an hour. He taught his sons this procedure, neglecting the constraints. During the month he also learned a smattering of Spanish.

Personal Adjustment and The Transparent Self

Personal Adjustment had received enough acceptance as a college textbook for Van Nostrand to request a revised edition, published in 1962. The book was reviewed in *Contemporary Psychology* along with two other books on the topic of "adjustment."

> Here is a skilled revision of a book originally published in 1958. While retaining the unique core of personality-health and reality-testing, the author has performed a critical distillation, rearranged, refined, and augmented to effect a polished text for undergraduate course in personality adjustment.

The naïve searcher after a check-list for instant personality regeneration will find that this book definitely eclipses his Sunday-supplement expectations. Yet, despite its level of sophistication, the text is a highly readable one and the revision made it more so. The logical development, the somewhat analytic flavor, and the uncomplicated style further this unconventional approach.

Rather than mental hygiene *per se* the theme remains that of describing healthy personality symptoms together with means, resources, and prognosis for achieving personal adjustment. The book takes a dendroidal form with its roots in the manifold concepts of the healthy personality as implied and proposed by Freud, Adler, Jung, Rank, Fromm, Sullivan, the existential philosophers, Maslow, Rogers, Ruesch, Baltz, Allport, the Zen Buddhists, and by Jourard's own formulation.

The broad-brush, but judicious, orientation provides the reader with a philosophical-psychological foundation for the discussion of the modes of behavior that promote personality health. Upon this base, the trunk-section unites measures of evaluation of the individual as a totality to include his needs, cognition, emotions, body-concept, self-structure, and conscience. From this stock, there is a branching out to inspect man in his varied interrelationships, with emphasis on those elements that nourish him.

Chapter integration is more apt than that of the previous edition. The treatment of many topics is more encompassing than one would anticipate. The roles of emotion, conscience, guilt and interpersonal relationships are often neglected or treated in dilute fashion in the more usual books devoted to adjustment; Jourard's singular approach affords ample discussion of these topics. The chapters guide the reader in with short introductions that preview the material and formulate questions to be answered therein. Pertinent examples punctuate the more difficult-to-associate sections.

Succinct summaries tie up the chapters exceedingly well. Interest is sustained throughout with possible slight exception in the two chapters on interpersonal behavior and interpersonal relationships; here the flow ebbs considerably. The notes and references following each chapter are extensive and specific; separate name and subject indices add convenience.

The unusual goal of the text is ably achieved. This is definitely not a book built around a list of defense mechanisms. It has done much to silence the comment that texts and courses concerning adjustment are dilute, insignificant and inconclusive.[10]

American Association for Humanistic Psychology

The American Association for Humanistic Psychology held its first convention on August 28th, 1963 at the Sheraton Hotel in Philadelphia, with over a hundred attendees. Highlights were described in the first issue of the AAHP newsletter *Phoenix*. As the first elected president, Sid was asked to answer the question What Lies Ahead?

PHOENIX Volume I Number 1 December 1963

Objectives Outlined
by Sidney M. Jourard

It seems to me that Humanistic Psychology will be best served if it is undergirded with research that seeks to throw light on the qualities of man that are uniquely human, rather than on qualities that he shares with rats, pigeons, or machines. These qualities are most likely to emerge if the subject in a study is involved in a dialogic relationship with E[xperimenter], such that he has no vested interest in concealing or faking his experience and responses in the experimental conditions. Now it seems that much of the research conducted on human subjects has been done under interpersonal conditions that foster self-concealment and faking on the part of the subjects. The subjects are usually low-status people being tested or observed or interviewed by a high-status investigator. The latter often emits nonverbal pleas or constraints which influence the S[ubject] such that his responses tend to confirm the expectation of the E. Recent work published by Rosenthal at Harvard points to this implication.

If it is true that nondialogic transactions between E and S yield findings that conceal or distort S's "true" reactions, it follows that much of our psychology as written tells us little about man in his more open, less guarded moments. Rather, it may be viewed as testimony to S's susceptibility to or compliance with E's wishes and pleas as these are expressed verbally and in various nonverbal ways.

I wonder what our psychology of learning, perception, motivation, neurosis, and personality would read like if key studies were replicated, first with E and S in the usual capacity of impersonal strangers, and then with E and S in dialogue—in a relation of I and Thou—such that S dropped his defenses and communicated his experience fully. My hunch is that such replication is <u>feasible</u>, and that if it is done increasingly, it might provide a corrective to the often dehumanized portrait of man that we find in most psychology textbooks.

The Transparent Self

During his early years at the University of Florida Psychology Department Sid wrote and presented a series of talks at various conferences and symposiums. These and other writings were edited and assembled into *The Transparent Self: Self Disclosure and Well-Being*. Sid received a $250 advance on August 2, 1963 against future royalties from the book; six months later it was listed in the New York Times Books Today column as one of four new books from Van Nostrand. The process leading to the book's creation was recalled by Sid:

> I was publishing papers on self-disclosure, bunches of them, theoretical and data, and then somewhere along the line Hobart Mowrer asked me for copies of things, and we entered into a correspondence and he had published *The Crisis of Psychiatry and Religion*, a little paperback book, and after reading my papers he wrote me saying, I talked to my editor and he thinks maybe you could put together a book because it's a series [Van Nostrand Insight] that is looking for the growing edge of someone's work, and it doesn't have to be a book with a beginning, middle and end, so I put together my papers and edited them a bit, and submitted them, and dreamed up a title, and they published it with a cover—I was so furious.

Sid's fury was caused by an unauthorized change in the cover art. Every aspect of his books held meaning for him, including the title and overall appearance. *The Transparent Self* was Sid's first book with cover art, and he had chosen a graduate student who was also an artist to read the manuscript and devise a cover

> ...and he drew really a lovely picture and it showed two sets of naked feet and legs against a stark background and masks had been dropped, and I liked it. When the book came out they had changed the naked feet, they were Harlequin shoes, and I wanted to take the book away from Van Nostrand, and so on, but in spite of that the book caught on with astonishing reception and the most astonishing enthusiastic reception at first came from Protestant clergymen.

Sid's writing on transparency and self-disclosure had connected with the clergy and pastoral counseling, an acknowledgment of the timely nature of his subject matter and the scarcity of other writings in this area of counseling. A review in *Faith At Work* magazine from August 1964 provides an insight into this appeal and points out how his thoughts affirmed the religious concept of faith as something beyond body and mind:

This is one of the most provocative little books we have seen in a long time. A compilation of papers by the Associate Professor of Psychology at the University of Florida, it advances several lines of scientific support for the theory that physical and mental health depend a great deal upon self-disclosure toward the "significant others" in one's life.

You'll get a dozen new insights from the book, and we predict that they will all be helpful. Try this one, as a typical sample: Men in general die younger than women do because "manliness" inhibits self-disclosure and places on men a great burden of stress and energy expenditure.

Or this: The greatest help in psychotherapy comes when the therapist can simply be himself and responds honestly to his client, rather than slavishly follow some learned technique. The same goes for nurses, to whom Dr. Jourard addresses five of his sixteen chapters.

Or this: Man is more than body and mind. Science will someday confirm the existence of spirit. Even now "inspiriting" (or faith) is known to be a key factor in physical and mental health.

Dr. Jourard does not argue from Christian presuppositions, but his findings perfectly substantiate the experience of Christians who have found wholeness through open and honest relationship with both God and man. He calls his book "an invitation to authentic being," and we hope there will be many who are persuaded by him to answer the invitation. –W.H.

Meticulously Casual

A more guarded review ran in *Contemporary Psychology* a year after publication and brings up a theme common in criticisms of humanistic psychology's reaction to behaviorism and psychoanalysis: was it merely a complaint or was it offering a better model of human insight and motivation?

The Transparent Self. Princeton, N. J.; Van Nostrand, 1964. Pp. viii + 200. $1.95
Reviewed by ALFRED B. HEILBRUN, JR.

The author, Sidney M. Jourard, has very recently appeared in CP's columns as the author of Personal Adjustment *(CP Dec. 1964, 9, 488). He received his Ph. D. from the University of Buffalo in 1953 and is Associate Professor of Psychology at the University of Florida.*

This book is made up principally of a collection of talks given by Jourard at various workshops and scientific meetings which, when bound together, leave much to be desired editorially. As would be expected, there is no integration of content from chapter to chapter, but, worse, redundancy reaches annoying proportions. The public would have been well served if the ideas had been distilled and integrated by Jourard into a tidier package.

In fairness, however, this review must focus upon the author's unique ideas, for it is strictly in the ideational realm that this book will be applauded or dismissed. The main theme around which Jourard deftly weaves numerous variations is that people should learn to make their subjective nature known to others (self-disclosure). To do so is to avoid the restrictions of potential and fear of revealment which accompany the impersonal fulfillment of social roles and erection of false public selves. Stresses associated with remaining unknown to other humans are assigned a central role in the genesis of human ills, psychological and physical. Conversely, to be able to share a truly personal relationship (which requires full and spontaneous honesty of disclosure) allows for psychological growth and an organism which is unreceptive to neurosis or brucellosis alike.

Self-disclosure is not for the laity alone. Bedside manners of physicians and nurses and mechanically emitted behaviors of psychotherapists are taken to task as health-deterring for the patient and escape-hatches for the professionals. The premise here is that self-disclosure has curative properties for the patient, and the healer's failure to provide an opportunity for its occurrence by his own unwillingness to disclose (or even to listen at times) robs the patient of his opportunity for cure except by dint of placebo, spoken or medicinal.

Concepts that in the past have been more traditionally associated with the literary arts than with psychology are given feature billing in Jourard's cast of ideas. Human spirit, hope and faith are reexamined as they pertain to the processes of wellness, sickness and recovery. Their metascientific usage will elicit reactions in readers ranging from utter disgust to sympathetic interest, but at the least it can be said that Jourard has the courage of his convictions to linger outside the boundaries of rigorous contemporary psychological thought.

The reviewer's general responses to this collection of papers ranged from reluctant admiration to annoyance. Jourard's writing (or better said, speaking) style is meticulously casual in spots, but he's interesting. I also admire the fact that he is able to be creative in viewing human behavior when doctrinaire views provide safer haven. Yet in my opinion he has been insufficiently concerned with establishing evidence to support his ideas. Studies cited relating to self-disclosure offer results that are largely irrelevant to his broad proposals. Hopefully there will be those who, when exposed to Jourard's ideas, will disentangle them from their existential trappings, scrutinize them scientifically, and let us know whether his proposals are prophetic or merely polemic.

By the early sixties Sidney was enjoying a growing income from writing, teaching, speaking, counseling and publishing activities. His private practice provided not only income but helped him evolve his approach to the clinical setting through patient feedback along with application of ideas gained through reading, research and introspection. Several detailed and anonymous encounters between therapist and patient are presented in his writing to embody and illustrate his hypotheses regarding the benefits of self-disclosure. Publisher royalties from *Personal Adjustment,* steady publication in prominent academic journals, and the enthusiastic response to his presentations at professional conferences increased his confidence and reduced his ongoing financial concerns. In 1963 the family moved to a lakeside house just outside the city limits, on Bivens Arm Lake, a designated wildlife sanctuary. Canoeing around the lake provided a close connection to its natural beauty and a welcome break from academia. Two of Sid's friends lived within close walking distance: artist Hollis Holbrook, an Art Department faculty member and its first chair, and Frank Taylor, a novelist and English Department professor.

Impulsive

One aspect of Sid's nature was a certain impulsiveness, an irrational disregard for potential physical danger. One hot summer day I watched him finish mowing the lawn and promptly wade into the lake to cool off, then swim halfway across the lake and back in water populated with alligators and water moccasins. Although alligators are not normally aggressive toward humans this was not a risk-versus-reward scenario most would favor with a swim. In Sid, the dance of intellect and spirit often favored spirit over reason.

In March of 1964 Sid presented a talk at the university on ideas of masculinity, justice, the myth of the hero and the problem of the "nebish," a Yiddish word meaning "one who is fearful and timid, especially in making decisions and plans, in discussions, debates, arguments, and confrontations, and in taking responsibility." The Odyssey myth continued to resonate with Sid's thinking. An article published in the March 20th *Florida Alligator* college newspaper describes this presentation:

"Too Many Men Today Becoming Nebishes"

American boys are growing up to be nebishes instead of men because they have so few heroic males from whom to learn, said Dr. Sidney M. Jourard, associate professor of psychology.

Jourard made this comment while speaking on the topic, "Our Vanishing Manhood and Why" Wednesday night at the Florida Union.

"I am afraid men as men are too few in number," said Jourard. A man as Jourard defines the term is an educated male who finds himself completely involved in the pursuit of values.

"The values I speak of are challenges men live their lives for; a dedication to add something constructive to the world," explained Jourard, "Too often our males are dedicated to goals that are silly or dangerous, such as sex, money or power," continued Jourard.

An educated man does not necessarily have to have a college degree. Education, in Jourard's terminology, is displayed by the way one reacts to his world. "If one is confronted by injustice and is not moved to replace it with justice, he is not educated or a man, regardless of his degrees and social position," charged Jourard.

Jourard believes boys must be made into men through our families, elementary schools, and churches. Presently, according to Jourard, all these institutions are falling down on the job.

"Instead of the heroic man, boys are reared by Dagwoodian-like fathers who leave everything to the castrating mothers," charged Jourard. "At the elementary school level, the boy encounters women teachers who are too often working to help hubby out or for an extra spring wardrobe. And at the church level, the general clergyman is too ambitious or nervous about his future to allow himself to be a man."

Jourard's thoughtful solution to this problem comes from a revamping of the educational system. "We must first have men as examples before we can expect our boys to grow toward true manhood," contends Jourard. "I feel a good number of these men can be found in the 50-years-and-over age group."

If these men who are well educated and have been successful in their life's work could be recruited to teach our young children or to go into the ministry, then we would be on the way to ending our vanishing manhood problems, said Jourard.

This is a prime example of Sid at his most polemic and free-wheeling, as he presents a problematically vague definition of manliness, marginalizes and insults female teachers, refers to "castrating mothers" and describes fathers as bumbling Dagwood Bumstead characters (the husband of cartoon character Blondie), and then demeans much of the clergy.

An Uncanny Feeling

After seven years of teaching at the University of Florida Sid had earned his first academic sabbatical, a paid year away from the college with the intent to stimulate and refresh the intellect through pursuit of new professional skills and experiences. One such option for Sid was working with psychiatrist and Holocaust survivor Viktor Frankl, known for his book *Man's Search For Meaning.* However, Sid had been seeking a Special Public Health Service Fellowship with the psychiatrist Ronald Laing in England, and was accepted for a fellowship in the approaching academic year at the Tavistock Institute of Human Relations in London.

During the months leading up to the move to England, three of Sid's articles based on nursing college curriculum were published in *Canadian Nurse.* These brief articles address aspects of becoming a more effective nurse, a subject covered in five chapters of *The Transparent Self.* The titles "How Do People Learn?," "Let's Look At the Teacher," and "Personal Contact in Teaching" all have at their core the concept of dialogue between teacher and nurse, and nurse and patient. Sid based this concept on his reading of Martin Buber's *I and Thou,* believing in the power of a one-on-one encounter between two open-minded people taking turns actively listening to the other for mutual understanding and benefit. The teaching environment was a good place to explore this concept, and the three articles ran in consecutive issue of *Canadian Nurse*; a fourth was published six months later in 1965.

These articles are of no specific biographic interest with the exception of a revealing excerpt from "How Do People Learn?" regarding operant conditioning, a concept first introduced by B.F. Skinner in 1938:

> The students of reinforcement have discovered that, given a little ingenuity, one can gradually shape up the behavior of another person in desired ways by secretly, or openly reinforcing the behavior that approximates the idea you have in mind, and ignoring or punishing behavior that is remote from the plan of the trainer.

…I learned about this when I was a sophomore in college, and it gave me an uncanny feeling. I fell in love with a very pretty girl, and somewhere along the line, discovered it wasn't fate. She told me that she had had her eye on me for some time; she found out places that I haunted—the coffee shop, the beer parlor, the common room, the soccer field, debates, and so on, and she would just be there. Since I am a man, there is no problem in surmising what the reinforcements might be, but the behavior she wanted to elicit and then strengthen in me was "asking-for-a-date" behavior. Once she became part of the scenery, she vanished for a week or so. Then she reappeared, and I was rewarded by seeing her—and she smiled. That elicited the behavior she had wanted to elicit, namely, approaching and asking for a date. This behavior was reinforced by her acceptance, and the subsequent dates were also reinforced. So, while I was immensely flattered at her desire to know me, I was horribly shocked to feel that I was a victim of her strategy. Eventually, we broke up anyway, when her boy friend came back from Europe.[11]

Despite the personal nature of the encounter, this formative experience of disingenuous behavior enacted for the benefit of the deceiver went against Sid's intellect and spirit. Her behavior anticipated much of the content of the 1995 best-selling book *The Rules*, which outlines specific steps to attract a man through a set of behavior "rules" aimed toward the goal of marriage—after which the authors encourage you to finally reveal your true self.[12]

In the Psychology Department at the University of Florida Sid had found his place at last, and there were aspects of Southern culture and hospitality he found attractive, with reservations. He would sometimes comment that the South was a land of contrasts, a region of gentility and true Southern hospitality as well as its obverse, that in the South they "might invite you over for dinner, or then again they might just lynch you."

Europe   6

In August of 1964 The S.S. *Ruahine* sailed east out of Port Everglades, Florida and arrived twelve days later in Southampton, England, where Sid and family took the train to London and 6 Summit Way in the northern suburb of Southgate. Within walking distance was the Southgate subway station where Sid commuted weekdays to central London and the Tavistock Clinic.

Ronald David Laing (1927-1989) was a Scottish psychiatrist who had written extensively on therapy and mental illness.[1] Laing argued that much of what had been defined as mental illness, particularly schizophrenia, was a valid reaction to brutalizing realities and demands of society and family. Sidney had written on this topic in a more general sense in the chapter "Roles That Sicken" from *The Transparent Self*. Laing and Sid were somewhat similar in spirit, aware of the overarching power of culture and society to mold and influence one's personality, personal potential and character. Both were interested in applying existential thinking to psychotherapy. In Sid's words

> I spent the year with him, he and Aaron Esterson, just hanging around, and
> the ideas that they introduced me to, not so much their own, they got me
> reading existential literature and mystical literature, and I brought it back
> with me, and it affected my teaching and my thinking and my writing.

What Sid described as "just hanging around" may have felt that way compared to his teaching activities at the University of Florida, but he was continually observing, experiencing and absorbing the culture and people of London while engaging with a new academic milieu. Sidney was a natural-born people watcher, and the abrupt change from a small southern college town to a major European metropolis presented a fresh social environment for observation.

In 1964 Ronnie Laing was just on the cusp of becoming internationally known. He was charismatic, personable, ambitious; had begun espousing his social and psychiatric views in the midst of a growing youth counterculture (employing LSD as a psychiatric tool with his patients, among them the actor Sean Connery); and was being interviewed on television and print and radio on the topics of madness, family, the politics of experience, the enlightening power of psychedelic drugs. During the first few months of Sid's sabbatical year in London, Laing was in the United States lecturing, where he met Timothy Leary and Allen Ginsberg. In December Laing returned to England and lectured at Oxford. Within a year Laing had become the "best known psychologist (at least in the United Kingdom) since Freud and Jung."[2]

Laing, like Sid, was very much absorbed in himself and his intellectual pursuits, and, although both were on similar paths, their interactions were not the focus of Sid's sabbatical. Laing's views on the causes and definitions of mental illness differed radically from those of his contemporaries; Sid as a humanistic psychologist was also intrigued with the idea of society defining the individual in myriad, institution-serving ways. However, it was Laing's interest in existentialism and phenomenology that left a more lasting influence on Sid's thinking and subsequent work.

Existentialism

Existentialism can be viewed as a philosophical doctrine that affirms the existence of the individual person as a free and responsible agent of their own life, through acts of free will, another way of saying we humans are in control of our lives, in contrast to those who believe their lives to be controlled by other people, by God, by environmental stimuli or by suppressed and repressed early experiences.

Existentialism was born in Europe through ideas expressed by Søren Kierkegaard, Freidrich Nietzsche, Martin Heidegger, Jean-Paul Sartre and others. The famous (or infamous) statement "God is dead" by Nietzsche was part of the argument that there was no higher power in control of your life. This is not a denial of the power of outside forces such as poverty, exploitation, war, and economic environment; only an assertion that it is possible to transcend these forces. Sartre defended this possibility in his statement "existence precedes essence," meaning that your essence is not defined at the moment of your birth but is within your power to create or change. That this doctrine also brings full responsibility on you for your choices is what Sartre references when he says humankind is "doomed to be free." Sartre also acknowledged that many people choose the easier route of social conformity.

Existentialism further argued that all our acts ultimately try to avoid and disavow the ultimate "nothingness"—that is, death. Humans are the only form of life aware of their eventual death, and to fully grasp what it means to truly exist you need to be consciously aware that existence can be taken away at any time. Or, as Rollo May expresses it, one can "never escape the fact that death will arrive at some unknown moment in the future." But by confronting this primal fact of the human condition, "existence takes on vitality and immediacy, and the individual experiences a heightened consciousness of himself, his world, and others around him."[3] According to this view, to either deny death or to dwell morbidly on its inevitability are both improper stances, and, further, the balance of the two extremes is a workable life goal, expressed in Taoism as the yin-yang balance. In *Zorba the Greek* the protagonist says: "Two equally steep and bold paths may lead to the same peak. To act as if death did not exist, or to act thinking every minute of death, is perhaps the same thing."[4]

It seems that neither Sartre nor Kierkegaard were particularly joyous or cheerful personalities, and this extraneous fact may have encouraged a skewed view of existentialism as a gloomy, world-weary philosophical stance that seemed to border on nihilism. The titles of Søren Kierkegaard's two most influential books didn't help: *Fear and Trembling* and *The Sickness Unto Death*. These were not titles that pulled you in.

In contrast, Abraham Maslow's writings on the basic nature of humankind were viewed by many social scientists as entirely too optimistic. But to Maslow, the grimmer stance seemed a weak model for emulation:

> I don't think we need take too seriously the European existentialist's exclusive harping on dread, on anguish, on despair and the like, for which their only remedy seems to be to keep a stiff upper lip. This high I.Q. whimpering on a cosmic scale occurs whenever an external source of values fails to work. They should have learned from the psychotherapists that the loss of illusions and the discovery of identity, though painful at first, can be

ultimately exhilarating and strengthening. And then of course the absence of any mention of peak experiences, of experiences, of joy and ecstasy, or even of normal happiness, leads to the strong suspicion that these writers are 'non-peakers,' people who just don't experience joy. It is as if they could see out of one eye only, and that eye jaundiced. Most people experience *both* tragedy and joy in varying proportions. Any philosophy which leaves out either cannot be considered to be comprehensive. Colin Wilson distinguishes sharply between Yea-saying existentialists and Nay-saying existentialists. In this distinction, I must agree with him completely."[5]

Sid was a "yea-saying" existentialist. A common criticism of humanistic psychology included charges of naive optimism. It was as if the glum philosophers didn't want anyone arguing with their awareness of the inherently tragic aspect of human existence. What exactly *did* they have in mind? Dwelling on the ultimate absurdity of life through the knowledge that in every case life ended in death? Maslow had a point.

This writer remembers the experience of attending school in the working-class neighborhood of Southgate. My older brother Jeff attended Ashmole Secondary Modern, while my younger brother and I attended Osidge Elementary. We were initially ostracized and treated not merely as new students but new foreign students, taunted as "bloody Yanks," and Jeff was physically roughed up on the first day. We returned home that afternoon and reported our experiences. Sid was visibly upset, and said that after such treatment returning to school the next morning would be the bravest thing we could possibly do. This subtle psychological manipulation was effective, as we eventually integrated into the school culture and developed friendships.

In June of 1965 Ronnie Laing and associates established the Philadelphia Association, an alternative space to treat schizophrenia. Any interaction between Laing and Sid would have occurred in the first half of 1965. According to Sid's recollections, for a period at the Tavistock Clinic, every Thursday Sid would watch the actor Sean Connery walk past his open door and down the hall toward Laing's office for therapy. At the time Connery had starred in three James Bond movies, *Dr. No, From Russia With Love,* and *Goldfinger.*

The mysticism Laing introduced to Sid was reinforced by the popularity of Idries Shah's book *The Sufis,* published in 1964. Shah's book conveyed Sufi mysticism to a Western audience just as Alan Watts's books and lectures brought Zen and

In London 1964-5

Tao philosophies to a Western audience. In Sid's book review of *Final Integration in the Adult Personality* by A. Reza Arasteh,[6] he writes:

> I first encountered Sufi teachings in London, where Idries Shah's book, *The Sufis* was being widely read and discussed by intellectuals within and without the profession of psychology. I found it fascinating reading, so that Aresteh's book came to a prepared reader.
>
> The thesis is this—in Shah's book, in the volume here under review, in the books dealing with Taoism and Zen Buddhism, and to a growing extent, in books written by Western psychologists, e.g., Maslow, Jung, Fromm, Frankl—man is born, he is socialized, he conforms to the ways of his group, and then, if he is not aided, he languishes in a kind of behavioral trap.

In the classic sense, mysticism was another aspect of alternative consciousness as were psychedelic drugs, yoga, meditation, and various religious experiences as presented by William James in *The Varieties of Religious Experience*. James was an agnostic psychologist and philosopher who explored the vast number of documented religious experiences throughout history and explained how their existence reinforced his idea that *experience was reality* to the experiencer, whether it was acknowledged as "real" or not by others. James further argued that all religions were built around the personal religious or transcendent experience of a particular individual—Jesus, the Buddha, Mohammed. This aligned with Sid's concept of the ideal therapist being an exemplar of how to live in the world.

LSD Redux

Sid had previously experienced the effects of LSD in 1955, despite his complaints that he felt the dose he took wasn't strong enough. Ronnie Laing had been experimenting since the early '60s with the therapeutic value of LSD when administered to a patient under controlled circumstances. Laing guided his patients through a six-hour therapeutic session under the influence of the drug; and some patients claimed that one of these sessions was more useful than years of traditional psychoanalysis.[7] On a certain level the drug mimicked the effects of a psychotic breakdown by dissolving the usual structure of perceived reality; for this reason a knowledgeable and attentive guide was an important part of the therapeutic procedure, which for some could be a religious experience, for others a frightening and disorienting event.

Sid later wrote of an LSD experience under Laing's supervision, who is not named in the account. Details of this event were found in Sid's file folder labeled LSD: Myself, David Mycroft, London: June, 1965. Included in this folder is Mycroft's description of his LSD experience, which he prefaces by writing: "On Saturday at 11.50 Sid and I took l.s.d.; it started to take effect at about 12.15. From then until about 4.30 we stayed in a room, with shutters closed. … At 4.30 we went for a walk, finally going into a pub and playing darts over halves of bitter."

Sid described his LSD experience in a passage from one of his later books (the dosage was pharmaceutical Sandoz lysergic acid in single-dose glass ampoules):

> On the occasion of which I write, I was in the company of a physician who
> had himself, many times, taken the psychedelic trip. He was my guide and
> teacher. I took the dose of the drug in a shot glass of water and sat chatting

with the other, fellow travelers. Before long, I began laughing—it was a gigantic joke, a hoax but the laugh was on me. Everything I could see or hear or think seemed so arbitrary and unnecessary and it could have so easily been different. I could have been somebody else. There seemed no necessary reason why things fell when they were dropped; why not float, or scoot off sideways? Then, I noticed the wire of the telephone receiver, closest to my hand. A dim beam of light fell upon it, and it had an exquisite and fascinating iridescence. It seemed to give off a ruby glow. (Ordinarily, I am rather color-blind, or insensitive to subtle variations in hues.) I spent what seemed eons of time holding the cord, dangling and twisting it, fascinated with each new configuration that was produced. I felt as if veils had been lifted from my eyes, ears, nose, skin, and my sense of my own body. Sounds from the street would catch my attention, and it was as if I was truly hearing for the first time, as if wax stoppers had been removed from my ears. Everything was as important as everything else. I would note the feel of the chair against my backside, or the texture of a desk-top, and nothing else existed. Odors, taste, the sight of the flames in the gas fire— each of these presented itself to me, and I would note them, become them: my consciousness *was* these things and was *of* these things.

Perhaps an hour might have passed, by earthly time. I found myself flipping from the perceptual mode of experiencing to the imaginary mode. I could imagine something, and my image was as real as any perception. At a whim, I could transform my image of a person into a dog, cat, or locomotive; and each was as real as any perception.

Then I was truly swept away on a journey back through time. I experienced the sound of the song, "Ramona, I see you by a waterfall." Peculiar faces I couldn't then recognize, of very demure dandies, with fedora hat, bow tie, and devilish looks in their eyes, appeared and then disappeared. A phrase was uttered by somebody, some baby-talk gibberish I couldn't decipher. I experienced a period of my childhood, perhaps when I was two—a precocious peanut of a child, sentient, but regarded as a doll, like the midget in Günter Grass' novel *The Tin Drum*. The dandies were the teen-agers of the late 1920s—my older brother and his friends and an older cousin, who, when praised for their neat garb, would make a certain coy gesture. The song, "Ramona"; my mother would put me on the counter of our store and ask me to sing that song, "Ramona, I preshoo kanishiks"— and that was the babytalk. The elephants' legs: fat women in the store, me reaching to their knees, they in short dresses, stocking-tops turned down.

But I didn't stop there—I meaning my experience. From time to time,

I would experience what I thought was the universe—a spiral wave of nothingness that would move in a spiral path, cast itself into a configuration that I felt was the being of a whole millennium; then it would fold back on itself, only to flow again to cast out another, higher way for the world, for the people, to be. I heard a ghostly laughter, howling about what a joke it was to end one configuration—that everyone in it thought was God's plan—only to have it washed out of existence to be replaced by another.

In one of those moments of the universe's movement, I became a lion. I felt my claws tense—front paws and back; my mouth curled involuntarily into a snarl, that became a strangled gargle, finally to be released as a full-throated roar. The release of the roar was one of the most satisfying, and I think integrating, experiences of my life. I felt myself extending from my center right out to the edges of my body, perhaps filling it and living it for the first time. It is, I can assure you, a magnificent experience to feel your toes as your own, like talons, and as an integral part of yourself, rather than those little nubs experienced as "way down there."

From time to time, I would flip back into the mode of perception, and experience the world outside my own skin. It was constantly changing appearance, as if the edges of things—which ordinarily confined and contained their being—become waxy or actually ruptured, so that the insides were disclosed.

Several hours later, I and my fellow voyagers began to surface. It was like an experience of being reborn or reincarnated. At midnight, we went to a nearby Cypriot restaurant—a psychiatrist, a social worker, a writer, a young physician, and myself. We ate as if for the first time. The feel of jaws and teeth rending meat and bread was exquisite.[8]

Zorba the Greek

Greek author Nikos Kazantzakis was a novelist, poet and essayist who had studied with the philosopher Henri Bergson in Paris. Bergson and psychologist William James were mutual admirers. Kazantzakis's best-known work of fiction is *Zorba The Greek,* the story of a young Greek intellectual scholar who wants to transcend his bookish ways and achieves this through his encounter with Alexis Zorba, a man with a zest for life who works hard, fornicates, plays music, sings, philosophizes, drinks, seduces widows, lives life passionately, philosophically and recklessly, and when things get rough, he dances. This model had a certain appeal to Sid.

The narrator is a Greek college-educated man, tame and inhibited in his expressions and behavior. The movie adaptation with Anthony Quinn as Zorba was released during Sid's sabbatical year and at the start of 1965 the novel, the film and the best-selling soundtrack album were ubiquitous— you could not escape *Zorba the Greek* in all its multiplicity. The expression of freedom embodied in Alexis Zorba was close to the heart of existentialism and humanistic, person-oriented psychology; this appealed to Sid's intellect, while Zorba as a character appealed to Sid's spirit as a way to live; a powerful combination. Sid evidently identified initially with the narrator, a scholarly young man caught up inside his head, detached from the physical world. It's a reasonable hypothesis that Sid was finding his own way to loosen the powerful grip of growing up in Canada, with its own suppressive cultural mores. Sid's identity as an academic and a professor was at odds with his private, lustier self-image. Zorba was a model of a man meeting life head on with enthusiasm, energy and humor, existentially free and happy about it. As a novel *Zorba the Greek* was described by *Time* magazine as "plotless but never pointless," as there are Zorba's views on honor, war, religious hypocrisy, freedom, kindness, sexuality, awareness of death, and Bergsonian thought regarding the duration of time. It's all wrapped up in the narrative. Zorba:

> "Look, one day I had gone to a little village. An old grandfather of ninety was busy planting an almond tree. 'What, grandad!' I exclaimed. 'Planting an almond tree?' And he, bent as he was, turned round and said: 'My son, I carry on as if I should never die.' I replied 'And I carry on as if I was going to die any minute.' Which of us was right, boss?"
>
> He looked at me triumphantly and said "That's where I've got you!"
>
> I kept silent. Two equally steep and bold paths may lead to the same peak. To act as if death did not exist, or to act thinking every minute of death, is perhaps the same thing. But when Zorba asked me the question, I did not know.
>
> "Well?" Zorba said mockingly. "Don't worry, boss, you can't argue that out. Let's talk of something else. Just now I'm thinking of the chicken and the pilaff sprinkled with cinnamon. My brain's steaming like the pilaff. Let's eat first, ballast up first, then we'll see. Everything in good time. In front of us now is the pilaff; let our minds become pilaff. Tomorrow the lignite [mine] will be in front of us; our minds must become lignite! No half-measure, you know."[9]

Much of the character and the story resonated with Sidney. Zorba's views on organized religion, women as alluring creatures to be protected and adored, his ability to be in the natural world, to be in the moment, his hatred of war and violence; all came together in the speech and actions of one of the most iconic characters in modern fiction. As someone struggling with what being a man really meant in society and who himself was looking for such models of behavior, Sid found the character of Alexis Zorba appealing as a sort of modern hero-figure.

During this sabbatical year Sid visited his friend Nicholas Greville, a British orthopaedic surgeon. Greville was a lifelong sailor and during the winter they sailed the English Channel in his 34-foot boat *Trocar* and Sid fell overboard. Upon retrieval from the chilly sea he developed lockjaw from the severe cold. Nic had to pry open Sid's jaws in order to administer a warming brandy and Sid relished the retelling of this tale.

Literature and art described and dramatized the type of behavior and exploration of the human condition that was consciously left unexamined by behaviorists and neglected by psychoanalysts, and in reading fiction Sid was seeking both entertainment and models of what he later termed "magnificence." Heroes were of interest; the model he sought in literature was the individual as exemplar. Odysseus was one such figure, Zorba another.

Summer of '65

With the sabbatical year nearing its end, Sid arranged for the rental of a villa in Spain and the family drove to Dover in a Triumph Herald convertible, boarded the automobile ferry to Calais and continued through France to the Costa Brava of Spain where for six weeks they stayed at a series of villas in San Antoni de Calonge a few blocks from the Mediterranean.

When not drinking the inexpensive local wine, swimming, or otherwise relaxing, Sid wandered the small town mingling, talking and observing, employing his pidgin Spanish with curiosity and enthusiasm. I was with him when he asked a laborer's opinion of Francisco Franco, the current dictator of Spain. The man paused from his work of stuccoing a wall, said he hated Franco and possibly even more about the dictator. In mid-sentence, most of the plasterwork the man had been engaged in before the encounter collapsed at his feet. I don't know if Sid's questions distracted the man and therefore led to the accident but the conversation ended abruptly and we walked on.

Touching

This immersion in Spanish culture was another awareness-expanding environment for Sid. Having recently spent time immersed in British life, Sid began recognizing different levels of physical contact between persons in routine encounters in each of these cultures. He counted in the course of an hour the number of times a couple would touch one another while at a café. This was not a proper research study but merely an outgrowth of his curiosity. He observed this behavior in London and Paris, had done so the previous year in San Juan, Puerto Rico, and would continue his observations upon his return to the States. He was forming an idea about body-awareness versus alienation from body, reflecting on the touching taboos in different cultures.

What Sidney absorbed intellectually from this year abroad in Europe can't be quantified, but he had found that humanistic psychology was not held in high regard in the continent and was mainly viewed as an American development. John Heaton was a psychotherapist and phenomenologist at the Tavistock Institute during Sid's stay, and fifty years later he responded to my request for his recollections:

> Yes, I remember your father quite well. I cannot remember details but we had many talks together and I remember him as a pleasant person, very American!, who I got on with very easily. As for humanistic psychology neither I nor Laing were very taken with it. It was very American we felt, nothing wrong with that but we were not American; it was far too optimistic we thought and did not have much to say about the dreadful things people do to one another; just being a nice guy, as was Sid, was not enough. Humanistic psychology has not taken off in this country or Europe; another difficulty with it is that it has not much historical sense whereas we in Britain and Europe are steeped in it.[10]

Despite these views from colleagues, Sid was fully engaged during his sabbatical: he had lectured in Oslo, Oxford, Cambridge and London and at the British Psychological Society in Aberdeen in April 1965. In May he submitted the results of his research in body-accessibility to the *British Journal of Social and Clinical Psychology*, and it was published a year after his return to Florida in the September 1966 issue. This paper includes the first published description of his café observations regarding the level of touching between two people in a public space during a specific time period. The overall focus of the paper is on where people touch others and where they allow others to touch them, based on four relationships:

mother, father, closest friend of same sex, closest friend of opposite sex. Included in the paper is the following comment:

> I watched couples in coffee shops in San Juan (Puerto Rico), London, Paris and Gainesville (Florida), counting the number of times that one person touched another at one table during a one-hour sitting. The 'scores' were, for San Juan, 180; for Paris, 110; for London, 0; and for Gainesville, 2.

Later he writes:

> It is time for systematic study of the parameters of touching. I suspect that many people suffer from deprivation of physical contact during their adult lives, but there is no way to prove this without knowledge of normative and desired touching patterns, and their sources of variation. The present study was undertaken as a first step in this direction.[11]

In the latter half of August the family returned to the United States on the SS *Oriana*. Sid's experience with LSD, the philosophy and style of Alexis Zorba, the months immersed in British culture and academia, his introductions to existentialism and mystic experience, Sufism—these collectively stimulated and shaped his intellect and opened him up to new ideas. Many concepts were already interrelated. Henri Bergson's concept of life being constant movement and change and the ceaseless "becoming" nature of life resonated with Sidney's thinking. Bergson and William James, who created the term "stream of consciousness" were mutual admirers of each other's writing, and Kazantzakis was admittedly influenced by Bergson. The acknowledgment of the multiplicity and diversity of human behavior was what unified these people, along with their appreciation of the aspects of consciousness that made humans different from animals.

Harmless Noise

Soon after resuming his teaching back in Gainesville Sid received a series of letters from the landlord of the house at 6 Summit Way in London. A scholar returning from two years in India, Mr. Hardy was unhappy with the state of the house upon his return and, convinced that the second tenant (Sid) did all the purported damage, wrote letters, including one to J. Wayne Reitz, the president of the University. Hardy was demanding a sum of money for items missing in a household inventory. Sid's eventual response provides both an insight into his view of such behavior and an example of a clear, direct writing style.

1506 SW 35th Place
Gainesville, Florida

September 7, 1965

Dear Mr. Hardy,

I am at a loss as to how to construe the barrage of letters you have addressed to me at various places, and then, incredibly enough, to the president of a University and the chairman of a department. The latter personages, quite properly, regard the matters of which you write as something between two private individuals. The letters are not reasonable, indeed, they are not wholly truthful; more charitably, they impress me as the solitary fuming of a man who feels, wrongly, that he has been wronged.

My wife has responded in considerable detail to some of your rather wild and free-swinging charges. I endorse the whole of her letter to you. Mr. Hardy, your petulant and irresponsible missives should not have been mailed.

You are not on sound legal bases. Indeed, if I were less kindly disposed, in principle, to a fellow academician, I would think seriously of charges of libel, slander, and other irresponsible threats to the reputation of a reasonable man. I am angry that you saw fit to write to my departmental chairman and to the University president, but since it is harmless noise, I can only feel a little sad that you lost so much perspective, in your pique, to send such letters.

What really angers me is the impact of your groundless charges on my wife. She is a stable, even tempered person with a good sense of humor. But your letters were sufficient to shake this, and to leave her upset until we were able, finally, to get resettled at home, and to answer you....

I don't know what to add to my wife's letter to you. I see no justification for the 100 pounds which you seem to feel we owe you, not on legal grounds, not on moral grounds, and not on any conceivable grounds of common sense. Rather, I would request on all of these grounds that you return my 25 pound deposit, for reasons which my wife has shown in her letter to you.

It is not my disposition to be vindictive. However, you must realize that if you continue with your fanfaronade of hysterical charges, I shall have to begin to think of recourse. I have not yet mailed a letter to the University Housing Bureau, to suggest that prospective tenants might find more reasonable landlords, nor have I even composed a letter to address to someone in your place of work comparable to the chairman of my department or the president of my University. Mr. Hardy, grow up! When a man lets his house to living human beings, to two sets of them over a two year period, he cannot expect to find his house exactly as he left it. Moreover, he cannot, with impunity, level charges to the effect that any observed wear and tear is the responsibility of the second, and not the first set of tenants.

Let me tell you, Mr. Hardy, that if you believe that Mr. Greenfield arranged a partnership between you and I, and thereby arranged a mismatch, I agree fully! This woolly-headed bungler almost arranged that you should be without a tenant. However, we did manage to move into your house in spite of his incompetent dithering. I was never wholly apprised, in any clearly understandable way, of the terms of the lease. After you violated your own lease by an unannounced visit, to inform me later (from Pakistan) that I had violated the clauses relating to dogs and the re-arrangement of furniture, I was prepared then and there to leave your premises. We had other housing available. I told you of my readiness to do this. I did not conceal anything. One of the reasons for staying on was my empathic realization that it is a disturbing thing to be in a far-off land, and have one's house vacated, with the inevitable lapses in mortgage payments that this entails. Of course, this is something you do not appreciate.

Now I am in the middle of something like reverse "culture shock," the experience of returning home after being in another country for a year or more. My own house is not as I left it. I am involved in getting it back into shape for me after my year-long tenant vacated. Perhaps your letters to me represent your version of culture-shock. I cannot take them seriously as an expression of anything else.

I paid you a fair rent for your house. I paid in addition a deposit of 25 pounds. For reasons made abundantly clear in my wife's letter, I feel entitled to repayment of this sum, or if you wish to quibble, of the sum less anything we truly owe on the telephone account, and any shillings of indebtedness for breaking a dish or two.

This is as much time and thought as I wish to devote to this matter. Get over your unwarranted tantrum, Mr. Hardy, stop demeaning yourself by writing silly letters to me and anyone else. This letter to you will be between you and me. I want no more of this twaddle. There is more for both of us to do with our time and passion.
Yours sincerely,

S.M. Jourard

Hardy's response began as follows: Dear Dr. Jourard, "You are very right and I am very wrong," closing with: "Diagnosis: paranoia."

New Directions

7

IN THE AUTUMN OF 1965 American culture was in a state of rapid transition. U.S. military presence in Vietnam had escalated, students were marching in protest and burning their draft cards; the militant human rights activist Malcolm X had been assassinated, Martin Luther King, Jr. was becoming the leading spokesperson for the civil rights movement, and the word "hippie" appeared for the first time in print in the *San Francisco Examiner*.

In the dozen years since receiving his doctorate, Sid had produced a large number of research studies on a variety of subjects, including: ego-strength, self-image, a person's body self-satisfaction or dissatisfaction in relation to body size and to images of the ideal female figure, the traits and aspects of healthy personality; self-disclosure in relation to a person's age, race, gender, and their religious denomination. The year abroad included exposure to new subjects: existentialism, mystic and religious experiences, and his second and seemingly profound experience with LSD. Sid was reading psychologist William James's *The Varieties of Religious Experience* with its discussions of mysticism, repentance, conversion, saintliness and the inclusion of excerpts from personal reports of such experiences throughout human history, unexplained by science but profoundly real to the recipient. Other books of influence to Sid's thinking included Alan Watts's *Psychotherapy East and West* that drew parallels from Buddhism, Taoism and Yoga to psychotherapy, and *The Joyous Cosmology: Adventures in the Chemistry of Consciousness* in which Watts describes his own pursuit of altered states through psychedelics. These books explored experiences outside the mainstream of scientific thought and explanation. Sid's exposure

Sid in Gainesville, circa 1966

to existentialism and the works of Jean-Paul Sartre had been broadened by Ronald Laing, who had co-edited a book on Sartre's work.[1]

Soon after his return to Florida Sid spoke at the Invitational Conference on Independent Learning in Milwaukee. He was assigned the task of addressing the problem of independent learning from the standpoint of Personality Theory, but he instead became engrossed with the question of fascination itself: what is independent learning and why is it a problem? Sid presents his hypothesis

> that independent learning, the embodiment of the state of being fascinated, involves six stages. The first is the experience of the impasse. The next stage we will provisionally call the stage of detachment, a kind of dying. The third is immersion in oneself—an entry into one's center, one's source of experiencing. Next is an emergence, or rebirth. Fifth is the experience of new possibilities. Sixth is the selection and pursuit of one of these.[2]

Sid's recent return after a year abroad is viewed in such a light:

> It has just occurred to me, after completing a year of sabbatical leave in
> England, that the process I just described is a sabbatical leave of one's mind,
> of one's personality structure. The academic sabbatical is a removal from
> one's usual surroundings, but I discovered it is easier to get out of one's
> surroundings than to get them out of oneself so that new surroundings can
> invite one into encounter. Many of my American colleagues in England
> successfully shielded themselves from fascination with and involvement in
> the English experience, because of the panic they felt when invited to let
> go their usual preoccupations. They carried America with them. Indeed,
> the phenomenon of "culture shock," long noted by anthropologists, is
> another dimension of the experience of leaving, not just one's country, but
> one's mind. One has to let the American in one die in order to become a
> participant in a new experience, to be reborn.[3]

An Objective Look at Subjectivity

Phenomenology is a school of thought that focuses on the objective study of topics
usually regarded as subjective: consciousness and the content of conscious experiences, such as judgment, perception, and emotion. Although phenomenology
seeks to be scientific, it doesn't approach consciousness from the perspective of
clinical psychology or neurology. Phenomenologists attempt this study through
systematic reflection on the essential properties and structures of experience. From
a phenomenological view, experiences are reality to the experiencer. Experiences
such as a religious feeling of connection to a higher power or force, an unexpected
ecstatic feeling not physically-based—these reports from the experiencer could
not be wished away by the argument that such experiences weren't scientifically
detectable and that without quantifiable measurement they didn't exist. William
James believed that all religions are built from the personal religious experiences
of the founders of such religions.

Phenomenology chooses as a starting point for research persons in their environment, with the view that human experience cannot be isolated from the environment. According to the German philosopher Martin Heidegger, a more precise
name for a human being was *being-in-the-world-with-others,* which acknowledged
each person as a network of interpersonal relationships.[4] The two poles of self and

world are dialectically related. Self implies world and world self; there's neither without the other, and each is fully understandable only in relation to the other. From this viewpoint, stating that a person is *in* an environment, or asking what influence the environment has *on* a person are both simplifications. The person and the environment are an integral whole.

Six months prior to his LSD experience in London, Sid had written a brief essay, "The Mystical Dimension of Self"[5] wherein he discusses the ability of the artist to "flip out" into a different consciousness in order to create, then return to a social state to refine and present the art. Some artists stay in the mystic state of creation constantly; others can move in and out of the state at will and with success. The history of art provides examples of both, from Van Gogh to Picasso.

California Beckons

Intellectually and culturally refreshed by his year abroad, Sid's attention became drawn to certain centers of learning on the West Coast exploring ideas that resonated with his own. Sid became aware of a self-described growth center on the northern California coastline in Big Sur Hot Springs that eventually became known as the Esalen Institute. Founded by two wealthy Stanford graduates, Michael Murphy and Richard Price, the mission of the Esalen Institute was to host workshops led by writers and therapists interested in humanistic psychology.[6] Esalen became a well-known site for many counterculture and human potential gatherings involving encounter groups, consciousness raising, psychedelic drug experimentation, body awareness, and yoga, a wide range of activities that merged comfortably with the hippie culture that grew in the latter half of the nineteen-sixties.

Two months after his return from England Sid drove from Florida to California to participate in the programs of the Esalen Institute:[7]

> Esalen Institute at Big Sur Hot Springs announces November 12-17 *Sidney Jourard* (University of Florida) and *Gerald Goodman* (University of California) will discuss theory and research on self-disclosure and related concepts in "A Psychology of Intimacy." Demonstrations and workshop.

Out of My American Mind

A lecture taped for Big Sur Records[8] provides an insight into Sid's thinking following the intellectual stimulation of his year abroad. The topic was "Human Uses of Behavioral Research." He begins:

> I'm a psychologist by trade; supposedly a psychologist is a scientist
> who aims to study human behavior, and the purpose of studying the
> human behavior and experience, according to the various textbooks, is
> to understand man's experience and behavior in order to predict it and
> control it. This supposedly is the charge that we psychologists have, except
> that I renege on it. I've been trained, like most psychologists—and I see
> my mission as one of understanding man—to find out what are the things
> that determine his being and his behavior and his experience. But it's at
> this point that I draw a sharp division between myself and some of my
> colleagues, most of my colleagues. I want to find out what are the things
> that could determine man, in order to subvert them, transcend them,
> in short, to study man with a view toward maximizing his *freedom* from
> determiners, his ability to transcend his past, his genetic endowment, social
> pressures, and to discover what his possibilities might be, and to fulfill them.

He then questions the premise of psychotherapy as an approach to healing the patient, and comments on his experiences of the previous year, recounting his view from abroad:

> For years past I was very much uncomfortable with the whole field of
> abnormal psychology and psychiatry. I used to teach abnormal psychology,
> it was one of the most popular courses at the University of Florida; I'm a
> good lecturer. But I came gradually, through a number of experiences, to
> realize that what they call abnormal psychology, or psychiatric nosology,
> is actually a very peculiar kind of politics, an invalidation of those ways
> of behaving and experiencing that for one reason or another don't fit the
> existing social system. It's as if each society decides what range of human
> possibility will be regarded as sane and good for that time and place, and
> everything else that doesn't fit those criteria of what's sane and good are
> going to be disqualified and punished and regarded as evil and insane.
>   This growing realization that psychiatry and clinical psychology
> and to some extent social work and the ministry that concerns itself
> with pastoral counseling—the realization that people who practice this

counseling and psychotherapeutic art, that these people are political counter-revolutionaries, that they are the velvet glove at the end of the steel fist of social control—came most sharply to me in the past year when I went out of the country, spent a year in London both studying existential phenomenology and just being away from what I usually do. In that time and place being out of the country and at the same time out of my American mind, it became apparent, as a very serious professional student of man, committed to enlarging his possibilities, that if I wanted to do my job the way I was beginning to see it, I would have among other things, to reread the Marx that I studied when I was an undergraduate. Not to become a Marxist revolutionary but to reacquaint myself with Karl Marx's perspective on how social systems work, how they come to be stratified into classes with a minority dominant class and a larger mass of people who were socialized and trained to fit certain roles in social systems that they would have to fit in order to keep the social system going in turn, to perpetuate the privilege of the few against the mystified being of the many.

This excerpt brings some clarity to Sid's interest in maximizing a person's freedom from various determiners that include his past, his genetic endowments, social pressures (as mentioned above) and to "discover what his possibilities might be, and to fulfill them." The word "possibilities" seems abstract and vague, until Sid clarifies how he views the force of social conformity. The year overseas provided an objective look at the forces in American culture that worked against this maximizing of freedom. The subject of existential freedom, as theoretic as it can sound, was a core philosophy of Sidney's life stance.

One of the things that occurred to me in my period of meditation on what I'd been doing for twenty years, was this: that the institutions have the wealth, and they hire the behavioral scientists, and they don't spend money unless they get something in return. So you have psychologists, psychiatrists, sociologists for the *institution*. They study man for the institution. Well, who then, is the student of man for the individual person? Who is the psychologist for the person? Well it turns out to be the psychotherapist, but the psychotherapist has priced himself way beyond the range of the individual. And so a very worthwhile mission is for more and more physicians, psychologists, psychiatrists, sociologists and anthropologists to study man for the individual instead of the institution.

Birds of a Feather

At the start of the 1965 academic year at the University of Florida Sid met Thomas Hanna, the recently-arrived chairman of the Philosophy Department, who became Sid's closest friend.

Hanna received his doctorate at the University of Chicago and had written *The Thought and Art of Albert Camus* and *The Lyrical Existentialists,* and was editor of *The Bergsonian Heritage.* His best known works were yet to come: *Bodies in Revolt* (1970) and *Somatics* (1988). In Hanna's words:

> It was back in 1965 when I came to Gainesville the first time, and I arrived during the summer when they brought me down to be the chairman of the Philosophy Department.... it was late summer and I got a phone call one morning about 11 o'clock from a fellow with a very nasal twang to his voice. He said he had heard about me and knew I had written some books about existentialism and phenomenology and he was very interested in these things and he was a psychologist, and why didn't we get together at a bar called the Windjammer, which I'd never been to.

After they met and ordered drinks Sid began to share some of his recent experiences in England regarding

> someone named Ronnie Laing that I didn't know about. And he talked about being in Great Britain and he talked about existentialism—he talked about a lot of things, and the main thing that came through to me about this fellow who introduced himself as "Sidney"(and I always called him Sidney from that point on) was that Sidney was a man of enthusiasm. He had a tremendous amount of enthusiasm, and in fact we were both rather enthusiastic and we talked about things, it seemed that every one of which we held in common, and we had one interest after another, and we became rather fascinated with each other, but the feeling about the whole first encounter was enthusiasm.[9]

Hanna continued to chair the Philosophy Department before his move to San Francisco in 1973, where he became the director of the graduate school at the Humanistic Psychology Institute (HPI). Sidney had found a kindred spirit in Tom Hanna.

If Sid had created a Latin motto to best describe his life stance it easily could have been Labor Gravis, Libertas Absoluta: Hard Work and Total Freedom. His goal, and the goal he espoused for others, was total freedom, to the extent that this freedom did not encroach on the freedom of others. The Golden Rule was an integral aspect of this philosophy, but not using the active verb as in "*do* unto others what you would want done to yourself" but the more altruistic version attributed to the Greek rhetorician Isocrates: "Those things which provoke anger when you suffer them from others, do not do to others." Sid devoted his energy and intellect toward developing a body of knowledge that he hoped would help others to achieve a greater measure of freedom in their life without diminishing the freedom of others.

One source of this knowledge for Sid was literature, including the classic writings attributed to Socrates, Plato, Aristotle and Epictetus. The Homeric poems, particularly The Odyssey, embodied for Sid the metaphor of the human journey into the world, gaining knowledge through experience, then returning home to share new knowledge and awareness. The circular nature of the journey away from home and then back was the classic quest tale, with the return from the quest an integral aspect.

This quest is addressed in "An Odyssey Within," a talk Sid presented at the Language and Life Seminar at the University of Florida in 1966.

> Whenever Western man has felt stalemated, at the end of his tether, his first impulse has been to burst through and out and push farther west. He has searched the outside world for freedom, resources, love, distraction and fulfillment. He has found many of these, but inevitably, no matter where his voyage led him, he has then found himself again experiencing entrapment. Like Homer's Odysseus, or like the boll-weevil, he has been looking for a home, but once he finds it, he finds it a trap. Then he may try to drink himself out of boredom, blast himself into orbit out of this world, or consult psychotherapists for help in finding out what is wrong with him.
>
> Now when this man or woman was en route, on his <u>quest</u> for a home, he was magnificent—vital, alive, eyes snapping and dancing, sexy, fit, cunning, inspirited. The man had only to stand in the presence of the woman, or she in his, and they turned one another on. He paused in his quest, perhaps confusing her with his quest, and married her; together they made a home and eventually had it made. Once ensconced in Ithaca, or the suburbs of Ithaca, they began to die a spiritual death. There seemed nothing more to quest for. The outside world seemed stagnant, and so did they. They might have traveled abroad, only to find they couldn't leave the suburbs behind them. They carried them within and compared everything they saw abroad with the way they were at home.

This is a caricature of a kind of modern western man (I've seen him here and in Britain and in a few places on the continent), but it's not entirely inaccurate. He always looks <u>outside</u> when his life becomes stagnant within.[10]

It is easy to read the opening paragraphs as autobiographical. Freedom, boredom, drinking, spiritual impasses, sexuality, magnificence—these were areas of experience and enquiry consequential to Sid as a person.

Later in the talk, after describing his London experience with LSD, Sid qualifies the long-term value of such extreme questing for new experiences:

> But the intimation of what is possible, when induced by drugs can be, I believe, a false and possibly dangerous path to liberation, to fulfillment, to Ithaca. It is like cheap grace, effortless non-attachment. …I am now fascinated with the possibilities of abetting everyman's Odyssey without drugs. I'm grateful for my drug-induced experience of my usually repressed possibilities, but I can also see some danger in reliance upon drugs for liberation. In fact, I now believe that repeated doses of LSD destroys a person's ability to commit himself to projects that take longer than five minutes to complete. Such a person becomes project-less, and hence world-less. I've had a number of acid-heads consult with me, as part of their effort to find values worth committing to, to make a world for themselves that has futurity. It's a challenging task—I don't think Tim Leary has been an entirely responsible messiah.

Sid thought Timothy Leary's motto "Turn On, Tune In, Drop Out" was limited and self-serving, a withdrawal from societal involvement and toward an experiential cocoon. In contrast, Sid valued dialogue, encounter and interaction.

1966

In 1966 Sid co-edited *Reconciliation: A Theory of Man Transcending. (From the Work of Franklin I. Shaw, Dec.)*, published "An Exploratory Study of Body-accessibility" for the *British Journal of Social and Clinical Psychology*; "The 'Awareness of Potentialities' Syndrome" in the *Journal of Humanistic Psychology*; "Some Psychological Aspects of Privacy" in *Law and Contemporary Problems*; contributed a chapter "Toward a Psychology of Transcendent Behavior" for *Explorations in Human Potentialities*; and in the journal *Voices*, Sid recalls an early training experience that most likely occurred in 1958, although for reasons soon revealed, the specifics of date and locale were not included.

You Can Do Whatever You Wish Here

This happened at a workshop, where about fifty trained psychotherapists were gathered for a week of encounter. At one point in the week, everyone went to a nearby mental hospital, to meet selected back-ward patients in groups (of therapists) of five or six. In our group, there were two women therapists, three men therapists including myself, and a graduate student who was studying psychotherapy, and who had a theological background.

Our patient was a male schizophrenic who had been in the hospital since 1946—over twelve years at this time. He was of Brooklyn Irish extraction, wore a brownish-blonde crew-cut, and had an eager-beaver, ready-to-please expression on his face. He was brought into the room where we all sat awaiting him. He sat down, and put himself at our disposal. One of us began the interview, identifying the group members to him, and then asking how we might be of help to him. I recall wondering how he liked staying in the hospital, and asking if he didn't want to get out? He replied that the hospital life was pretty good, three square meals a day, light duties in the laundry, enough money to buy smokes and candies, etc. Others asked him questions, and when he spoke, the atmosphere was dripping with permissiveness and acceptance. At one point someone, I think it was one of the women, told him he could say or do nearly anything he wanted.

I broached the subject of women to him—didn't he miss contact with girls, the chances for sexual pleasure. He blandly replied that there was enough of that in the hospital: the boys in the ward would pull you off or blow you, and then of course, his mother came to visit him every month, and he and she would go at it in the shrubbery... all this spoken in a cooperative, even eager way. Then, the patient said, "All this talk about screwing has got me randy. Does anyone mind if I jerk off?" and without awaiting an answer, he unzipped his fly, and revealed a substantial and erect penis. At least two of the therapists present said, "Go ahead if you want to," when he asked his question. I was, myself, embarrassed, angry, confused, and amused, and said nothing. I thought, as I looked at my colleagues, that they did not look to me as permissive as they wanted to appear or sound. However, the patient took the words at face value, and set about his pleasurable task with unselfconscious gusto.

Soon after he began, he asked one of the women present if she would come and pull him off. With her clinical *persona* slipping, she said with effortful composure, "No, I don't think I should." He countered by saying, "Well, would you mind if I played with your tits?" Again she demurred, and so he resumed his solitary task under the watchful "permissive" eyes of the therapeutic masters.

The hilarious and grotesque features of this whole fiasco was that, as he was throbbing away, several of the therapists continued to ask him questions, and, moreover, between sighs, he answered them. The atmosphere was electric, as I experienced it anyway. Then, I evolved the courage of my experiencing, and said something like, "Look, I don't know about the others, but I find this very embarrassing and it makes me angry to have you pull off here. I don't think this is the time or the place for it. Put it away and zip up your fly." (I was apprehensive, as I said this, lest my colleagues think me something of a square.)

The patient said, still pulling away, and breathing more heavily, "Yeah, I wouldn't mind stopping, but you can wait a minute, I'm just about to come."

Here, in the silence and uncertainty, I displayed a true, gentlemanly *savoir faire* –I said with great understanding, "Oh, if you're just about there, then go ahead and finish; *then* put it away." He did both.

Shortly after he folded his handkerchief and put it in his pocket, the time was up, the patient was returned to his ward, and we sat, somewhat stunned, I think. Then we went out on the lawn outside the building, to discuss how we had permitted ourselves to be had in this way. I think we reached some kind of consensus that we had been taken by an expert manipulator (I use the term advisedly), and I for one had an object-lesson in what happens when one tries to seem to be like some cliché of the therapist instead of being the person that one *is*. I suspect the patient is still laughing, if he's not weeping.[11]

Determiners and Freedom

What was Sidney attempting to achieve through his reading, writing, reflection, and research? Did he have a specific model in mind such as Maslow's Hierarchy of Needs or an overarching theory of personality as did Freud, Jung and Wilhelm Reich? For Sid, it appears that the core issue was freedom. "To the extent that psychologists illumine human existence to bring it under the deliberate control of someone other than the person himself, to that extent they are helping to undermine some person's freedom in order to enlarge the freedom of someone else."[12]

Sid despised being conned on any level—the confessed psychological game played on him by the woman in college remained with him as a lived experience of human motivation and its resultant behavior.

Thus, advertisers, businessmen, military leaders, politicians, and salesmen all seek to learn more about the determiners of human conduct, in order to gain power and advantage. If they can sway human behavior by manipulating the conditions which mediate it, they can get large numbers of people to forfeit their own interests and serve the interests of the manipulator. Such secret manipulation of the masses or of an individual by some other person is possible only if the ones being manipulated are kept mystified as to what is going on, and if their experience of their own freedom is blunted.[13]

The potential financial rewards of such manipulation are obvious. Sid's view regarding the purpose of psychological research practically guaranteed no grant research money from any organized enterprise reliant on the very information Sid refers to: advertising in all its forms, car sales, marketing, marketing focus groups. If the procurement of money drives much of human behavior, Sid's role is that of a prophet shouting to an uninterested crowd. As he puts it

Psychologists face a choice. We may elect to continue to treat our Ss [Subjects] as objects of study for the benefit of some elite; or we may choose to learn about determiners of the human condition in order to discover ways to overcome or subvert them, to enlarge the Ss'—that is, Everyman's—freedom. If we opt for the latter, our path is clear. Our ways of conducting psychological research will have to be altered. Our definition of the purpose of psychology will have to change. And our ways of reporting our findings, as well as the audiences to whom the reports are directed, will have to change. We shall have to state openly whether we are psychologists-for-institutions or psychologists-for-persons.[14]

It's all there: the primal emphasis on existential freedom, the wholesale rejection of behaviorism's approach to the person, and a stance firmly against psychologists collecting such knowledge to generate profits for a business. Sid had read, and then reread Marx. It was the argument of labor versus capital in another form.

Learning how to transcend the specific determiners in your life—to engage that potential for freedom—formed the basis for much of Sid's research. He was well aware of how the knowledge of determinants of behavior could be applied and by whom. An excerpt from Sid's talk at the Esalen Institute in the fall of 1965 reveals this stance:

As human beings, we're subject to limits, to biological pressures, social pressures, the momentum and inertia of habit, the kinds of things that the behavioral scientists investigated pretty thoroughly, but we also are as Sartre puts it, "condemned to freedom," and from this perspective, we face an option: we can be in this world, as determined beings, or we can be in this world as free, transcending beings. Behavior scientists have to function like other scientists: mainly, to find out and measure just what *are* the determiners in this world. To this extent, I'm like any of my colleagues. I'm a disciplined investigator, I try to find the determiners, I try to measure them and I try to weigh them, one way or the other, but it's at this point that a choice arises: once you have specified determiners, you then have an option. You can conceal the existence of these determiners from the people whom they affect, and this puts you in a position of being one up on them, and once you know what they are you get a lever on them, you can manipulate the determiners and hence manipulate behavior—just read Skinner's book *Science and Human Behavior* for the most forceful, brilliant analysis of how this is possible and how in fact it's being done.

And the other option is to call it to somebody's attention that these determiners exist and it's really up to you whether you acquiesce to them or play judo with them and maybe invite their thrust behind you in the pursuit of your own freely-chosen projects. I happen to see, we'll call it humanistic psychology, as serving this mission. It's identical, up to a point, with the mission of Division 3 of the APA [Society for Experimental Psychology and Cognitive Science] and the Psychonomic Society [A society for the experimental study of cognition], to find out what are the determiners that affect behavior and experience, and at that point we part company, because they exempt themselves from political and philosophical questions, [Sid now switches syntax from 'they' to 'him'] for him they've been settled. He's a positivist, and usually an upwardly-mobile middle class man; or else he separates his political and religious and ethical views from science, so in effect he is a colluder with the status quo, or he's an employee of the space administration, General Motors. Or he takes another position and says alright, I have a privileged glimpse of the undoubted determiners that affect man. I can study them, and in fact I ask subjects to show themselves to me so I can find out what these determiners are. Then I have a choice, I can either keep him in the dark as to what I found out, and whisper it to the people who have underwritten my grant, or I can say look, you have shown me how you learn, how you pursue, you've told me about your past, your marriage, or whatever, you've told me your secrets or you've showed them to me. I'm a trained man, I discover certain determiners that are affecting your existence, I'm now going to point them out to you so that if you find that these determiners are getting in your way of enlarging your existence, discovering new possibilities and so on, this is what you might do to get around them, and in fact one can apply fully-developed sciences of transcendence, let's say expanding your ability to learn, expanding your ability to read, enlarging your capacity to remember, enlarging your capacity to enter into dialogue with another human being. These are applied sciences that only work because somebody has discovered what the determiners are…as fast as we discover determiners then instantly it becomes possible to transcend them.[15]

Disclosing Man to Himself

In his interview for the CPAA Sid recalled "In 1968 I put together a bunch of my papers beyond *The Transparent Self*, called *Disclosing Man To Himself*, and that in some ways is the better book, although it was never as popular." The book was Sid's second with Van Nostrand, its thesis outlined on the dust cover:

Psychology, as a science, has devoted itself to discovering determiners and limits of human behavior. Knowledge in the field has expanded at a tremendous rate. Unfortunately, this knowledge has become too much a tool to direct, even to control, the destiny of men. Psychology has been used by corporate organization, by those who have things to sell, by the few who would control the many.

In reaction to this state of events is *Disclosing Man to Himself*. This book, and this psychology, treat the human being not as an obstacle to total institutional control, not as a possible error factor in experimental procedure, but as an end to himself—an end to be fostered.

Disclosing Man to Himself is a book that is, or at least illustrates, this turning point in the profession of psychology. Its goal is to help man enlarge his grasp of his situation, to make him more conscious of his freedom and of his capacity to grow in awareness. There are suggestions for some new dimensions for psychological research and some new ways to be a psychotherapist. There is an overall redirecting of psychology. This new direction is toward the *service* of man.

Sid's philosophy, combined with his clinical observation promotes a psychology in service to humans to enlarge their grasp of their situation, to make them more aware of their freedom and of their capacity to grow in awareness. This easily sounds vague and fuzzy to contemporary ears but the wording can be analyzed on a deeper level. "Grasp of the situation" implies the approaches of existentialism, and phenomenology; "aware of freedom" is certainly existential and "growing in awareness" encompasses many levels of meaning, from self-awareness to becoming more cosmopolitan and less provincial in outlook. Sid makes this clear in the book's Preface:

> This book continues themes I presented first in *The Transparent Self*. There, I explored the meaning of self-disclosure for wellness, growth, and personal relationships. Here, I have tried to develop a few steps further the "humanistic" approach in psychology. I have tried to show laymen and students and colleagues one view of what psychology might look like if psychologists tried more directly to show those whom they study what they have learned.
>
> A lot of knowledge about a lot of men, if it is possessed by a few, gives these few power over the many. Psychologists seek knowledge about men. Men consent to be studied by psychologists. The question is, who is being helped when psychologists study men? If I have knowledge about you, I can use this to my advantage, and against yours. If I have knowledge about myself, I can increase my freedom and my power to live my life meaningfully. If you have knowledge about me, I would like you to enlighten me, not control me. And I would like to know you.
>
> The book is an invitation to psychologists (and physicians, psychiatrists, teachers, clergymen, counselors, and psychotherapists) to disclose themselves to men, and man to himself, rather than to one's colleagues alone, or to institutional leaders. And it is an invitation to those laymen who are studied by or consult psychologists to ask for as much transparency as the professionals ask of them.

The chapters are divided into four groups: A Humanistic Perspective on Psychological Research, Psychotherapy for Growing Persons, Experience: A Neglected Dimension in Psychology, and Some Conclusions and Prospects for Humanistic Psychology. In the first section Sid introduces the idea of *dialogue* as expounded by Martin Buber's *I and Thou*,[16] an encounter distinctly opposed to mystification and purposeful deception between the participants.

The next section defines a healthy personality as a growing one, and defines the growth cycle as (a) an acknowledgment that the world has changed, (b) a shattering of the present experienced "world-structure," and (c) a restructuring retotalization of the world-structure which encompasses the new disclosure of changed reality.

In the third section "Experience: A Neglected Dimension in Psychology," the approach of phenomenology is explored. According to Sid's historical perspective, beginning in the 1920 behaviorism dominated psychology from the successes of Pavlov and Watson's research. "Consciousness, mind, experience—these were regarded as extra-scientific realms, not suitable for study by hard-nosed, tough-minded investigators." Those were the precise areas of Sid's deepest interest. The widespread adoption of psychoanalytic theory also discounted the value of experience:

> According to the psychoanalytic view, man, while he can be free (or freer),
> is mostly a vessel driven by instinctual urges and irrational super-ego
> prodding. And his conscious experiencing is not investigated for itself,
> but rather for the glimpses and hints it may afford of the subterranean
> unconscious mental life.
>
> The upshot has been that the reporting and description of human
> experiencing has been shoved out of the realm of science, and relegated
> (or elevated) to the province of the arts and humanities. Novelists, poets,
> painters, playwrights, musicians—these have been the people who
> investigate human experience in its myriad forms. The only scientifically
> oriented people to take a serious interest in experience per se have been
> the philosophical phenomenologists, and a scattering of psychologists
> who began to read literature in the tradition of existentialism and
> phenomenology.[17]

Phenomenology focused on the importance of experience, an oddly neglected aspect of life yet the very definition of what it is to be alive, a participant in the three-dimensional world of people, interaction, events. In further chapters Sid explores learning, growth and creativity from the phenomenological point of view.

In the final section, Sid discusses the challenge of automation: how he viewed the future for humans when most work is done by robots and automated manufacturing, and how people could find meaning beyond work. This is prescient but in a different way than Sid expected. Through automation and outsourcing many employment positions and retail business models have become obsolete, leading to a shrinking middle class as the wealthy become wealthier and the poor remain poor.

The Epilogue reiterates the main thrust of Sid's research. He wants to make psychology more relevant to the fuller development and individuation of *persons*.

Counterculture

Disclosing Man To Himself was published the year after the Summer of Love, 1967's coming-out party for what became the Hippie culture, a reaction against the status quo of American consumer and military-industrial power. Along with this culture came recreational drug use. Sid's view of recreational drugs went beyond their customary use as pure recreation. There were possibilities of expanded consciousness and alternate realities available through the use of psychedelics and marijuana.

In an article from the University of Florida college newspaper *The Independent Florida Alligator*, Sid presents his views on marijuana:

Marijuana Panel Raps Pot Users

The danger of developing a nation of "potheads" is not as great as that of developing a nation of fascism, Dr. Sidney Jourard, UF psychology professor, warned in Thursday night's marijuana forum in the University Auditorium.

Jourard explained that "the intense measures of violence used in the military-like crackdown on drugs are more dangerous than their use."

The forum was held despite a reported request by a member of the Board of Regents that "forums debating topics that were legislated against such as murder, drugs, and stealing should not occur on campus."

...Jourard also said, "Consenting adults should be able to seek their own pleasures, but marijuana should be subject to the same taxes and laws on its use by people under 21 as is alcohol."

"People who use marijuana are expressing some form of social protest," Jourard explained.[18]

Due to the aggressive enforcement tactics of narcotics officers and the law enforcement agencies in central Florida, marijuana possession was actively prosecuted, especially outside Gainesville's city limits, and there were tales of persons serving a one-year term in state prison for possession of a single joint. Sid, who was by now familiar with the political ramifications of drug prosecution, announced to me and my two brothers that if we chose to smoke marijuana, either by ourselves or with friends, to do it only at our house. This approach to the problem was not common among the parents of our friends.

Demystify, Enlighten, Transcend   8

DESCRIBING SID as a humanistic psychologist is accurate but incomplete, as he was a writer of books, a university professor, lecturer and speaker, and a practicing psychotherapist. A bigger challenge lies in describing humanistic psychology. Beyond what humanistic psychology rejected— behaviorism and psychoanalytic theory— what was it *for*?

With linguistic roots in the word *humanism*, humanistic psychology shared foundational values described in Humanism, an ethical view that emphasizes the value of human beings and of reason and critical thinking over supernatural beliefs or dogma as embodied in organized religion. In "Reason With Compassion," H.J. Eysenck describes humanism's opposition to religion as originally inspired "by the fact that where Humanists put their faith in reason, religious people put their faith in faith."[1] Eysenck wrote that reason was vital to science, the rational attempt to solve problems posed by nature or by human behavior: "Humanism is the use of reason in human affairs, applied in the service of compassion." Sid was attempting to combine his intellect and his spirit in a similar way, using insight into the human condition gained from the scientific method and applying it to the larger issues of life, in pursuit of the eternal verities—truth, compassion, wisdom, love, justice, beauty. On a certain level, Sid was an idealist.

Because Humanistic thought focused on what made humankind *different* from animals, the behaviorist's study of animals to gain insights into the human condition was problematic for humanistic psychologists on several fronts.

For starters, animals lacked imaginative and subjective experiences inherent in self-conscious awareness. As a result, experiments involving dogs that salivated at the sound of a buzzer, pigeons trained to peck at certain colors of a disc in order to receive a pellet, and white rats learning to run a maze were all decried by Abraham Maslow, who commented:

> In animal psychology, the stress has been on hunger and thirst. Why not study the higher needs? We actually do not know whether the white rat has anything to compare with our higher needs for love, beauty, understanding, status and the like. With the techniques now available to animal psychologists, how could we know? We must get over the psychology of the *desperate* rat, the rat who is pushed to the point of starvation, or who is pushed by pain or electric shock into an extreme situation, one so extreme that human beings seldom find themselves in it.[2]

A Human Psychology

Another aspect of the humanistic approach to the study of human behavior was identifying what Sid called "symptoms" of extreme wellness, something beyond the lack of disease or the ability to fit into various acceptable societal roles, referred to as adjustment. The concepts of spirit-level, inspiration, vitality, courage, were purposely neglected in psychological discourse because they connected the relatively new science of psychology with its ancient parent, philosophy. Understanding the levels of these qualities of spirit in a person was one such avenue of research from a humanistic approach; there were others: inner needs, fulfillment, the search for identity, and other distinctly human concerns.

It was easy to doubt the possibility of the measurable scientific study of such amorphous subject matter, and this raised questions about the purposes of science. Maslow discussed "peak experiences" and had developed the theory of the hierarchy of needs that, if fulfilled, would lead, on a perfect day, to greater "self-actualization." These ideas and other writings attracted a group of like-minded therapists, psychologists and others in the social sciences who eventually became aware of each other through Maslow's mailing list. The list grew into a journal and a newsletter, *Phoenix.* The newsletter's first issue in December 1963 contained a report of the first convention of the American Association for Humanistic Psychology, held August 28, 1963 at the Sheraton Hotel in Philadelphia, including this note from a discussion group that included Rollo May, S.I. Hayakawa and Sid:

The term "Human" rather than "Humanistic" was suggested. Research implications of humanistic orientation included such approaches as replicating studies where the relationship between E[xperimenter] and S[ubject] is one of experience and familiarity, rather than the usual condition of being strangers. It was suggested that the limitations on man's potentials are set by man's imagination and we need more dreamers.[3]

Sid's preferred term Human Psychology was not chosen. In later years Sid had grown beyond using the word "human" in any context when referring to psychology; in a 1974 interview for the CPAA, in response to the interviewers comment that the psychology department in University of Toronto was humanistic, Sid replied "psychology is a humanistic discipline, it's redundant."

The debate over psychology as a natural science or a human science was ongoing. Data-driven behaviorist experimental psychologists not only dismissed the idea of measuring feelings, they apparently had no interest in the feeling side of human experience whatsoever. Sid wrote:

Man's *self*—yours and mine—has proven to be a vexing problem for psychologists. To be a self is to be, not an object, but the subject of one's own experiencing. And psychology has not dealt as neatly and systematically with subjectivity as it has with behavior. Yet my behavior embodies and encodes my subjectivity. To study my behavior without trying to discern what I mean, what I intend by it, is to strip it of its meaning-for-me. Studies of my behavior that neglect consideration of its meaning-for-me presume that its meaning-for-you, the researcher, is all that is important for scientific comprehension of my behavior and experience. To ignore or deny my experience is to deny something that exists. This is bad science.[4]

Despite the unified front against the tenets of behaviorism and psychoanalytic theory, the humanistic psychology umbrella was so large as to make agreement about much else difficult. When questioned in a 1971 interview "Do you think the humanists will ever get it enough together organizationally to present an institutional alternative to say, the behavioral engineers? Or is it by nature a fragmentary movement?" Sid answered "I don't know. Humanism is a very loose term. You get ten humanists together, and you will find it very hard for them to agree on anything but the necessity of pluralism."[5]

Even psychologists working within a narrow range of interest rarely agreed fully on anything, as their theories could be and were criticized by psychologists in the peer-reviewed journals.

Many of the areas of activity and research that interested Sidney his entire life were all built around connection, the relationship of therapist to client, of spouse to spouse, parent to child, teacher to student; the interaction of humans with the environment, with themselves, with others. This was one of the tenets of phenomenology, that a person or subject cannot be accurately assessed or studied separate from the context within which the person or subject functions, as behavior is built around relationships with others and with social culture, and the study of humans should be about the current situation of humans, and the desire in others to define you or attempt to do so, as he described in his paper "On Being Persuaded Who You Are."[6]

His writings for the *Journal of Humanistic Psychology* were often accompanied by a short autobiographical note in a section called "The Persons Behind the Ideas." In the April 1968 issue Sid describes his stance this way:

> If I identify with any systematic view, it is that anti-system system, the "humanistic-existential-phenomenological" approach, that of the "HEP-cats" as my department chairman calls it. I arrived at this position by way of earlier training in behavioristic and psychoanalytic perspectives, reaching beyond them, to the *person*, as the challenger of systems.
>
> The present work grew out of the realization that self-disclosure to another person and letting another person touch you, are both ways of letting him know you.

Counterculturalists

Around Gainesville in the late '60s it was hard to miss Sid as he went about his business, the very archetype of a liberal psychology professor. His hair, never flowing, grew somewhat longer and he drove a Triumph TR3 convertible, repainted butterscotch yellow, a color chosen by Sid, who was colorblind. He dressed casually while teaching and consulting, only wearing a suit and tie when necessary for appearances at conferences and other higher-profile professional settings. He once said, while packing a gray suit for an upcoming lecture at Ball State University in

Indiana, "You see this, son? This is my 'sincere' suit. I wear this whenever I am being paid a thousand dollars to speak at a university." Sid was adept at role-playing when the situation called for it. His beliefs remained consistent but what he wore was chosen for the setting.

In November of 1965 Sid spoke to a group in San Francisco at the time that the hippie counterculture began to unfold, although the word "hippie" was not in general use yet. In this talk Sid mentions "beatniks" and "squares" as the two opposing cultural camps, with the beatniks not buying into the squares and their cultural package of America and material gain, money, traditional family values, etc.

Eight years later he reflected on the role of those who run counter to social mores and customs:

> There probably is a sense in which they used to be called bohemians, or beatniks, or hippies but really the artists in our society have been sort of leaders, almost therapists. They provided a scene where if you didn't fit in your neighborhood in Winesburg, Ohio, or a suburb of Pittsburgh, you could either experience yourself as neurotic, or crazy. And then once you bought that game, then it was just an escalation of all kinds of treatment. And the other is, if you had some help from your friends, you could be smuggled out of Winesburg, Ohio to Greenwich Village or San Francisco or California, and instead of being crazy, you would have a chance to explore other ways of living your life.[7]

Sid's choice of Winesburg was not random, as Sherwood Anderson's novel *Winesburg, Ohio* presents various characters struggling with communicating their feelings and confronting their isolation and desires.

Being the child of Jewish atheist freethinkers who embraced Marxist philosophy and the concept of universal equality, Sid fit right in with the growing hippie counterculture of the late sixties, and Gainesville was a relatively liberal environment for a southern town. The liberation movements embraced by the counterculture appealed to this former Canadian in his early forties who had his own inhibitions and constraints to overcome.

For many years Sid taught an introductory psychology course to a class of two to three hundred students in a large auditorium. Initially viewed by many undergraduates as a soft science "easy A," students soon found it was difficult to even earn a C without study and good writing skills. Sid read and graded the tests himself, correcting grammar with a red pencil. "These students would come up after receiving their papers and say 'Lordy Dr. Jernad, I didn't sign up for no grammar class!'" He had no patience with imprecise writing and was particularly critical of poor spelling. In a 1974 lecture Sid commented that, even among many graduate students, grammatically correct English was a second language. Words were his modus operandi. He took seriously the effective use of written English language as a tool of communication, echoing the statement of the poet Wallace Stevens that "technique is proof of seriousness."

As this was the late sixties, the Age of Aquarius and the hippie culture abounded, and freedom was a core value of the counterculture: freedom from the views of their parents, of the government, and from many cultural norms. This fit neatly into the academic reaches of existentialism and was in concert with Sid's philosophical views. The college setting and this congruence allowed Sidney to connect socially with the youth culture while still retaining his academic standing. Sid enjoyed his reputation among students as a "hip" professor and thrived on the variety of observable human behavior to be found in a small college town.

Therapist

Connecting and communicating with his clients in therapy was one such setting. Sid had been a practicing psychotherapist since the early fifties during his latter years at the University of Buffalo. As a source of income this private counseling was a necessity in his early years; now he used it more as an opportunity for a real life patient-client dyad that allowed him to try out his ideas and gain immediate feedback. However, his obligation to teaching and writing books made his private practice small by design.

Sid was developing his own hybrid approach of therapy that did not involve a school per se, as in a Rogerian approach, psychoanalysis, or any clearly-defined technique. His exploration of the "dyadic effect"—that self-disclosure inspired and invited the other person's self-disclosure—opened his clients up to him, allowing the therapeutic process to accelerate and human experience to be more fully revealed. Sid viewed this process as dialogue, based on the concepts of Martin Buber, whose *I and Thou* was a seminal book in Sid's therapeutic approach. He saw a partnership between therapist and client, as did Carl Rogers with his client-based therapy, but he believed a conscious effort was required to determine the precise balance of disclosure and listening that maximized the effectiveness of such an approach. Sid wrote of his growing awareness of a different, less objective client-therapist relationship and he seemed to tailor the therapy to the particular patient, as the following three examples illuminate:

Now in psychotherapy, I found myself for a long time trying to heal my patients by faithfully and self-consciously practicing technique as I learned it. It was only after reaching insurmountable impasses in my therapeutic work that I began to grow from novice technician into psychotherapist. It was as if I had been invited by my teachers and preceptors to be attentive to their example and to hew to it—to impersonate them, really. Grotesque situations arose with patients in which it was as if they weren't sitting with *me*; rather they were speaking to an analogue of Carl Rogers, or Sigmund Freud, or—more immediately—my therapy supervisors. The sound of my voice, on tape recordings of sessions, was most unnatural, as if I were not myself, but "the therapist." In time, with fear and trembling, and as testimony to my resolve to be helpful to patients rather than to imitate the acts of someone who once had helped patients, I let my patients teach me how to be a therapist with them. I found myself transcending my technique. Here are some episodes which helped me discover that to be a psychotherapist means that one can be as flexible, inventive, and creative as law, ethics, and the dignity and integrity and well-being of oneself and one's patients will allow. And that leaves much elbow-room.

* * *

An attractive, even stunning, woman in her early twenties consulted me. She wore a tight yellow sweater and an equally tight skirt, both of which garments she filled exquisitely. She sat in the reclining chair in a most provocative way, telling her story. I was hardly listening. Suddenly, she asked me, "Would you like to go to bed with me?"

I replied, taken aback, "You're wondering whether I want to be more intimate than a therapist." "No, I asked you if you'd like to go to bed with me," she insisted. I replied, in a panic, trying to get her back into what I then thought was the proper role for a patient, "The reason you ask this is because you aren't certain about your desirability." (In fact, both my comments, taken in context, were relevant and technically sound.) She said, "I keep asking you and you won't answer." I said, in growing anxiety, "No, I couldn't go to bed with you, it's not ethical." "You couldn't?" she insisted. Finally, I blurted out, "Look, Miss X; I find you very attractive. But

I don't want to go to bed with you." "Why not," she asked, "since you say I'm attractive?" I continued, "because If I did, I'd be so scared and guilty I wouldn't enjoy it, and moreover, I'd run the risk of being disqualified in my profession." She breathed a huge sigh of relief, sat in a more prim posture, and proceeded to tell me of her experience with men whom she had enticed into situations she couldn't cope with nor could they.

* * *

A man in his late twenties, very obsessed with his own manliness, consulted me for help when he found he couldn't finish a thesis on which he was working. We proceeded through the beginning stages of therapy swiftly enough—he told me about his present situation, his earlier life, his complicated relationship with his father—and then we reached an impasse of intellectualized chitchat. During one session, when the chitchat died out, there was a period of silence; and the patient sat there, with a look of desperation on his face. I felt an impulse to take his hand and hold it. In a split second, I pondered about the countertransference implications of such an act and debated whether I should do such a thing. I did it. I took his hand and gave it a firm squeeze. He grimaced; and with much effort not to do so, he burst into deep, racking sobs. The dialogue proceeded from there.

* * *

A nursing student was referred to me by her instructor. The girl became nauseous and faint whenever she approached a patient to give him an injection. None of the efforts of her teachers or fellow students to help her availed. She was in danger of being asked to leave the nursing program. She was obviously a tense young woman. I interviewed her and learned something of her family background and her experience at the University as a nursing student. She could be diagnosed as an hysteric, on the basis of her disclosures, but that thought was not very helpful in the urgency of the present situation. I pondered whether to take her on as a patient for intensive psychotherapy, but there was no time. I decided to try something different. In the third meeting, I asked her to get a hypodermic needle and show me how to use it. She could perform an injection on herself, in the arm or thigh, without fainting; and she could receive one from another. She filled a hypo with saline solution and showed me how to hold it; and with dispatch, I performed an injection in her forearm. I didn't do it at all badly, if I say so myself. Then I asked her to inject me. She brought the needle to my upper arm, trembled, blanched, and said, "I can't do it."

In the next session we were talking about her hobbies—she was a swimmer and kept herself physically fit. She prided herself on it. I asked her to do some setup exercises—touching her toes, deep-knee-bends, and push-ups. She thought I was crazy. I agreed, but asked her to proceed anyway. She did so. Then as she stood beside my desk, panting, I took up the hypodermic needle, handed it to her, and asked her to prepare it again for an injection. She filled it with solution; and when it was ready, I said firmly, "Now give me an injection." She came over to me, plunged the needle in, pressed the plunger, pulled the needle out—and then stood up, almost dazed but not blanched, saying, "I did it, I did it. God damn it, I did it!" She showed up on the wards that day and gave injections wherever her instructor told her to. She continued effectively with her studies. I did not have further sessions with her, since she did not wish it. I am not sure one could call these sessions "psychotherapy," though the outcome was evidently psychotherapeutic for her.[8]

On The Road

Sid's personality was of a singular nature that is difficult to encapsulate, so it is of value to learn of how others experienced him in various roles and settings. In "What Sid Jourard and Timothy Leary Were Like In Person" Len Bergantino provides this candid 1970 view of Sid from the perspective of a younger scholar:

> It was the next to my last year of doctoral work at the University of Southern California (USC). I was a licensed marriage, family, and child counselor, and I signed up for a weekend workshop with Sid Jourard at Lake Arrowhead. Jourard had recently written a book that was hot in the humanistic-existential department at USC, entitled *The Transparent Self.* Jourard's plane came in late from Gainesville, Florida, where he was a full professor in Psychology, and he took the podium about 9:30 pm Friday night instead of 8 p.m.
>
> People began to ask him questions…such as Are you married? How many children do you have? How many times a week do you have sex with your wife? Do you have sexual relationships outside of your marriage? It went about that far, and then Jourard stunned the audience by saying "I am going to talk to you bastards about privacy! Just because I wrote a book about

transparency you think you can rape me psychologically up here!"

He dressed in blue jeans and a pullover shirt and his belly hung out some. There was a party—a mixer—given after the Introduction, where the audience had a chance to socialize with Dr. Jourard. I remember he kept belching in people's faces but that did not seem to dissuade them, including myself, from pursuing him. He was quite charismatic in an unconventional way.

Sunday about noon he closed his presentation and I brought a tape recorder over to his cottage and waited for him. It was my intention to hire him for an hour and tape a psychotherapy session with him doing therapy with me being the patient, and to get a bird's-eye view of what he actually did. I was with a girl I was dating named Rachel who was very attractive.

Jourard walked in, saw the tape recorder plugged in, had a small fit, and pulled it out of the wall before he asked me what I was doing there. When I told him, he said he had no interest in doing that, but if Rachel and I wanted to drink wine with him for the next several hours he would be glad to spend time with us. Years later I was able to surmise that this was his way of doing psychotherapy from a humanistic-existential point of view. He was being as fully Sid Jourard as he could possibly be and that was the therapy, belching and all. He made his point. That was 1970.

I met him another time when he came out as a guest professor at United States International University in San Diego and I was living down there working as a clinical / counseling psychologist for the VA Outpatient Clinic. Dr. Jourard introduced me to his students as a young and courageous psychologist and it meant a lot to me that he respected me....

Afterthoughts: Sid Jourard told me that while he was a full professor at the University of Florida in Gainesville, he did three hours of psychotherapy per week. I asked him why so few, and he said something like "Doing more than three hours of private practice a week drains the life force and life energy out of me!"

The highest honor one could receive as a psychologist as a journeyman after five years of licensure is a Diplomate from the American Board of Professional Psychology. Hearsay then was that he had flunked the ABPPs five times in a row on the same issue. They asked him to reference and quote the literature in clinical psychology, and he kept saying "I write the literature, I don't read it!" For better or worse, that was Jourard, true to himself.[9]

In a question-and-answer period following his presentation in Ithaca, NY in May 1972, Sidney responds to a question regarding his psychotherapeutic approach. The question is in reference to Sid's idea of a therapist being able to share a sense of what he calls "magnificence" in order to encourage similar feelings in the patient:

Q: Because of the issue of authority, I was wondering if somehow you could have people [therapists] that were actually magnificent heroes, and yet wouldn't come down in such a way so that when the person gets some change occurring he can attribute it to himself?

A: I make this assumption for myself, that the other person has much more power than he ever dreamed he has. When he consults with me, he is arguing, "You are strong, I am weak." And I'll say, "You don't seem weak to me. You've got the strength of a horse." "No, I am sick," he might reply. "You don't seem sick to me. You seem bewildered or confused or befuddled or timid." He attributes characteristics to himself that I disagree with and I attribute characteristics to him that he disagrees with. And we have a kind of argument going. If he wins the argument, he loses a great deal indeed, because he is saying over and over again, "I cannot, I cannot." And I'm saying essentially, "You can, you can. I have done it. He has done it. We are human. You are human. You probably may be able to do it." And so on.[10]

Sid continued to write and publish. In 1968 he contributed the opening chapter in *Ways of Growth: Approaches to Expanding Awareness*.[11] The following year Sid contributed the chapter "Sex in Marriage" in *Readings in Humanistic Psychology*.[12] His writing was now being anthologized and reprinted, as the article was written seven years prior. A lengthy chapter in *Current Topics in Clinical and Community Psychology* documented research by Sid and ten of his research colleagues on the effects of experimenters' self-disclosure on the behavior of subjects. In "The Invitation To Die," his chapter in *On The Nature of Suicide*, Sid addresses the theme of suicide from the point of view of existential phenomenology:

A person lives as long as he experiences his life as having meaning and value, and as long as he has something to live *for*—meaningful projects that will animate him and invite him into the future or entice him to pull himself into the future. He will continue to live as long as he has hope of fulfilling meanings and values. As soon as meaning, value, and hope vanish from a person's experience, he begins to stop living; that is, he begins to die.

I am going to propose that people destroy themselves in response to an invitation originating from others that they stop living.[13]

This contribution became a chapter in the revised edition of *The Transparent Self.* Sid trafficked in ideas and by collecting these ideas into books he presented themes that could be seen through the overarching concepts of existentialism, phenomenology, and humanism. In the journal *Voices* that same year he contributed "The Therapist As Guru,"[14] using a term popular at this time through a growing awareness of Indian spiritual beliefs. The Beatles had recently meditated with Maharishi Mahesh Yogi and a guru was a wise man, a spiritual adviser. The egocentric nature of this metaphor fit in with Sid's growing idea of a psychotherapist being an exemplar of a healthy person, evolving the patient's self-concept by way of example. This was not a traditional role for a therapist and it did not lend itself to introduction as a practical approach for most practicing therapists, whom Sid would criticize repeatedly in years to come at conferences as not "guru-ready."

Passport photo, 1969, Crescent Beach, Florida.

South of the Border

In the summer of 1969 Sid traveled to Mexico to visit Thomas Hanna, who was on a sabbatical leave to write *Bodies In Revolt* on a scholastic grant. Hanna recalls the visit:

> I don't think he liked Mexico, he thought it was kind of crazy and it made him feel uneasy, but I always put him in situations of danger and he thought "Well, if Hanna will do it it must be O.K…'cause probably Hanna wouldn't risk his neck." So he would go to these strange places, and risk strange foods, and strange environments, and in both cases when he was visiting me in Guadalajara and Cuernavaca he did that. But the thing that was fascinating was to watch Sidney in a foreign clime where they didn't speak his language, where people were very different. And what he did was literally, was have a kind of banquet of observation of people. If you just left him alone for a minute he'd sit down, lean against a wall and start watching people in Mexico. In Guadalajara all he did was watch. [I'd say,] what are you looking at Sidney?" [He'd say] "Look at that guy over there! The guy who's selling the tamales! And look, look how he moves his eyebrows as he hawks his tamales. Look at his shoulder. Watch him!" Because they were people he'd never seen before, they were types that were new to him. And it just blew his mind.[15]

On his second visit to Hanna, in addition to observing people Sidney ingested peyote. In making this decision his intellect and spirit were in close accord.

> The descriptions of "psychedelic trips" provide one with a more dramatic portrayal of the openness to experiencing which occurs with "letting go." On one occasion, I ate a fist-sized peyote button. Its taste was absolutely hideous, and the effort to keep it in my stomach after swallowing each bite was heroic. The content of this cactus is an alkaloid poison, and so as fast as I was eating it, my stomach was reflexively attempting to expel it. Nevertheless, I held it down for about two hours before I finally yielded to the need to regurgitate. I was in Mexico at the time, and a trusted friend was sitting with me on the roof of his house. About an hour after I vomited, I began to shiver from an experience of cold. I huddled in my chair. This ended after a short time, and I felt energized to an extraordinary degree. I began to dance with rhythms which my friend said were African or Indian. I looked at lights from the street, and they had intense blue

auras. The heavens appeared to me as they might if one were living inside a volcano, with only the cone open to the skies. I believed I could see the Aztec serpent god *Quetzcoatl* flying through the air. During the plant-induced surges of energizing, my perceptions of distance were altered; the street appeared only a footstep away, whereas the actual distance from the roof was more than twenty-five feet. I recall telling my friend, "Peyote is definitely not for children, or unstable people; I can see how someone would believe he could fly, or step from a building to the ground, and then go ahead and do it, only to die. I at least know that my experience is from the peyote."

During the period of strength and energy, I broke a piece of tile about an inch thick with my bare hands, and I pulled a foot-long metal spike from out of a brick wall and bent it. (Next morning I could neither break the tile nor bend the spike). I believed then that I could get into the "rhythm" of bricks and metal, and by such contact, perform what looked like superhuman feats.

After perhaps two hours of such goings on, I became exhausted and lay on a cot; the period of quiet began a voyage in time to my early childhood, perhaps the years between two and four. I re-experienced some of the vivid visual and auditory memories from that time, which I also had done some five years earlier, when I took lysergic acid (LSD) under the guidance of a physician experienced in those matters. I also could recognize myself again as various animals, for example, a lion, an eagle, a snake, and a dog. After another two hours or so, I slept. On awakening the next morning I discussed the experience with my friend, and found it enlightening.

I do not believe such drug-induced experiences are growth-enhancing for everyone. If a person is of narrow perspective, immature and incompetent, and not responsibly engaged in work and personal relationships, I believe that powerful disengagement from his customary identity can be disturbing, even destructive to his capacity to cope with the world. The other "natural" ways of disengaging are more self-regulating, in that the person can get no further "out" of his identity and his customary experience of the world than he authentically "earns."[16]

By the end of the nineteen-sixties Sidney was thriving academically, his writing career was firmly established, and seven years after the initial publication of *The Transparent Self* the book's success was evident. Sid began work on a revised edition just as the seventies arrived.

International

9

FOR SID, 1970 was a year of teaching, publishing, travel, and the revision of *The Transparent Self*. He contributed "The Beginnings of Self-Disclosure" to *Voices*, the journal of the American Academy of Psychotherapists; an essay on suicide for the *American Journal of Nursing*; and chapters in two publications, one on reinventing marriage and another on "Confronting the Realities of 'Them' and 'Us'" for the National Education Association. Sid and an assistant compiled an annotated bibliography of research in self-disclosure, a subject he had been exploring for fifteen years.

Three articles co-authored by Sid describing the results of self-disclosure research were published in the *Journal of Personality and Social Psychology*, the *Journal of Counseling Psychology* and the *Journal of Humanistic Psychology*.

These co-authored articles were a way that research in self-disclosure could be integrated into the stream of current thought in the varied psychology journals where they appeared. Sid was well aware that his research did not attract grant money from large corporate interests. He explains his approach to research:

> A lot of my students were doing Masters. I worked out a policy when a
> student would do a Masters [thesis] with me since I was hot in the area, we
> would negotiate, it would be in an area, self-disclosure usually, or something
> to do with body and things, and the student would work out what fascinates
> them; it would be either that area or something else, and we would work out
> a compromise, reconcile the two interests, and I would have my idea about
> what is a worthwhile next step in this research program, because I had no
> grants, so I did my research program in this way and the agreement was that,

with a few exceptions, with a study to be published, I would be the senior author making it perfectly clear that this was the student's masters thesis, and their doctoral dissertation was their own, that was their maiden song—not a swan song—their maiden speech. So we put out a lot of really good provocative papers, and then I put them all together as a chapter in a book.[1]

Israel

As the son of agnostic freethinkers and with a growing interest in mysticism and in the undeniable power of belief—- he found the effectiveness of medical placebos compelling—Sid approached the Old Testament not as religious text or true history but as metaphor. Ted Landsman, friend and psychologist at the College of Education, encouraged this new interest in Jewish culture, and at Ted's suggestion he, Sid and Stan Lynch traveled to Israel, arriving during Passover week, April 20-28[th,] 1970. Also in Israel at that time on a separate research visit was Fred Richards, a graduate student of Sid's. Fred's wife Anne describes their encounter:

> A trip with a handful of educators was arranged by Dave Aspy, allegedly to do research on Israeli schools. When they arrived, however, all the schools were closed for Passover and they had to find other things to do. (Clearly, no one with any knowledge of Israel arranged this trip.) Fred was walking in Tel Aviv. He passed by a café and someone called out his name. He turned—and Ted Landsman and Sid were sitting outside the place. Sid said that he had just made a bet with Ted Landsman that someone Sid knew would walk by within a half hour. If this happened, Ted was supposed to pay for his sandwich or whatever they were eating. Fred was the one who walked by— so Sid won the bet and the three of them had a great time visiting with one another. The serendipity of the moment made it an utterly delightful experience for all of them…
>
> As to the reason Sid was there . . . Ted was very attached to his tradition of Judaism and kept encouraging Sid to explore his Jewish heritage because he thought it would resonate with the things Sid cared about.[2]

Sid later told me that while facing the Western Wall— the Wailing Wall—he felt himself spontaneously beginning to rock back and forth in the tradition of devout Jews, a movement known in Yiddish as *shuckling*.

The visit to Israel was consonant with his growing interest in the power of belief and faith and the role of religion in human life and the role of the prophets in the Old

Testament. By substituting the word "Life" for God, Sid explored a new meaning in the Bible, described in his essay "One of the Names of God Is 'Life Itself.'"[3]

In August Sid flew to Amsterdam for the AHP international conference at Vije University where "In his featured address on psychotherapy, Sidney Jourard spoke of the necessity in inviting people to 'reinvent' themselves. Jourard led the conferencees in a didactic encounter session, utilizing both verbal and non-verbal techniques of relating to a partner."[4]

Directly after the conference Sid flew to Miami for the annual meeting of the Association of Humanistic Psychology where he participated in two panel discussions, "The Hidden Image of Man" and "Behavior Control: The Psychologist as Manipulator" in which "...opposing points of view on the topic of behavior control are debated and discussed, with audience participation."[5]

World Conference on Scientific Yoga in New Delhi

Sid was an enthusiast of varied experiences. He was taking flying lessons at the Gainesville Regional Airport and received his medical certificate for flying. The years following the 1967 "Summer of Love" revealed increasing interest in America of non-Western ideas that were being explored by the youth counterculture. Alan Watts had popularized and introduced to Western readers the worlds of Zen and Buddhism through his books and lectures. Sid had already experienced psychedelic drugs. He had read George Ohsawa's book *You Are All Sanpaku*, recommending a macrobiotic diet to increase health, and Sid subsisted solely on brown rice for two weeks and enjoyed the results.

He discovered Rolfing and commuted to Jacksonville for a series of treatments from a Rolfer who had studied directly with Ida Rolf.[6] I recall him telling me, "Today they worked on the muscles under my armpit. It was excruciating!" After the series of sessions he showed me how his most comfortable sitting position was with a straight back; his posture did improve. Although never an adept, he had been practicing yoga for some time when he was invited to participate as a western psychologist in the World Conference on Scientific Yoga in New Delhi during the last week of 1970.

The conference was organized by Christopher Hills (1926-1997), an English author, philosopher and scientist. In December 1970, Hills, his son John, and Kevin Kingsland organized the world's first World Conference on Scientific Yoga in New

Delhi, bringing fifty Western scientists together with eight hundred of India's leading swamis, yogis and lamas to discuss their research and ostensibly create a World Yoga University. Sid was a featured "western psychologist" (listed in the program as "from Miami, U.S.A.") along with Dr. Stanislav Grof, a psychiatrist and founder of the field of transpersonal psychology; other participants in this singular event included the Indian philosopher Krishnamurti and Swami Satchidananda. Attendees included musician Alice Coltrane, widow of John Coltrane, and the actor James Coburn. I was present at this conference because I asked Sid if I could come along with him. We arrived in London and went to Centre House in Kensington, described by Hills as a self-discovery and human-potential community, where he had arranged for members and interested parties to travel as a group to New Delhi and the conference.

The ten-day trip that followed allowed me to view Sid not as my father but as an internationally-recognized social scientist invited to participate in a cultural exchange in India. It was informative to watch Sid's various social interactions. From London the group flew on Aeroflot to Moscow and then to New Delhi where we stayed at the YMCA.

During the opening ceremonies at the Constitution Club of India there were speeches from various officials and monks and swamis. After an hour or so Sid observed the increasing restlessness of the audience, and when his turn came he spoke exactly five words: "Greetings from America—more later." At one session of the conference Alice Coltrane played harp. One evening the Indian philosopher Krishnamurti spoke in a tent across from the conference site. He denounced the concept of following any guru. In a later panel discussion Sid stood up and said the conference was half over, and there were too many egos going around—in other words, no one was accepting the other person's philosophy. This comment received wide applause.

Sid found amusing the behavior of various gurus, saddhus, holy men and yogis who were used to being surrounded only by their followers or students, now being forced to confront one another along with a perceived threat to their autonomy; Sid claimed to have overheard a heated argument between two such gurus over which was more ego-less. These holy men had rarely met others.

In one presentation I watched Sid describe how changing one's perspective—either figuratively or literally—could change one's experience of reality. His moderate yoga skills brought forth an idea. To demonstrate changing perspective, he

Sid in New Delhi, December 1970

stood on his head on the table in front of him. I recall the sound of the coins in his pocket clattering to the tabletop just as he straightened his legs to achieve full upright position.

The Indian audience members found his extroverted personality intriguing but intimidating. In another presentation he had audience members pair off randomly as in an encounter group and said, now, one of you give the other a foot rub. No one moved. He said, "Well, if this *were* an encounter group, one partner would begin by...." Sid was exploring the boundaries of self-disclosure in many ways.

After a few days of the conference, a well-known saddhu/guru was seated in a outdoor garden area of the event site for a meditation event. If you wished to meditate in his presence you approached him to be touched and then found a spot to sit, assumed a lotus position and began meditation. He was squat, bald, and wore a gruff or neutral expression. Sid approached him with the others. The guru offered Sid a rose petal and indicated that it should be eaten. Sid later told me that, although intellectually he understood the purpose of eating the rose petal was an acknowledgment of submission and connection to the spirit of the guru, he found a place to sit and immediately went into a deep meditative state. He confided that he was astounded at his reaction.

Sid with Attendee, New Delhi, December 1970

Sid, L to R: Ed Elkin, unknown, Stan Grof. India, December 1970

After the conference Stanislav Grof organized a five-day trip by car to surrounding areas of interest, hiring an Indian driver and car to negotiate the primitive roads that were shared by automobiles, herds of goats, bicyclists, cattle, and pedestrians. We visited ashrams, the Taj Mahal, viewed the erotic bas-relief sculptures of Khajuraho, and returned to Gainesville shortly after New Years Day 1971. There was no Second World Conference of Scientific Yoga.

The Current Rate for Insight

A few days after returning to Gainesville, on January 5th Sid was participating in a symposium at Michigan State University. A series of three letters exchanged in advance of the event between Sid and the head of the symposium committee reveal an example of free-market economics in action. In August of the previous year Sid had rejected their offer of $350 per day for the three days and asked for $500 per day. In a letter the next month Bruce McCrone writes "Our budget for the symposium would not cover that amount…The committee and I are hopeful that you might reconsider and find that you are able to come. I realize that this is an imposition, but because you are respected by the committee and the students I feel I must make the effort to try to induce you to come to our campus for the symposium."

A week later Sid received this response: "I appreciate your acceptance of our offer to be with us for the Symposium January 11, 12, 13 for the fee of $1500.00 [approximately ten thousand dollars in today's funds]." On a letter later received from McCrone describing travel arrangements Sid has written extensive notes as to his schedule for each day, including a radio interview, press conference, four addresses, three discussion forums, and a meeting with graduate students. He tinkers with the title of his main address, finally settling on "Unpolluting the Human Environment: A Social World for Humans to Grow In."

Sid was now twenty years into his career. The synergy of his ideas and effective communication skills had brought him success as a sought-after speaker, and his books were in the mainstream of contemporary psychology and social thought.

The Transparent Self   10

In 1971 the revised edition of *The Transparent Self* was published with much new content. The first edition had brought Sid's findings on self-disclosure to an audience beyond academia that included pastoral counselors. He recalls

> I put out a revised edition of *The Transparent Self*, which I always thought
> was a terrible book. It was repetitive, a lot of redundancy to it; so I took
> out about nine chapters and the ones that were left I tightened and moved
> things from one chapter to another to make it a better piece of writing,
> although I think the ideas were very good ideas.

The Women's Liberation movement had coincided with other liberation movements active at that time—Gay, Black, Native American—and in the words of one humanistic psychologist, Richard Farson, "Humanistic psychology, like all of psychology, was dragged kicking and screaming through every liberation movement. It was embarrassing how far behind the curve we were."[1]

A letter from a "practicing female and a practicing psychiatric social worker" sent to Sid through his publisher and referring to the first edition may have had an influence on the revision. After identifying herself in the manner above, the letter continues:

> I must take exception with your rather distorted conception of women
> as demonstrated in your book <u>The Transparent Self</u>. I am writing this to
> you because I feel that your bias detracts from an otherwise valuable and
> perceptive book.

I am particularly concerned by your sardonic description of "the centuries-old techniques employed by women to make men see, feel, believe and do what they want them to." (p.59) Surely, you must be aware of the centuries-old manipulation of women by men for the purpose of keeping women down, in their place, in the home, etc. Even "subliminal advertisements" on television tell me "You've come a long way baby." In a previous chapter you demonstrate deep understanding of "Some Lethal Aspects of the Male Role." I wonder about your ability to treat women effectively if you do not understand the "lethal" aspects of the female role, particularly in modern American society. Perhaps you need, in fact, to reevaluate your ability at self disclosure in terms of your feelings about women.

I am, of course, writing this because of my general feeling that what you say is so terribly important to me as a person and as a therapist...[2]

It seems almost certain that Sid's comment regarding the "centuries-old technique" referred to the woman from his undergraduate days in Toronto who admittedly used techniques on him to see, feel, believe and do what she wanted—to win his attention and affection. Sid deleted the passages referred to by the letter-writer and rewrote much of the chapter.

One key aspect of Sidney's literary approach was that much of his writing originated as spoken presentation for lectures and papers, written in the knowledge that it would be read aloud at academic conferences and symposia. In regarding the source of much of the book's content, he says "Everything in it was spoken, all those were papers that I prepared for oral presentation so that in writing them I was speaking, that's a spoken book."

The titles of new chapters reveal the scope of his interests and the differing approaches in presenting them: "Self Disclosure and the Mysterious Other"; "The Experience and Disclosure of Love"; "Self-Disclosure, the Writer, and His Reader"; "Sickness As Protest"; "Education for a New Society"; "Psychedelic Drugs: The Impotent Protest"; "An Invitation to Authenticity"; "Resistance to Authenticity in the Psychotherapist." These are variations on a theme of dialogue or the lack of dialogue, approached from different viewpoints.

The redundancy and repetition Sid found fault with in the first edition is still there, but this can be viewed as a writing approach with parallels to aspects of artistic expression, particularly the simultaneous perspectives of Cubist paintings and the music of Erik Satie, a French composer known for writing works in groups of three or more that presented different facets of a musical idea, as in his three

Gymnopedies, six *Gnossienes,* and five *Nocturnes.* In both these art forms—painting and music—a single subject or theme was perceived and presented from multiple directions and viewpoints.

The most lyrical of Sid's writing is in Chapter 6, "The Experience and Disclosure of Love," beginning with quotes from several folk songs on the subject of love:

Ol' mas' loves wine, and Miss loves silk, the piggies they love buttermilk,
The kiddies love molasses,
and the ladies love a ladies' man.
I love to shake a toe with the ladies,
I love to be a beau to the ladies,
Long as ever I know sweet sugar from sand,
I'm bound to be a ladies' man.
     Folk song, Southeastern U.S.

Love, O love, O careless love….You see what careless love has done
     Folk song, U.S., 19th century

Plaisirs d'amour, ne durent qui'un moment. Chagrins d'amour durent toute la vie.
     Folk song, French, very old

I sowed the seeds of love, and I sowed them in the springtime.
I gathered them up in the morning too soon, while the songbirds
so sweetly sing.
     Folk song, British, about 16ᵗʰ century

Amor patriae Motto
For the love of God…*Sometimes a prayer, sometimes not.*

Eros and agape. *Gemeinschaftsgefühl.* Love as an art. Love as behavior. The beloved as a "reinforcement magazine." As sex object. As an object of worship and reverence. What does it mean to love? I will discuss love from the perspective of existential phenomenology. From this vantage point, love is a state of being, it is an experience, it is a commitment and it is a relation.[3]

In a footnote to this statement he elaborates on this perspective:

> Existential phenomenology is the systematic study of a person's way of *experiencing* his world. It is concerned with determining how the world which is common to all is perceived, thought about, remembered, imagined, phantasied, and felt about. I study yours by asking you to disclose yourself to me. For a more systematic introduction to this discipline see W. Luijpen's book *Existential Phenomenology*.[4]

For this revised edition of *The Transparent Self* Sid deleted the subtitle *Self-Disclosure and Well-Being*. Van Nostrand created a cover design that Sid found satisfactory, a luminous purple image of a man's face and upper body on a black background, the face internally repeated four times in diminishing size, the hollowed-out white typeface of the title emphasizing the concept of transparency.[5]

Sid in 1971

The Journal of Pastoral Care reviewed the book soon after publication:

> Originally published in 1964, this is a much revised edition of the successful writings of the well-known humanistic psychologist, now Professor of Psychology at the University of Florida. "Self-disclosure between men," writes the author, "reduces the mystery that one man is for another. It is the empirical index of an I-Thou relationship, which I … see as the index of man functioning at his highest and truly *human* level rather than at the level of a thing or an animal." Driven by this conviction, the author writes a dramatic and fascinating volume, filled with relevant challenges for many areas, including pastoral care and counseling.[6]

This revised edition of *The Transparent Self* remained in print for twenty-four years.

Self-disclosure had been caricatured as incessant divulging of information about oneself while oblivious to the level of attention or interest on the part of the recipient, with little regard for the appropriateness of such behavior, referred to at the time as "letting it all hang out." Today the acronym TMI—Too Much Information—captures this type of disclosure. Sid's view was much more nuanced, as revealed in an interview following the book's release:

> That's something peculiarly cultural about the U.S. as I've discovered, and I think about Canada too, a sort of built-in or trained-in incapacity for dialectical thinking. I see it most clearly in my writing about self-disclosure, which became popular because people said oh my goodness, non-disclosure is bad; disclosure is good, so let us then disclose, and with the same compulsivity. Of course, what I see as desirable is to be able to be utterly open in relevance, and be utterly private in relevance; to be able to swing both ways. And that's true of every other polarity.[7]

In 1971 another of Sid's book projects came to fruition through publication of *Self-Disclosure: An Experimental Analysis of the Transparent Self*, a sort of companion volume to *The Transparent Self*. In it Sid assembled and organized much of "twelve years of continuous research on the factors involved in a person's willingness to let others know his experience."[8] The book was a compendium intended for psychology students and clinical psychologists involved in therapy research and consisted of descriptions of twenty research studies in self-disclosure. Included in the Appendix were twenty-two research tools: various questionnaires designed for specific studies, a disclosure game, paired-associate word lists and other experimental apparatuses. The *Journal of Pastoral Care* provided this brief review:

> Operating under the assumption that advances in any new field are made when suitable techniques for measurement are discovered, the author provides us with his instruments designed to measure self-disclosure as well as his empirical findings over the past decade. Jourard's major theories that self-disclosure follows an attitude of love and trust and is characteristic of healthy personality are given empirical muscle in this collection of research findings. Those fascinated by *The Transparent Self* may find special pleasure in this more technical volume. Besides providing considerable empirical findings, the book is an excellent model to demonstrate how research gets done.[9]

Another book reviewer commented

> It is Jourard's contention that there is an urgent need for all of us to become more disclosing, more open, more transparent, even while recognizing the courage that such behavior will require. This book attempts to build a case for the "transparent way" by marshaling the evidence for the relationship of self-disclosure to significant variables.
>
> …The specific results obtained in the reported studies are not the most significant contribution of this book, nor is Jourard's questionnaire methodology. Its importance lies in the implications he raises for the construct of SD for such areas as psychotherapy, psychological assessment, and for mental health itself. Unfortunately, these implications are sprinkled throughout the book, rather than developed at greater length in the final chapter, which is specifically devoted to implications of SD research.[10]

In support of Sid's own statement regarding the importance of relevance in self-disclosure, the reviewer comments that

> …a suggestion buried in a footnote implies that the choice of the target-person for disclosure is at least as important as the total amount of material disclosed. This would seem to fit in with the clinical impression that the individual who too readily discloses personal material in public is probably as maladjusted as the tight-lipped non-discloser. However, equating SD with repression and with mental health may be a gross oversimplification of the complex problem of adjustment.[11]

Encyclopaedia Britannica

Sid was approached by the Encyclopedia Britannica to write on the topic of Personality Adjustments and Maladjustments. The editor had requested a 10,500 word article on that topic, to follow an outline provided by them. A letter from the General Editor of the encyclopedia, Warren E. Preece, centered on a conflict between what the encyclopedia required and Sid's view of what should be written. An excerpt makes this clear:

February 19, 1971
Dr. Sidney M. Jourard
Department of Psychology
University of Florida
Gainesville, Florida 32601

Dear Doctor Jourard:

I have just had my first opportunity to read your manuscript PERSONALITY ADJUSTMENTS AND MALADJUSTMENTS. I have, frankly, two reactions: first, it is a well written, stylistically bright article — it reads very well indeed — and second, I do not think that we can use it in its present form.

You will recall that in May, in a telephone conversation with Mr. Goetz, my Executive Editor, you told him that you had not found it possible to "relate to the outline" we had provided because it was "about ten years out of date." Mr Goetz told you at that time that he could not comment on the assertion but that if you had done a good job of reporting the state of knowledge in the field for the readers of a general encyclopedia, it was probable that the manuscript would be usable.

Frankly, then, here is the problem. We do not find that your manuscript is an adequate report of the state of knowledge about this field. I concede that in this area we may be in a state of very rapid transition. I concede that humanistic psychology may be the wave of the future and may, in fact, be already here. It is tempting, in such areas, to say let us ignore the past and take a flier on the future. As a general encyclopedia we do not feel we can do this. For some time to come lay readers will turn to the Britannica for information about personality adjustments and maladjustments. There is a fairly recognized body of traditional knowledge about these fields and we do not believe that we can satisfy our obligation to the reader by, in essence, telling him that it may be more important to worry about adjusting society and less about adjusting the personality.

This does not mean that we should not deal with the transitions and trends now in progress…

The letter continues by asking if Sid would be willing to revise his manuscript to "meet this quite real encyclopaedic need."

Sid was not willing, and his original submission was not used.

A New Division of APA

The American Psychological Association (APA) is organized in various divisions, currently fifty-four. In 1971 the association officially recognized Humanistic Psychology as a viable field of research and created Division 32 for this category of research into human motivation and behavior. After more than a decade of exploration using this perspective, the event was a milestone in acknowledging the validity of the humanistic view of humankind as a component of the social sciences.

Life Bound

In August of 1971 Sid was invited to participate in Life Bound, a teen-oriented two-week survival and personal growth program held in southern Colorado, a humanistic variation of the popular Outward Bound survival courses. Invited at Sid's suggestion were myself, my younger brother and my cousin. All of us hiked, rappelled, engaged in "rap" sessions, experienced a two-day solo retreat away from all others, ran six miles, and spent a few days learning city survival skills in Boulder. Sid was offered this experience in exchange for providing guidance during the program's interpersonal encounter and personal growth exercises, aspects of the overall curriculum designed to augment and enhance the vigorous outdoor activities.

Prophets and Psychotherapists

In September Sid participated in the APA annual meeting "Psychotherapy as a Secular Calling" in Washington, D.C. where on September 4th he presented his paper "Prophets as Psychotherapists, and Psychotherapists as Prophets."

In this talk Sid explored the parallels he saw between the role of the Biblical prophets in ancient times and the role of an effective psychotherapist.

For many years I prided myself on my secular approach to the understanding of human suffering and my intervention therein. But the thinker whose work most influenced me beyond my initial training was Martin Buber, and so in spite of the fact I had no formal instruction in being a Jew, there was and remains an Old Testament flavor to my thinking, writing and ways of being. And, so, after a recent visit to Israel, I began to read the Old Testament for the first time. I am finding it a fascinating, extraordinary document about the struggle of some prophets and leaders of a recalcitrant people to become human beings freed from the idolatry of place, tribe, family; whose worship of their deity is not in words, sacrifice or ritual, but through *living in a way,* a way that is informed by Divine Ecology, Divine Public Health, and Divine Interpersonal Science. When this stiff-necked people fell away from living in the way prescribed by *Jaweh,* their punishment was swift and terrible. I prefer, however, not to regard defeat in battle, famine and disease as evidence of the Lord's wrath; rather, they seem to be outcomes of not paying attention to long-range consequences of one's present ways of treating the weak, the lowly, the strangers in one's midst, the soil, the waters, the animals, and oneself.[12]

In a later passage Sid makes the connection referred to in the title of the talk:

One of the defining characteristics of the Old Testament prophets was the idea that the one true God, *Jaweh,* spoke through them. This, I believe, is a metaphor signifying that the prophet was able to achieve a perspective on his culture, on the behavior of self and others which enabled him to see what those embedded could not see. The psychotherapist in modern days must be capable of achieving such an outsider's perspective, of attaining what Buber calls "distance," but he must also have the capacity to "enter into relation," in order to have his vision and message heard. In modern terminology, an effective psychotherapist, like an effective prophet, can detach himself from prior ways of being and then return into community with one other, or many others, and share his vision. But I hold the hypothesis that the prophetic psychotherapist and the psychotherapeutic prophets are effective to the extent to which they embody, in their very *being,* the ways to live that are most compatible with life together in this time and place. It is not possible, I argue, for a true prophet to preach one way and live another. This may require that the psychotherapist in his prophetic function (which is not incompatible with healing) may be, for the moment, a very irritating, infuriating person who discloses the truth that hurts, that fosters guilt, anxiety, and intense suffering. But, like the prophets, he does not confront for the joy of inflicting pain, but out of profound concern. If the therapist, like the prophet, is angry, it is because there is something to be angry at. We can view Carl Rogers's wrath at certain dehumanizing aspects of graduate and undergraduate education and his promulgation of encountering as "a Way," as a case of a therapist "gone prophet."[13]

PSY 300

All during this time Sid was employed as a professor at a large state university, and since arriving in Gainesville in 1958 he had taught classes; kept a small private practice as a therapist; written books, articles and research papers; and traveled throughout the country and occasionally overseas on speaking engagements and attending conferences. He was a demanding professor and his advanced undergraduate courses illustrate the level of involvement he expected from students. In the Fall of 1971 one such course was PSY 300, "Healthy Personality: The Approach of Humanistic Psychology." As defined by Sid in the introductory paragraph of the course syllabus "'Healthy personality' is the term used to refer to ways of being a person in the world which yield personal growth, and physical and psychological well-being as outcomes." Included in the course were two hours of lectures each week, a laboratory-discussion session and two exams that made up half the grade, the other half based on assignments in the discussion group such as a term paper or book-review. Students participated in two hours of experiments, with bonus points for each additional hour up to five.

Each of the six lecture topics in the syllabus refers to chapters from two of his books, *Disclosing Man to Himself* and *Personal Adjustment*. Teaching from your own writing is a normal aspect of academia; of greater interest is the section labeled Additional References: "Here are some books that I have found absorbing and quite relevant to the aims of this course." Recommended but not required, the list reveals the scope of Sid's reading and the interest he hoped to spark in his students. Included among the thirty-four listings are books by social scientists Gordon Allport, Eric Berne, Martin Buber, Viktor Frankl, Freud, Erich Fromm, Jung, R.D. Laing, Maslow, Rollo May and B.F. Skinner, and novels by Herman Hesse, Aldous Huxley, Nikos Kazantzakis ("Zorba the Greek; anything else of his"), George Orwell, Henry Miller, and Colin Wilson.

All of these texts were of a piece to Sid; all addressed the human condition and their inclusion was a reflection of his own reading and an understanding that fiction could serve a purpose beyond entertainment.

In, Out and About   11

SID'S ACTIVITIES IN 1972 were varied. By now he was receiving international recognition as a figure in the growing field of Humanistic Psychology. He had presented a paper at a major conference every year for two decades. His ideas about humankind's ability to transcend limitations placed upon them by heredity and social constraints kept him in demand as an engaging speaker.

Words were the tools he used to communicate his ideas, either spoken or written, with colleagues, students, therapy clients, and readers. His ability to communicate clearly through the spoken word had served him well, both personally and professionally, and he took advantage of this skill through speaking engagements in the U.S. and overseas at universities and other learning centers. As his second academic sabbatical leave was approaching, Sid was in full academic mode, with lecturing and teaching responsibilities at the University along with a steady writing output that included correspondence, articles published in academic journals, book reviews, and chapters in anthologies.

Psychology had grown to be a popular college undergraduate major in the 1970s, a trend consonant with the ardent but earnest search for meaning explored by the counterculture, the hippies, and the human potential movement, a broad orientation that hoped to promote positive social change and bring happiness, contentment and fulfillment. The freedom sought by such existential and humanistic thinkers was a good fit with the then-current youth movement and the varied protest and liberation groups in existence at the time.

Through a classified ad in the AHP newsletter[1] Sid sought a like-minded colleague to join the Psychology Department. The ad reveals his areas of interest as well as the salary for an assistant professor at a state university in the early '70s—another indicator of why money was a lifelong concern for Sid and a further motivation to write books:

> WANTED: assistant professor, Psychology of Personality, with especial emphasis on existential, phenomenological and humanistic perspectives. The candidate should be knowledgeable about the existential-phenomenological approach to the study of man, including principles of personal growth, and an interest in developing rigorous methods for the study of personas and states of consciousness. Strong research impetus is desired, to lend strength to our developing program in personality and humanistic psychology. Reasonable teaching load, and an opportunity to explore experiential approaches to teaching. Salary — $12,500. Write:

> ++ Sidney M. Jourard
> Department of Psychology
> University of Florida
> Gainesville, Florida 32601

There, in his own words, are Sid's current research interests.

In early April, Sid spoke in Kristiansund, Norway as a participant in the Scandinavian Conference on Humanistic Psychology. Following the conference he was in Nottingham, England where he read "Psychology: Control or Liberation?" to the British Psychological Society.

The topic of control versus freedom was central to Sid's belief that the knowledge obtained through psychological research should be "given away" to promote humanity's self-awareness rather than be used against persons for the political or economic gain of those who obtain such knowledge. The opening statements of his talk make this point clear:

> *Sartre* described a scene in which a voyeur peeps through the keyhole into a bedroom. Suddenly, he is discovered by another, and becomes, thereby, an object for the other, and for himself. His experience of his freedom oozes away. Whenever a person is caught in the act, when someone hitherto

concealed is seen, then the looker turns the one looked at into stone. Psychologists have been inviting the subjects of their research to become as natural objects, like stones. The surprising thing is that the subjects have cooperated. For the life of me, I cannot fathom why, because I do not know of *any* good that has accrued to the subject as a consequence of *being a subject*, that is, an *object*. This is a strong statement for me to make, because I am a psychologist, with twenty-five years of my adult life dedicated to this discipline. I really do not believe that the humans we have studied, in the ways that we have studied them, have benefited from our research! I do not believe that the quality of personal life has been improved by the results of eighty years of the scientific investigation of human consciousness and action. In fact, there is more basis for me to believe that the knowledge of man that we have acquired has been used to control and limit him rather than to enlarge his awareness, his dignity, or his freedom.

In research, as most psychologists have practiced it, subjects are recruited and asked to make themselves available to the psychologist for observation, interviewing and testing. He records their speech, actions, and reactions with various kinds of equipment. He analyzes the findings, and publicizes them. Typically, the psychologist defines psychology as a scientific discipline which seeks to *understand* the behavior of man and other organisms. Proof of understanding is evident when the psychologist can *predict* the action or reactions under study, by pointing to signs, or by bringing them under some kind of deliberate *control.* Great pains are taken to insure that the observer does not influence the behavior he is studying, so that the persons or animals under study will show themselves "as they really are." Ideally the subjects would not know that they were being watched, because the experience of being observed affects action.[2]

The remainder of the paper explores the idea that when the cost of psychological research is borne by private or public agencies, they will not "willingly countenance research which will undermine their power over people. A pharmaceutical firm is unlikely to spend millions of dollars in the study of placebos, so that drug use in medicine will be diminished."

The theme of control versus liberation is continued in a description of research in self-disclosure and how disclosure on the part of the researcher encouraged disclosure on the part of the subject to a startling degree—the dyadic effect— bringing into question the accuracy of much of the data gathered by psychological research in which this approach was not taken. He concludes with a statement embodying the reason why Sid's research was not underwritten with grants from corporate America.

> I suppose that the project is to give it away — [because] as fast as man is studied by natural-science psychologists (to learn about the determiners of his experience and action), humanistic psychologists (who can be natural-science psychologists too) can make apparent to all, the ways in which their freedom is being eroded by hostile nature or hostile people.
>
> Psychological research, from this perspective, becomes an enterprise wherein the subject becomes privy to the aims of the researcher, and wherein he is free to learn about the researcher as the researcher learns about him.[3]

The idea of the researcher clearly stating the purpose of his experiment in advance to the subject remains controversial and goes against the normal process variables of researchers at that time and in contemporary research—an approach that includes treating the subject as Other, deceptive methods, undisclosed confederates as part of the experimental process, and purposely misstating the true purpose of the study. These techniques are defended as the only way to receive accurate data untainted by the goal of the researcher. Sid argued that subjects have little reason or motivation to provide honest responses, bringing into doubt the value of the considerable amount of data collected under such a hypothesis.

Sid was a radical thinker and many of his statements regarding human motivation and behavior can be experienced as idealistic and polemical. Yet he thrived in his chosen profession of psychologist even while criticizing the standard approach of much psychological research.

In April he was in Chicago for the Midwest Regional AHP Conference. In May he was in Ithaca, NY presenting "Changing Personal Worlds: A Humanistic Perspective" at a symposium at Cornell University.

The result of this symposium was a book—*Humanism and Behaviorism: Dialogue and Growth*—with contributions from nineteen other authors, but centered around a series of papers by and dialogues between Sid and Joseph Wolpe, a South African psychiatrist and a proponent of behavior therapy.

Wolpe had become famous for his treatment of Post-traumatic Stress Disorder (PTSD) through "systemic desensitization," a behavior modification approach that was highly successful. Sid, who in reference to therapy said "being able to do two things is always better than only one," understood that there were times when behavior modification was the most effective approach to curing certain mental disorders.

Sid's opening sentence gets directly to his argument:

> Everything depends on what you believe man is like. If you assume that man is something like a machine, that assumption is, in a way, not an assumption alone. It is sort of an invitation and a prescription to man to be in the world in ways that mimic a machine. Man seems to me to be a very peculiar creature: he can conform himself to all kinds of images, because he doesn't have any rigidly fixed nature or design to determine how he will be in the world, how he will act, and how the world will be for him. Now, if you assume that man is a being like a monkey or a pigeon, then that too is a kind of invitation that a person may accept.[4]

What Wolpe and Sid had in common was they were both exploring the ways in which personality change occurs. In discussing the approaches of behavioristic psychologists, Sid writes "It's unclear to me yet how effective these men are at attributing power to patients. I think they believe power resides in the idea of behavior modification, or the various conditioning theories and techniques. What I found most fascinating about the whole field of behaviorism or behavior science is that its appeal is to those who are most fascinated with the problem of management and control of somebody's behavior."[5] To an existentialist such as Sid, this was anathema.

Yet, in a story involving himself and his colleague Henry Pennypacker, whose work focused on behavior analysis, Sid describes a behavior modification technique he employed to help end his long-term addiction to tobacco.

> Pennypacker and I are very good friends and colleagues and have been for the past ten years; we each were compulsive smokers. He and I both were smoking two ounces or more of pipe tobacco a day every day, inhaling every puff. We were totally addicted. About two years ago I decided to quit. But as an addict, I had withdrawal symptoms. I became terrified. I asked myself, "How can I quit? I know what, I'll do what Hank Pennypacker does, I'll count something. I'll count puffs, chart it, and establish a base rate.
> I then said, "The hell with it, that's for children and animals, and I'm

neither. I will trust in my own theories." I was interested in yoga, and I developed this technique for stopping my smoking out of a Hatha Yoga exercise. I kept my pipe in my hand at all times; every time I got an urge to smoke, I would take a slow yoga breath. If the urge persisted, I would do another one. That first day I had to do about fifty cycles of that but then the second day it was cut to twenty-five, and the third day about a dozen, the fourth day about half-a-dozen and the fifth day two or three. That was it, there was no more. I have not smoked for two years now, and I have had no urge to resume.[6]

This approach resonates with a scene from the novel *Zorba the Greek*. Zorba describes his own father as a *palikari*, a sort of warrior:

Well, he had all the vices but he'd slash them, as you would with a sword. For instance, he smoked like a chimney. One morning he went out into the fields to plough. He arrived, leaned on the hedge, pushed his hand into his belt for his tobacco-pouch to roll a cigarette before he began work, took out his pouch and found it was empty. He'd forgotten to fill it before leaving the house.

He foamed with rage, let out a roar, and then bounded away towards the village. His passion for smoking completely unbalanced his reason, you see. But suddenly—I've always said I think man's a mystery—he stopped, filled with shame, pulled out his pouch and tore it to shreds with his teeth, then stamped it in the ground and spat on it. "Filth! Filth!" he bellowed. "Dirty slut!"

And from that hour, until the end of his days, he never put another cigarette between his lips.

That's the way real men behave, boss. Good night![7]

Bored and Restless

This biography focuses on Sid's academic career, but he was also a person with his own libido, frustrations, responsibilities, and passions oftentimes at odds with the traditional mores of society. The personal freedom he defended as an existentialist was not a perfect fit with the more traditional view of marriage. What brought stability for some was constrictive for others. Sid was also becoming bored by his life, and by his own admission, boring. His closest friend Thomas Hanna recalls Sid's view of most people being "hypnotized" by the common cultural motifs:

He despised anything that as he always put it, hypnotized. He said, "the world is full of hypnotism, and most people go about hypnotized." And those people bored him. And as I say they were ninety percent of people. And I think that as he got older his tolerance of those ninety percent diminished. There's no question about that because he got increasingly bored. And of course he became with that boyish enthusiasm increasingly popular, so he would be invited to various things and he would go to them and he never stopped talking. I'd say "Sidney you talk too much," and he'd say "Yes, it's true. You're quite right. But," he says, "I'm the only one interesting enough to listen to. So that's why I talk. The rest of these people bore the shit out of me!" So he talked, and he entertained, and in some sense the more he got bored with people the more he talked and the more he entertained, and in those last years before I left [1973] he was more and more bored, he had reached a stage in his life where I think he really wanted to do something else. And I think he would have probably ended up in California, I think he would have moved in that direction, just for the hell of it, just for something different to do. Cause he pretty well had had a triumphant career at the University, he'd had all the success you could want as a psychologist, as a psychotherapist, as a writer, as a lecturer; he had that. He said "Soon," he said, "Wait till [Carl] Rogers dies," and he said, "I'll be El Numero Uno," and he saw El Numero Uno looming in his future, and he enjoyed the whole project."[8]

Sid's intellect was fully intact but his spirit was searching and he was becoming stale to himself. A sabbatical leave was looming. Sid needed to get away from the quotidian nature of the academic routine, marriage, parenting, and home responsibilities. He was also intent on revising his first book *Personal Adjustment*, already in its second edition.

A Modern Odyssey $\qquad$ 12

SID BEGAN HIS sabbatical at the start of the 1972 academic year with, as before, no specific academic responsibilities other than the enrichment of his mind; his salary for the year was provided by the University of Florida.

In a fitting move for a man who admired both Homer's *Odyssey* and Joseph Conrad's sea tales as literature and metaphor, Sid participated in an ocean voyage excursion developed by Chapman College in Orange, California. Faculty and students created a college semester on the 584-foot SS *Universe* as it headed westward into the Pacific. In Sid's words:

> I had been asked by the publisher to revise *Personal Adjustment* and I had gone through many changes in my expansions, shifts in my thinking which were reflected in my teaching and so on, so I thought it's time, so with this sabbatical I went on a ship around the world, called Chapman College World Campus Afloat, and that disengaged me from a lot of professional and personal and family hassles which were really—they were rough, and they were naturally demanding of my time, and I settled and arranged things as well as I could well enough—my wife was working, my kids were all fairly well ensconced, and I felt good about leaving them, and I went around the world. I was ship shrink, as they called it, officially Coordinator of Counseling on this boat, and taught a couple of courses, and there was time to begin revising my book, and I knew that I had gotten all my hassles behind me when one day between Suva in the Fiji Islands and Sydney, Australia, I put a sheet of paper in the typewriter and wrote down Chapter

One and started off saying, I don't know if I'm able to get my thoughts together to begin this revision. However I am—I'm typing all this out, because the way to begin is to begin...and I began, and I did a vast amount of editing, and I wrote four chapters for what was still called *Personal Adjustment*, and I ripped out a lot of material and put a lot of new material into chapters and produced a book of which I'm quite proud, and I gave it a new name—I called it *Healthy Personality*, and there is a story there because I wanted to call the first edition, back in 1958, *Healthy Personality*, and the publisher prevailed upon me and I yielded—a terrible mistake. They wanted to call it *Personal Adjustment*, but it wasn't a book about adjustment, it's a book about healthy personality.

Sid spent one hundred days at sea and various ports with the SS *Universe*, departing California in early September, crossing the Equator September 17th, with stops in Sydney, Singapore, Malaysia, India, Tanzania, Kenya, South Africa, and Ghana, arriving in south Florida on December 17th. He later related that he had bought two cases of South African wine during the days the ship was at port there, intending to bring some home, but they lasted about "a week."

Carl Rogers Was Not Intimidated

After Christmas his sabbatical continued during the winter quarter with a teaching position at United States International University in San Diego, where he met David Mearns, a Scottish psychologist who recalls their experiences together:

> My time with Sid Jourard was while I was Visiting Fellow (1972/73) at the Center for Studies of the Person in La Jolla, just north of San Diego. Sid was on sabbatical in the same area. In fact, he had also applied for one of the two Visiting Fellow positions at CSP, but had not got one. I puzzled over why they would have taken a young Scottish psychologist with no reputation over Sid Jourard. My conclusion was that part of the reason was that they wanted to use the experience to stimulate developments in other parts of the world, but more of the reason was that they were probably intimidated by Sid's ability and dynamism. Carl Rogers was not intimidated—I brought Sid to the Center and Carl got on famously with him.
>
> I was pretty unwild and Sid was really wild. We were complementary to each other and genuinely enjoyed each others company. I was shy as a rule, but he brought me out. We went to a lot of parties—I never discovered how

he found out about so many. He was interested in the therapy work I was doing with traumatized patients. Clearly he would have loved to have the freedom to work in that kind of intense therapeutic contact with hard-to-reach patients.

We audited two courses together at United States International University (USIU) in San Diego. One was given by Viktor Frankl. We dropped out of it after the third seminar. His prison experiences were powerful, but he was not an easy communicator. We quite liked Frankl, but we truly hated the other presenter who had better remain nameless. We hated him so much that we went to all his seminars. Though there were about 250 other people attending, we felt a kind of personal responsibility to stay the course in order to try to block the wilder excesses of this presenter's intellectual and emotional bullying of women. In every session he would invite someone up on the stage to be his "client." Inevitably, several would volunteer and the presenter always selected a woman. Sid and I, and a few others, would groan at the prospect of yet again witnessing the disempowerment of a woman at the hands of the bully.

After each seminar we would retire to "happy hour" at our favourite bar and plot our destruction of the presenter. Sid was much more involved in this than I was. The only times I ever saw Sid impotent were in relation to the abuse served up weekly by this presenter—Sid was genuinely distressed. Now it should be said that Sid was a hugely attractive guy and not averse to the kind of casual relationships that were almost inevitable in Southern California in that era. But he was also a basically honest and good man—utterly non-manipulative and genuinely respectful. The presenter was not that man—Sid accused him, not in his presence but in our bar, of satisfying his perverted sexuality with his public bullying of women. One happy hour I said to Sid, "There is nothing for it—next week you have to be the volunteer!" We stayed long after happy hour fantasizing the many ways that Sid could use that client role to gain revenge on the Bully.

But, fearless Sid chickened out at the last minute. He said that he would be recognized, if not by the presenter, then by others. "True," I countered, "but so what?" He then rationalized that the presenter would not take him as a volunteer because he preferred women. "Not if you're forceful and physically walk up on stage—anyway, he is finding it more difficult to get volunteers now," I argued logically. But Sid wanted out. I had never seen him scared before. This bullying really got him in a deep place—we talked about that long beyond happy hour that evening. So we never enacted that great revenge on the presenter. Perhaps, if Sid had carried out the plan, that presenter would not have retained his reputation throughout the rest of his life. Instead, for the last seminar, we bombarded the presenter with countless critical questions and observations.

For this we sat, not together, but on opposite sides of the room, taking it in turns to mount our challenges and each keeping his own record of "success," or, in my case "failure." We were little boys together, each trying to surpass the other with our audacity. Four times I tried to ask the presenter about his absence of research evidence, but Sid knew the presenter's work better and could actually get him on the internal logic of his theory. The attacks got more personal when I pointed out that his series of seminars had been highly repetitive in their content and were not being appreciated nearly as much as Frankl's (here I inflated Frankl somewhat for the purpose). But Sid finally won the game with a clear knock-down when the presenter went into his usual section where he asked for a volunteer client. "I hope you are not going to choose a woman to abuse again," came a voice from the opposite side of the room. It was a strong voluminous voice, as Sid's always was. There was only calm in the voice—that calmness made it all the more threatening. All eyes turned to him and there fell a deathly hush. The presenter was dumbstruck. Slowly Sid got to his feet and left, closely followed by me.

We walked silently to our bar. Happy Hour had not started, so we told the barman we would wait the thirty minutes until it did. He shook his head and poured us our usual half-price drinks. Soon we were laughing hysterically – we were literally crying with laughter for the rest of our evening.[1]

Sid did not keep a personal journal but his 1973 pocket calendar provides an itinerary of the activities of his sabbatical leave. Sid was a people person and along with his previous contacts there are over a hundred names and addresses of people met during the year. In January he was in San Francisco, April in Quebec City and St. Louis, May in Council Grove, Kansas, attending a conference on Altered States of Consciousness (Council Grove Conference), Berkeley, Redwood City, Fullerton, and Laguna Beach, then back in San Francisco for the annual AHP meeting.

Food For Thought

Sid's lecture[2] to a symposium presented by the Philosophy Department at Cal State Fullerton, California on May 15th provides a window into the sources of his thinking and his current views at that time.

In this talk to a gathering of philosophy undergraduates, his themes include freedom, the dominant role of family, school, religion and popular culture in conflict with this freedom, the conflicting roles of education and mass media, and how philosophical views of humankind can act as self-fulfilling prophecies.

[Sid]: I'm not going to give comments on *The Transparent Self*, which I'm supposed to do according to the program, what I'm going to do is to talk around the theme of the human situation, which grows out of a course that I did teach, last winter, in San Diego. This is a sabbatical year for me, and as was pointed out, I've gone around the world and discovered how provincial most of us are. Being away from the place where I usually live and work has sort of liberated me from other people's expectations, and my own expectations of myself, and has given me the chance to review the situation; the human situation: mine, and possibly, yours ….

The first theme that I'm going to speak to is the question, how then, shall we think of man? And that includes yourself: how shall I think of you, and how shall I think of myself? And the overarching theme of this first topic could be stated this way: "Be careful how you think about man, because it's going to come to pass." Be careful how you think of yourself, because that's a self-fulfilling prophecy. And be careful to whom you listen, when they speak about man, because before you know it, you may find that your perception, whatever it might have been, has subtly been replaced by somebody else's perspective, so that when you live out that view of yourself, you are draining your own substance to nourish and enrich some beings other than yourself.

How shall we think of man, including ourselves and nature? We are dependent on witnesses. When we live these views of man, what is the quality of the life that we're living? And what is the impact of our action as we live out somebody's vision of us: on us, the person who is acting, and equally important, what is the impact of our action, as we live out our view of our possibilities, what's the impact of our action on the other human beings in the midst of whom we live, and the grass, and the trees, and the flowers, and the animals, and so on.

The first view that has a great deal of scientific prestige behind it is the view of man as a determined organism and that view is most strongly presented by my colleague B.F. Skinner, who has written a most influential, and I think in many ways a demonic book called *Beyond Freedom and Dignity*. Now, Skinner is a superb writer, and is able to reason very closely from the premises that man is indeed a natural organism, and like all organisms in Nature is subject to determinism. And so he has written the way in which this is the case: that man is a product of his reinforcement schedule, and the tendencies for reinforcement that are locked up in his environment . . . .

When you describe a human being, it's really an invitation to him to be the way which you describe. Because no matter how you describe me, two minutes later, I can be different, if I choose to be. There is one image of man, that I think is the most sellable to large organizations that are most interested in how to manipulate, predict and control individuals and large groups of people. So that naturally, research that grows out of this kind of image of man— as a kind of animal who can be trained and controlled the way any zoo animal can— is of keen interest: to the government, to the military, and to business and industry, the captains of all of which hold human beings in utter contempt, and view them as animals to be trained. And they have a large-scale apparatus to carry out this kind of conditioning and training.

Another view of man that I think at least grants man a little more dignity and a little more freedom than the view of man as a determined organism, is the view connected with Thomas Szasz and the late Eric Berne and the late Alfred Adler and that is to view man as a creature who is in the world in the fashion of a player of games. Those of you who know your Latin could speak not of *homo sapiens* but of *homo ludens*. Man the player of games. According to this view, man isn't seen as an organism or as an animal, he's really not defined, but he is in the world playing the games that are equated with social living: playing the game of being a mother, being a father, and the "games that people play" that Eric Berne described with a lot of wit and penetrating insight.

But if you view yourself as that creature who plays games, that too can ultimately rob life of the qualities of intensity and meaning. Because if you're persuaded to see all your involvements in the world as nothing more than "games," then it's difficult to see how you can generate any kind of passion or intensity of experience because "after all, it's only a game."

Now for some people, that may be good therapy, to realize that one's role, let's say, as a wife or a husband, is not necessarily a matter of life and death, it's a game, and if you happen to play the game badly, well you get that game stopped, and you find another player, and play the game again.

The view of man as a game player *can* be, in short, life-giving, but it can also be devitalizing.

Sid then touches on views of human life-drives, as seen by Freud (seeker of pleasure and freedom), Viktor Frankl (seeker of meaning), Otto Rank (as creative artistic self-author), and the Eastern approaches of yoga and Buddhism (as seeker of enlightenment and liberation):

> There are some representative views of man in general, and then you can all find views of yourself in particular, that are referred to in some jargon as your self concept, sense of your own identity. To get rid of the high blown jargon, I can ask you: just who do you think you are? And who do you think you can be? And what does your mother think you are? And your father? And your spouse: who do they think you are? And who do they think you can be? And whose view of *you* do you take to be the case? Your own, or your mother's? There's a sense in which every one of the men here is the reincarnation of his maternal grandfather, if your mother liked her father. And she may have shaped you up, so that *there you are*; the old goat is dead but you're carrying on his way of experiencing the world and pursuing values in the world without ever having a chance to decide who you wanted to be. Well, the real challenge is, you can be damn near anybody that you've got enough passion or courage or creativity to envision yourself to be. But having envisioned it, there begins the work of becoming it.
>
> …Nobody gladly gives up power. The way every social system works is to keep that social system from changing. Because the way that it is presently organized—according to this perspective that I am speaking from right now—is a kind of utopia for a minority but not necessarily a utopia for the majority, but the minority try to persuade, or mystify or befuddle the majority into believing that they are living in a utopia. But this utopia, this "good society," the "best of all possible societies in the history of mankind"—the one we are living right now, for example—is not necessarily seen as a utopia by blacks, or by women, or by young people between the ages of about fourteen and say twenty-two, it turns out to be a utopia primarily for people in positions of power who have been schooled in the world outlook of Orange County, [laughter] and who are over the age of forty, and who are men.
>
> Now: there's the utopia and how do you persuade everybody who isn't over forty, male white, Anglo-Saxon and Protestant, sometimes with a Germanic name…how do you persuade everybody who doesn't fit into that rather restrictive category? Which I use metaphorically, because there are a lot of other counties than Orange, and a lot of other countries, like South

Africa…white South Africa is very much like that, it's not a utopia for many, many of the citizens who live in South Africa.

How do you persuade the people for whom it's not a utopia that it *is* a utopia? Well, there are two ways: bribery and threats. You can use technical jargon, but here are some of the ways in which bribery and threats are used by people who have access to the means of influencing people, in order to keep them from discovering that they are being exploited, mystified, used, lied-to, in order to keep a status quo.

Organized religion has traditionally functioned to bribe people with promises of a better life in the hereafter and to somehow persuade them that you render unto Caesar the things that are Caesar's and render unto God the things that are God's, but one of the things you're not supposed to do is to criticize the organized status quo of your society.

Hardly any of the organized Protestant, Catholic, or other churches have been at the vanguard, in the history of the Western world, of liberal movements, or revolutionary movements. It's much more common for the organized churches to be in direct collusion, one way or another, with the power structure, with the military and with the large economic interests. This of course is especially clear in the more dictatorial countries like South Africa and Spain. But it's clear enough, if you learn how to look, in this country. I remember in May, in the *Gainesville Sun*, a little small-town, university town newspaper, there was a little squib explaining that over three hundred million dollars of the endowments of the four or five major Protestant churches of the United States were invested in prime war stocks, prime war industries. Nobody seemed to bat an eye. Of course, the Vietnam War was on.

All right. So religion is one of the befuddling means of keeping people from being aware of the human reality of their situation and of the possible ways that the situation could be that would make it more life-giving or more utopian for other than a small minority of living things. As a matter of fact, this world, or this country, is not utopia for fishes, it certainly wasn't a utopia for the buffalo, it's not a utopia for dolphins or whales. As I reviewed the situation I realized we've got to broaden our conceptions of space and time, and ways to live life. The mass media clearly, are absolutely mad. No—we are mad, for putting up with the mass media. Because on the one hand, some number of billions of dollars are spent every year for institutions that are called educational institutions—elementary schools, high schools, colleges and universities, that nominally are supposed to exist in order to induce a respect and a love and passion for truth, justice, and beauty in the people who go through them; but of course all that happens is that you socialize Americans.

There's a difference between a typical product of our school systems and someone who is committed—passionately—to truth, beauty and justice. Let's say if we spend eight billion dollars on these institutions which don't do a good job, considerably more billions are spent on advertising, the aim of which is to get people functionally decorticated, so they can't tell the difference between good, real value and beauty, and sham. I consider that absurd, it's almost like that scene in *Catch-22* where this dead man is encased in plaster; they pour fluids in at the top and drain them out the bottom, and then they rotate bottles, without recognizing that the man's been dead for some time.

It could give one food for thought to realize how much money is spent to teach people how to think, and reason, and recognize truth and beauty and justice, and how much is spent to prevent that from happening. And of course, we've put our money where our truest commitments are. Television and movies, be very careful about watching television, or listening to the radio, or going to the movies, because all the time you're watching those or listening to them, your perspective is constantly being bombarded with efforts to persuade you how men, women and children, ought to be, how the world ought to be, and so on. And what happens then, in a very subtle way as you read the comics, or watch any of the movies, since man doesn't know how to be, he has to copy the examples available to him. And if there's one thing that's come out of some of the sounder psychological research, it's this: that human beings, since they don't know how to be, copy the models or the examples that are available to them from sources that they take to be authoritative. Now that might give one food for thought.

The mass media, the movies, TV, radio, music, lyrics, painting: all these represent an invitation to man to envision the world in certain ways…more than an invitation, they are a subtle persuasion that this is indeed the way the world is, which doesn't do much to enlighten you, but instead it inserts a perspective into you, that as you live out that perspective, once again, you're not necessarily nourishing your own well-being and growth but your actions may well instead be serving to maintain a status quo. Which is more a utopia for one little group than it is for the rest of the people in it….

Although Sid is reading from a syllabus, this is not a prepared talk but an elaboration on his key points reviewed near the end of the talk:

1. Conceptions of Man.

2. How people get socialized to be the way they find themselves when they take the trouble to look.

3. The psychology of persuasion and influence.

4. The human cost of being in that way.

5. Prophecy, visions of other ways for the world to be and people to be in it. False prophets have negative effect.

6. What it takes in order to get on with growth.

Sid's test for a true prophet is simple: examine the environment that results from following their beliefs. If people flourish and are healthier from it, the ideology is good. If they don't, it is bad. Sid offers the following example:

> It's too bad there are no Aztecs around, to ask them, "When the first Catholic fathers appeared, bringing to them the message of the loving savior, Jesus Christ," they're not around to answer the question, "Now do you *really think* that your life was improved by converting, from that pagan Aztec faith to the 'true' faith?" There is a remarkable correlation between the advent of Christian and Islamic-Mohammedan missionaries, and genocide, which is food for thought, at the very least. And it is certainly food for historical study and analysis. Why is it that a nation can be flourishing and living in a reasonable ecological balance with Nature at Time 1; and at Time 2, contact is made with another culture which purports to have a better cosmology and ethical system, and epistemology, and moral philosophy; and what then happens is that the people who lived there, die. Or else they become menial labor. That's food for thought.

The themes of control and freedom were present in his talks, his writing, in casual conversation with colleagues. Viewed with objectivity, Sid was an idealist, a social critic who confronted people with a broad, at times over-broad descriptions of the cultural forces that molded and controlled them—Skinner would call them behavior reinforcers. In one way Skinner and Sid were discussing the same idea but their stances regarding these reinforcers were in opposition. Skinner claimed man was merely the sum of them. Sid clearly did not.

Later in the talk is Sid's prescription for self-healing:

Now to whom do professional psychotherapists turn for help when they find themselves in some sickening or dispiriting impasse in their lives? Do they seek yet more analysis or client-centered therapy or behaviour modification or Gestalt psychotherapy? I don't. Instead, I pull back, I withdraw from the ways in which I'd been living up to that point and through meditation or conversation with an honest friend or travels to get away from the scene, try to get a perspective on my situation. I try to reinvent my situation and my ways of being in it some enlightening ways. This takes time, so I need to be able to put up with depression and boredom and some anxieties. I'm glad to get all the forbearance from friends and family that I can get during this time of withdrawal in order to reinvent myself. I don't want to be healed. I just want to be left alone or talked to as a human being. If I turn to psychotherapists it's not because of their technical orientation but because I knew them as persons, and I respect their prowess at coping graciously with dilemmas which presently overpower me.

In August Sid led a workshop entitled "The Psychotherapeutic Dialogue and Personal Growth," at a Holiday Inn in Montreal ($35, all proceeds to benefit AHP). Sid, whose father belonged to and supported various business and fraternal organizations, now found himself running workshops to help support his own professional association.

The Value of Experience

Self disclosure is a route to well-being when the disclosure is appropriate to the setting. Sid had no resistance to sharing appropriate information, an example being his response to a question from conference participants in a Crisis Telephone Services Summer Workshop conference call.[3] Each participant had been given copies of Sid's article "The Invitation to Die."[4]

> I know one time I tried to kill myself. It was nearly twenty years ago [1954] and I was in terrible despair. There were personal complications; I couldn't see my way out of it. And sitting there in despair, drinking brandy and mulling over my miserable lot, I decided to end it and turn on the gas. I sat in this little apartment where I was living at the time, waiting for it to happen. I got headachey and I had to have a leak, so I went to the toilet. I was standing there urinating, with my glass of brandy in one hand, and I looked in the mirror and saw my grim face. Now I really intended to kill

myself, but I looked at my face and I looked so grim and dramatic that I burst out laughing and I flushed the toilet, turned off the gas and went out to the out-of-doors. I breathed good, fresh air, and for weeks thereafter I was in a panic. Suppose I had had too much to drink. Suppose I had fallen asleep. I would have been dead. This experience taught me a hell of a lot about what it means when one dies. What is one trying to kill, anyway? I saw clearly that I was almost metaphorically killing off one of my ways of being me that had culminated in disaster. And it was a beginning of another way of being me. If, through some fluke, I had succeeded; if I hadn't had to take a leak at that very instant, I would have missed a vast amount. That personal experience has given me some personal credentials to talk to other suicidal people, I rather think, just like drug addicts trying to get rid of their addiction to drugs—they're very good at helping others. I think this is almost a basic truth involved in helping: that the ones who are effective in helping are the ones who have conquered and who have continued to struggle effectively with whatever it is that is bringing the person down. I would think, in other words, that crisis center people ought to be ex-suicide attempters.

Humanistic Psychology?

One of the great challenges of what psychologist Amedeo Giorgi wanted to call human science was that of generating data. In chemistry and biology and other "hard" science, data is quantitative, theories are proved or disproved with numerical data. Psychology has an aspect of subjectivity, as the subject is the human condition. One of the advantages of behaviorist approaches to psychology is the hard data generated with its methods; Sid was on a different, perhaps wider search. In the introduction to a joint interview on the subject of education with fellow "humanist" Arthur Combs, it was pointed out that Sid had "…contributed chapters to many texts in the fields of medicine, psychology, education and sociology." Sid's theories and research results included shared areas of interest in each of those fields.

In congruence with his comments about education in the previously mentioned Fullerton lecture, when asked if he had an idea about how adolescents could be better taught in high schools and how schools could become more humane institutions, Sid said:

> I think I would lower the age at which children can legally drop out of formal schooling to about twelve. My stream of association runs something like this: Well, why don't we put education and training on a free enterprise

basis, instead of letting the taxes do it. Governments can't leave such minimum indoctrination to chance. I think there's some wisdom in having compulsory education up to a certain level. I have a stereotype about the French. French education is strict as hell, and people who come out with a high school education there are very learned, skeptical human beings. They succeed in ways where we fail, despite cruddy classrooms, irascible teachers. Can you imagine Jean-Paul Sartre teaching high school in this country? Teaching philosophy? There's a case where I think, at least part of their required, public education works. Without any particular enlightened permissive this or that, or packaging. Thinking of educational alternatives, I know some young people who are trying to open up learning communities that don't have curricula, and I think it's grand to have such available against a backdrop of structure. I think if compulsory education limited itself to reading, writing, arithmetic, language, and thereafter people sought what they want, whether it's how to become a mechanic... I think that would be an advance.[5]

By September 1973 Sid had completed his sabbatical year through traveling around most of the world on a university's Semester at Sea program, followed by his time in California teaching, studying and interacting with colleagues. He then returned to Gainesville with—at least in theory—a refreshed mind, ready to resume his activities at the University of Florida.

Academic Dialogue

The status quo was anathema to Sid, and there was more than one status quo. Within the free-for-all that was psychology in the early seventies, his views were not universally shared within the landscape of humanistic approaches to science. As Sid said, to get humanists to agree to anything other than the necessity for pluralism was indeed a struggle. The humanistic psychologists had no unified voice or stance, and humanism by Sid's description was a loose term. Opinions within the entire field of psychology could seem as varied as the persons espousing them.

A window into this view is provided through a sequence of comments and responses following a book review by Sid of Amedeo Giorgi's *Psychology as a Human Science: A Phenomenologically Based Approach.* Sid's review was in the July 1972 issue of *Contemporary Psychology* and the following letters and their responses appeared in four issues over a period of fifteen months.

Men Are Like Me, Not Like Rats[6]

Psychology as a Human Science: A Phenomenologically Based Approach. New York: Harper & Row, 1970. pp. xv + 240. $3.50 paper.

I must confess to mixed feelings about Giorgi's book. He is a competent historian and knowledgeable critic of established, natural-science experimental psychology. His first chapter is a model of clarity and erudition. He is a master of the existential-phenomenological literature. But I am impatient with those who are arguing that psychology can become a human science (I agree), but who have not then gone on to demonstrate that their way of doing psychology more nearly makes sense of man and helps him to fulfill more of his possibilities than some other position. Actually, the day I started to write this review, I received a volume of papers called *Duquesne Studies in Phenomenological Psychology, Vol. 1,* which Giorgi and his Duquesne colleagues, W. F. Fischer and R. von Eckartsberg, edited. These papers are a pledge that the methods sought by Giorgi can bear some fruit.

The papers in that book are a step toward a science of persons, a human science rather than a science of behavior. Science is a way of making subject matter intelligible to man. The ways of making matter, or chemical phenomena, or the behavior of animals intelligible to the inquirer do not make man *as man* intelligible. Animals behave, man acts! We try to make animals or physiological processes intelligible in order that *we* might tame *them,* and "use" them for our goals. It is inappropriate for us to make a man intelligible to us (but not to him) so that we might use him. It is appropriate to help a man become intelligible to himself so that he can free himself from control by other men, by natural processes, and other "determiners" which would limit and subdue him.

The best way to make a man intelligible to himself and to another is to ask him to disclose his experience of his situation. This he will do, in truth, when he trusts his audience. In the process he learns, as does his audience, what aspects of the "natural" world he has had to yield to in order to live and which he has transcended in pursuit of his free projects. Exemplary biography, autobiography, and fiction, it seems to me, are human science at its best. When a man shows and tells his action, and then tells us why he did what he did, and *how* he did it, he is letting others know *their* possibilities. Just as the findings in a natural science laboratory experiment have a range of generalizability, so do accounts of man's experience generalize to other men. Men can recognize their own possibilities for action in the reported experience of others. And, for man, the direct determiner of action is *his experience of his situation.*

I am willing to guess, and to try to make my guess a self-fulfilling prophecy, that the advances in humanistic psychology, or a human science of psychology, will consist in perfecting the art of biography and autobiography, so that men will be able to share their experience at taming facticity, but not at taming their fellow men.

If I, and others, pursue psychology as a human science in the ways I have just mentioned, then Professor Giorgi's book can be regarded as successful; I was stimulated to think more about the problem of defining a humanistic psychology by reading his volume. Perhaps the next generations of students will take his volume as a challenge, to do better human science than Giorgi and his Duquesne colleagues have done, than [Arthur] Combs had done, and, for that matter, than this reviewer has done to date.

Four issues later, *Contemporary Psychology* ran this letter:

RESPONSIBILITY DEFINED

Sidney Jourard's review of *Psychology as a Human Science: A Phenomenologically Based Approach* (CP, 1972, 22, 407-408) was no review at all. He simply expounded his own ideas. Some readers may be interested in his ideas, but I think the majority would rather know something about Giorgi's book. All we know from the review is the author, name of book, publisher, price, and number of pages. This information is provided in the Books Received section of CP. It is the responsibility of the reviewer to inform the scientific community of an author's main points and to critically evaluate them. In this regard, Jourard's review is woefully inadequate.

RUSSELL D. CLARK, III
The Florida State University, Tallahassee

JOURARD'S REPLY TO CLARK

I agree with Clark, that I did not inform the scientific community of the author's main points, nor did I critically evaluate them in an explicit way. I did react to Giorgi's fine book in a way that Giorgi perhaps appreciated. Perhaps other readers might be moved by my "review" to see what I reacted to, to read the book themselves.

SIDNEY M. JOURARD
University of Florida

The next issue ran this letter:

In a recent review of a book by Giorgi, Jourard (CP, 17, 7, 373-374) seems to be using the terms "humanistic psychology" and "science" so broadly as to make them indistinguishable. Here are two examples:"Exemplary biography, autobiography, and fiction, it seems to me, are human *science* at its best," and "advances in humanistic psychology, or a human science of psychology, will consist in perfecting the *art* of biography and autobiography..." [italics mine]. While not denying the importance of biography and fiction as sources of knowledge, surely we will have fewer communication problems if we continue to regard the form of literature known as the novel as art rather than science. And, with no intent to discourage the advancement of humanistic psychology (in fact, it is because I'm concerned about the epistemic health of this approach that I've written this brief comment), I submit that if the quotations indicated above are not, in fact, contradictory, they at least *appear* to be so (see italicized words).

Unfortunately, this kind of conceptual confusion is all too typical of writings in humanistic psychology (i.e., Jourard is not a special target.) Elsewhere I have argued that the major source of difficulty is an epistemic one—that is, that there is insufficient awareness among specialists of the epistemological foundations of their disciplines (Royce, 1964), and, more specifically, that scientific psychology (although it involves metaphorism) relies primarily on the underlying epistemoligies of rationalism and empiricism, and that humanistic psychology (although it also involves rationalism and empiricism) is primarily dependent upon metaphorism (a primarily nonscientific epistemology) (Royce, 1965; 1970.) Please note that no major point here is merely that humanistic psychology is not science. (If it is, we would not need the term "humanistic" since it would "reduce" to science.). Thus, we get knowledge via this approach—but it is humanistic or metaphoric knowledge, *not* scientific knowledge (Royce, 1967; 1973).

I am aware of the Germanic usage of the terms science (Wissenschaft) which equates it with the term knowledge, but I'm assuming this is not the intended meaning in humanistic psychology writings, and further, I have assumed that such a move would be a retrograde step in any event. Finally, I recognize the legitimacy of stipulating that "humanistic psychology" could merely refer to the human end of the science spectrum (e.g. from molecules to man), and that Jourard and other leaders in humanistic psychology might have something like this in mind. The main point is that the present conceptual foundations (logical, linguistic, epistemological) of humanistic psychology are in serious need of diagnosis and repair.

JOSEPH R. ROYCE
The Center for Advanced Study in Theoretical Psychology

JOURARD REPLIES TO ROYCE

I think that Royce (CP, 1972, 17, 764) makes a valid point in his criticism of my remarks about Giorgi's book, and about humanistic psychology and human science. The distinction between metaphoric and rational-empirical epistemologies is useful and clarifies some of the controversy between "natural-science" psychologists, and "human-science" psychologists. They are literally playing different games, with different rules and aims. Giorgi is exploring the further development of a psychology, the method of which (phenomenological) bears a closer affinity with the humanities than with the natural sciences. The disclosure of the world as it is for somebody (biography and autobiography) is an art. The question is, is *science* to be confined in meaning and method to natural science? Giorgi disagrees, and I am inclined to agree with Giorgi. A science of persons, of *human* beings is possible. Perhaps, in the interest of linguistic purity, it should not be called "science." Actually, the view of man as organism, which guides "natural-science psychology," is metaphoric. Harré and Secord (1972) are exploring the possibility of an "anthropomorphic model" for social psychology—thereby striving to reconcile the apparent contradiction between metaphoric and rational-empirical epistemologies. I have attempted something similar in my (1971) work on self-disclosure. Giorgi and his colleagues are engaged in a similar effort at reconciliation. I concur with Royce's last sentence: "The main point is that the present conceptual foundations (logical, linguistic, epistemological) of humanistic psychology (and I would add, of phenomenological psychology) are in serious need of diagnosis and repair."

SIDNEY M. JOURARD
University of Florida

Sid's non-review continued to generate comments from several who read it. Two issues later, an existential phenomenologist who worked alongside Giorgi at Duquesne wrote:

If I were to comment on Jourard's review of Giorgi's book, *Psychology As a Human Science* in the same style that he reviewed the book, I would never mention that review. For Jourard never reviewed that book. Obviously, he wasn't interested in conveying some notion of the content or flavor of Giorgi's book, since he never communicated anything about these points, but, rather, was intent on representing, once again, his own theory of self-disclosure, mixed in with his personal views of science.

Basically, Giorgi's book articulated a revolutionary concept of science that abandons many of the sacred cows of the conventional understanding of science. All of this was totally ignored by Jourard; but worse, he created the impression that Giorgi shared in his theory of science. For example, Jourard proposes that experience is the *determiner* of action—whereas Giorgi abandons causal thinking in human science. Most evidently, this difficult thesis cannot be either presented or defended here, but at least it should be noted, which Jourard didn't do, and shouldn't be distorted, which Jourard did do.

The matter is simple: a reviewer should review a work, and if, in so doing, clarification of his own views is necessary, fine, but the latter should be only an instrument in reviewing and should not usurp the reviewing.

Recently psychologists have been searching frantically for a framework that neither objectifies man, as do all the positivistic strains in modern psychology, nor fondles him, as does humanistic psychology. These psychologists may have turned to a study of Giorgi's book, had they been informed that precisely that framework is Giorgi's breakthrough. For some reason, Jourard refused to inform them of this.

PAUL F. COLAIZZI
Duquesne University

Preoccupied with the activities of his sabbatical leave, Sid responded nine months later in the November 1973 issue [18-11. p. 572:] as the great Giorgi Book Review Debate continued:

ANSWER TO COLAIZZI

Colaizzi is correct in some aspects of his review of my review of Professor Giorgi's book (CP, 1973, 18, 70-71). I conveyed very little, directly, about the content of that book, but I did react to it in a spirit that I still think is in keeping with *psychology as a human science*. I do not entirely share Colaizzi's view that Professor Giorgi has provided the definitive, breakthrough vision that "neither objectifies man ... nor fondles him ...." I think he has made a yeoman effort in that direction, and its fruit in future research and practice will be the test of the effort. I don't believe my review, or non-review, will deter interested psychologists, in search of a framework, from studying this fine book; perhaps it may be more widely read because of my report.

SIDNEY M. JOURARD
University of Florida

The above exchanges illustrate how psychologists could articulate their views and opinions through *Contemporary Psychology*, a monthly " journal of reviews" published by the American Psychological Assocation. There was no internet or email, and the journal provided a continuous forum for reviews, opinions of reviews, responses to opinions of reviews, and despite the possibility of infinite regression, this was by Sid's way of thinking a form of "dialogue" in the sense of Martin Buber's dialogic model…you "speak" (the book review), there is a response (letter), you respond to the response. These academics were not agreeing with each other, but they were listening to one another.

Forty-five years after this sequence of letters, Amedeo Giorgi responded to my request for his recollections of that time, and of any encounters with Sidney.

April 24, 2018
Dear Marty,

… I cannot give you much information about our encounters because there were very few of them…we met briefly, I think, at an APA convention and exchanged a few words but it did not lead to subsequent exchanges. Over time it probably would have because there were a group of psychologists at [University of] West Georgia…with whom I had many contacts over the years.

The situation was something like this. West Georgia was humanistic in outlook and was reaching towards existential-phenomenology. I was at Duquesne which was existential-phenomenological and was reaching towards humanistic psychology. In other words, our starting points were different but we were reaching towards each other. However, since the starting points were different there was no initial rush to get to know each other. That only happened over time. . . .

We were both arguing for a minority position in psychology and did not see right away that it would have been better for us to be together because we were emphasizing differences rather than similarities. That happens when one is young and it takes time to be more tolerant and accepting of differences. We are still very much a minority in psychology today even though we believe that the field would be much stronger if it followed our ideals. Psychology is a very amorphous over-extended field and it will take a long time for it to settle and become a more mature science like physics. . . .

Warmly,

Amedeo Giorgi

In an essay for *Voices,* the newsletter of the American Psychotherapist Association, Sid presents some far-reaching reflections on the human condition, followed by a response from fellow humanistic psychologist Robert A. Harper (who co-authored with Albert Ellis *A Guide to Rational Living,* the primary text of rational-emotive behavior therapy, or REBT).

A Future for Psychotherapy

It is a lesson, nearly but not too late for the learning. Man keeps forgetting, and perennially must be reminded he has no fixed essence. He is banished from the animal kingdom and the garden of Eden, and is condemned to freedom. He is blessed or cursed with the injunction to choose his future. Try though he many, there is no escape from freedom.

We all have taken refuge behind the walls we have ourselves constructed, walls that protect our naked beings from the scrutiny and touch of our fellows. We are lonely, but afraid. We look at one another as through the wrong end of the telescope, and touch, if at all, with carefully deodorized and sterilized gloves.

We feel ourselves lost in the other's definition of us. I am not who you think I am. I feel myself trapped in your view and definition of who I am. You see me as an essence, as essentially a man, of 47 years, of my profession, locked in my family roles. My deeds, my plans, my perceptions are to be those that befit a "biocomputer" with that programming. If I take myself to be more, or different, I terrify or infuriate you when you learn of my digression. I may know my difference, and conceal it as I would the crown jewels or a secret leprosy.

Women and children; blacks; the poor; homosexuals; madmen; foreigners; the elderly—all of us are discovering the horrible joke we have allowed to be played on us. Each of us is other than the one we were told to be, or believed to be. We do not have to put up with our past identities for another instant. We can choose a new identity and insert an authentic perspective into the world we all share just as readily as we assented to the other's definition of our promise and our limits.

God is dead, at least the little god envisioned by the timid, and those of little vision. The church is dead, at least that church which ministers only to those who have paid their dues in order to belong. The blacks of the West no longer are servile Uncle Toms, nor are the blacks of the Third World holding themselves to the limits of light and freedom defined by their colonizers. Women refuse to see themselves as silly, superficial, greedy and exclusively maternal. Schizophrenics decline to see their perspective as mad. Homosexuals insist on the right to speak to one another, and to "straight" people, as the people they are. Jews till the soil, fight battles for survival, and stand tall rather than crouched as did the timid inhabitants of ghettos. Deadening family structures have been challenged by Ronald Laing, Aaron Esterson, and David Cooper.

Race, religion, sex, age, family roles and occupational roles—all those efforts on the part of man to evade freedom and responsibility, to make his relationships automatic, programmed and contactless—have been melted away by man's hot realization that he is the embodiment of freedom and responsibility. If there is a future to human relationships, it will have to be a human or humanizing future. We can or must, choose, and the choosing is not in the head but in action. A human future consists in real encounter with another person. This starts authentic dialogue between the person I am—whom I show to you, whom I seek to know as you know yourself. Then, as I address you, you recognize yourself as the very person being addressed.

Everyone can be whom he chooses. He already is. Everyone can talk to everyone—there is no gap between generations, races, sexes, professions, nations, except as we choose it. There is nobody here but us, you and me. We can talk truly to one another, to find our common humanity and our authentic differences, to learn how to share this time and territory in life-giving ways, or we can choose to keep the world split into Us, and Them, with the implication that we must rid Our World of Them.

We cannot recognize Them as the rest of Us because we have emptied ourselves of our lust, our perversity, our rage, indeed, often our vitality, and dumped it upon them. Then we complain about their filth, and our emptiness and lifelessness.

When we recognize ourselves in the other, and the other in ourselves, we will have taken the first step toward ending war and exploitation, and toward making institutions fit for us to live in. We will do this because we will have opened our ears in order truly to hear the shrieks and murmurs of pain produced in them and in us as we live dehumanizing lives in dehumanizing families, schools, places of work, under dehumanizing political regimes. There is no one to save the world but you and me. The messiah is no one but ourselves in one of our possibilities. If he is not us, then he is nobody.

November 21, 1972, at sea

Response

By ROBERT A. HARPER

I am not an anti-authenticator, and I am all in favor of reciprocal self-revelation. When we drop our phoniness and, as persons, relate openly and forthrightly to each other, life is more interesting and enjoyable for me and for you. Such sincerity and self-disclosure probably has a therapeutic effect on the people to whom we relate in a clinical situation. A little, anyhow.

But I think Sid Jourard has written nonsense here about messianic psychotherapists who rise up and save the world by authenticating and self-disclosing and scrutinizing and touching selves all over the place. To humanize or rehumanize the dehumanized world institutions, much more is needed than for us therapeutic boys and girls genuinely to open our ears in order truly to hear the pain calls. More than savoring some kind of feel deal, many of us human beings—therapists and nontherapists alike—will need to undertake a lot of cerebrally and socially hard work (Nader's Citizen Movement and Gardner's Common Cause might be considered token beginnings.). Even to keep the human world alive, we are going to have to do a great deal of dirty, difficult, intelligently directed labor. We cannot effectively stand here letting our genuine therapeutic selves hang out.

Sid says either the messiah is us or he is nobody. Clutch tightly to your security blanket, Sid, because he's nobody. We must torturously problem-solve ourselves toward a slightly better (or barely surviving) world. There is no messianic magic that will save us the travail of moving there.

Psychotherapists as Prophets

Sid was drawn to the image of a psychotherapist as a prophet, whose role is to find the path for others to follow, both individually and as citizens within their culture. In a paper read at the Symposium "Psychotherapy As A Secular Calling" at the APA Annual Meeting in Washington, D.C. on September 4, 1971, Sid observes that a prophet,

> ... like Ralph Nader, told it like it was. They were like divine agronomists, military advisers, family counselors, ecologists, public health officers and muckraking journalists, pointing to, and reminding and showing others a better way, if not the "Right Way."
>
> The psychotherapist, according to this view, embodies part of the way of a prophet, that of being an exemplar of the way of life he wishes to invite others to follow for their own good, and, by implication, for

the good of the community. And he is a prophet when he points out the truth about destructive behavior. Old Testament prophets were desirous that the polyglot aggregation of Hebrew tribes might overcome their limited and autistic perspectives and become a people, a community called Israel, united under one God, living in exemplary ways as a beacon and example to all mankind. An extraordinarily modest ambition. A modern psychotherapist—insofar as he can see connections between and implications of usual ways for people to be and sickness, social disorganization and stultified growth and madness on large scale—can tell individual patients or seekers *what* he sees. And he can prophesy in market-places, before temples and in the places where people work; and modern prophetic psychotherapists have access to the press and the mass media—TV, movies, etc. to present their diagnoses and prescriptions.[7]

Later he states:

A prophet is, without compromise, committed to the highest good of which man is capable, and he mourns, castigates and incites in order that mediocre men might rise to those heights. Like the *outsiders* of whom Colin Wilson wrote, the prophet sees too much, hears the groans of pain to which others are deaf. Yet the prophets have a compassion for mankind and they seek to invite all men to take responsibility for the fate of man and life in this place and time. The prophets feel the blast from heaven, they inveigh against callousness, indifference and yet take no pleasure in the lot to which they have been called. Prophets are seditious, cranky, threats to the status quo.

After mentioning others whom he views as prophets (Wilhelm Reich, Brock Chisholm, Israel Charney, R.D. Laing and Aaron Esterson) Sid writes:

I presume to prophesy, as I have in print, that cosmetic family structures are responsible for physical disease, including cancer. I suppose I have had a prophetic function, too, in my writing about research and therapy as exploitive and adjustive disciplines, striving to find more humanistic and liberating ways for psychologists to be.[8]

Sid in front yard, Gainesville, 1974

Adventure and Misadventure 13

By 1974 Sid had been in private practice of psychotherapy for over twenty years, a university professor for fifteen, and was the author of several respected and much-cited books. In August, through the efforts of the psychology department of the University of Laval in Quebec, a French translation of *the Transparent Self* was published with the elegant title *La Transparence de Soi*.[1] Sid would modestly claim that he invented the term "self-disclosure" and popularized the concept of "transparency" in social interaction and its corollary the "dyadic effect" in that self-disclosure encouraged and drew out reciprocal self-disclosure. Research continued in self-disclosure (including its relationship to emotional well-being) and the results were published in academic journals of several social sciences.[2]

The main source of Sid's thinking was a continual process of reading, processing, integrating and synthesizing. His thinking led to writing and publication in academic journals and public speaking engagements. Through editing and organizing these talks and journal writings into thematic groups and with additional material, books had emerged: *The Transparent Self, Disclosing Man to Himself* and *Self-Disclosure* were all created in this way.

Healthy Personality

Sid revised *Personal Adjustment: An Approach Through the Study of Healthy Personality* and renamed the book *Healthy Personality: An Approach from the Viewpoint of Humanistic Psychology*. This revision included much new material.

As physical objects, books have the potential to last for many years, providing continual access to the author's thought. If there is a secular version of immortality in academia, published books are as close as one can get. It can be argued that authors of classic texts in prose, fiction, non-fiction and poetry are in a certain sense immortal. In *Inferno*, the first part of Dante Alighieri's epic poem *The Divine Comedy*, he placed personal political enemies in various circles of Hell depending on their crimes, where centuries later they continue to burn. Immortality of this sort is vastly appealing to the spirit, as humans are the only form of life aware of the inevitability of their death while alive.[3]

Healthy Personality was the third edition of Sid's first book, and a comparison of the various Prefaces is informative. The 1958 Preface states that

> The present work is an attempt to provide the reader with an explicit concept of healthy personality. Professional students of personality have succeeded in describing the diverse forms of unhealthy personality, but they have barely touched upon the problem of describing health.

Five years later, the second edition Preface read:

> To be "average" in personality means to suffer from various "socially patterned defects," as Fromm calls them. That is, the typical person in our society usually shows signs of premature arrest in his growth; he may carry symptoms of neurosis which are so widely shared in his society that he does not realize he is half sick. The simple fact is that in an age when space is being explored, and when man has the nuclear power to destroy this planet, average personality *is just not good enough*. We need to learn more about man's potentials for fuller personal development, in the hope that future parents and teachers will be able to rear generations of healthier personalities.

The Preface of the third edition has a much broader reach:

> Some ways of behaving in the world are life-giving to the person and not destructive to other people, to animals, or to the environment which supports us all. These are the ways I call healthy personality.
>   Not only do these ways enhance life and health for the person, they also stimulate, or at least do not impede, the growth and actualization of his more desirable possibilities. Healthy personality fosters personal growth and sustains health and well-being.

In this book, I have presented what we have learned in psychology—through clinical experience and through research in laboratories and natural settings—about healthy personality.

The point of view from which this book is written is that of humanistic psychology.

Humanistic psychology is the study of man based on the assumption that, as a human being he is free and hence responsible for his actions and their consequences to his well-being and growth. The humanistic orientation in psychology has flourished in the past decade, and I have sought to incorporate some of the vigor of that approach into my efforts to discuss healthy personality.

The new chapters address consciousness in the form of phenomenology; work and play; religion, and a description of the humanistic approach to the study and practice of psychology as a profession. Sid dedicates the book to Abraham Maslow.

Synthesis of Ideas

Sid's expansive and continuous reading, along with a perennial curiosity and the capacity to absorb and synthesize various views of the human condition had led him to a nuanced viewpoint that he named "HEP," a blend of humanistic, existential and phenomenological approaches to the study of humankind. In what looks to be a description of one of Sid's graduate seminars in Humanistic Existential Phenomenological Psychology he writes:

> There is as yet no such field as HEP psychology, but there will, of course, be. One aim of the present seminar is to help the participants become oriented in the area, and through their reading, to help others to become oriented. I would ask each of you to make 3 x 5 cards for titles of books and articles that you come across in your reading, including references in the bibliographies of those books and articles, that seem relevant to this broad area. In this way we can develop a library. The following references constitute a good beginning.

Sid lists sixty-one books, and the course outline reads as follows:

1. Foundations in Existential Psychology

2. Humanistic Psychology: Toward a Science of Persons, of Man, contrasted with Science of Behavior

3. A Psychology for Growth and Releasing Human Potentialities

4. A Humanistic-Existential View of "Mental Illness"

5. Humanistic-Existential Therapies

6. Research Areas, Methodology

7. Humanistic Psychology and Society: Toward a Humanistic Social Psychology, Sociology

What is HEP?

Sid read widely in the various psychologies and behavioral sciences, philosophy, sociology, religion and Eastern belief systems. In his writings he presented his views on such abstract yet germane human attributes as transcendence, freedom, change, dialogue, spirit, and authenticity, concepts difficult to quantify yet having deep connections with themes in human life. These views evolved as his sources deepened, widened and interacted. Each of these components—humanism, existentialism and phenomenology—influenced his current stance as a researcher.

Humanistic Psychology rejected many of the views of human motivation espoused by behaviorism, Freudian psychoanalysis and other depth psychologies. Existentialism argued that at birth a human has no predetermined nature—or as Sartre put it, "existence precedes essence"—and in the absence of a higher entity that frames humankind in a specific role, each person is therefore, whether they like it or not, free. In this view, the commanding value of life was *intensity,* embodied and expressed in acts of free choice, individual self-assertion, love and creative work, all of which were impossible to strive toward without the potential of anguish, suffering and risk.[4]

Phenomenology is the philosophical study of phenomena without an attempt at metaphysical explanation. In Sid's view, scientific psychology had *begun* with the study of experience, by Wundt in 1879, and by the 1920s this approach fell into disrepute largely through the success of the behaviorist approaches of Pavlov and John B. Watson, who stated "Psychology as the behaviorist views it is a purely objective experimental branch of natural science. Its theoretical goal is the prediction and control of behavior."[5] In *Disclosing Man to Himself* Sid writes:

Together with the domination of the psychological scene by behaviorism has been the widespread adoption of psychoanalytic theory. According to the psychoanalytic view, man, while he can be free (or freer), is mostly a vessel driven by instinctual urges and irrational super-ego prodding. And his conscious experiencing is not investigated for itself, but rather for the glimpses and hints it may afford of the subterranean unconscious mental life.

The upshot has been that the reporting and description of human experience has been shoved out of the realm of science, and relegated (or elevated) to the province of the arts and humanities. Novelists, poets, painters, playwrights, musicians—these have been the people who investigate human experience in its myriad forms. The only scientifically oriented people to take a serious interest in experience per se have been the philosophical phenomenologists, and a scattering of psychologists who began to read literature in the tradition of existentialism and phenomenology.[6]

For Sid, the values expressed in humanism, existentialism and phenomenology were a guide to understanding the human condition. He saw the synergy generated by the collective efforts of these approaches.

Intensity

A review of Sid's appointment calendars and scribbled personal notes reveal his activities and plans in minutae: a routine of teaching, a few therapy patients, hand-ball games, flamenco guitar lessons, in March two classes in transcendental meditation. Sid had taken flying lessons starting in 1970 and once described his first (solo) flight in a one-engine plane: the radio went dead while in landing descent and Sid had to safely land on the ground without the anticipated guidance of his instructor over the headset. The immediacy of that experience stayed with him.

In February Sid was in Wyoming for an event or presentation of which there is no documentation. The following month he led a workshop retreat in Cumberland Island, Florida for a group of dentists. In an interview with a fellow psychotherapist a few months later Sid mentioned this event:

> Interviewer: I've had patients who were dentists. I've been struck by several of them, who sort of come to in their late forties and say, what the hell am I doing, spending my life in other people's mouths? They've given it up and done something else they've always wanted to do.

Sid: The irony is that I am involved in a group of dentists in Florida who gathered themselves together into a group to perfect their professional skills and to learn how to make a lot of money, and having done that, they've arrived at the point where they're asking what in the hell is it all for, and as a group I have run weekend groups with them, and helped them to find... people like George Bach[7], and others to explore with them, what do you do with your life after you've had it made...

In April he was in Galveston; in May Sid chaired the Southeast Psychology Association meeting in Hollywood, Florida, with "Contributions to Personality Theory (Ways of Thinking About Man from Contemporary Lifestyle)." The next day he presented "Within Freedom and Dignity: The Tasks of Humanistic Psychology."

Crescent Beach, Florida, June 1974. Jeff, Marty, Leonard, Sidney

Peru

At the end of June and by the invitation of an anthropology graduate student (Anthony Oliver-Smith), Sid flew to Lima and spent eighteen days in Peru backpacking and hiking. In Oliver-Smith's words, there were three of them:

> Dave Healey an old friend of mine…and Sid and I. We packed for cold weather because the nighttime temperatures in the Andes are very cold because of the altitude, even though quite near the equator. We also packed all our food for the six-day hike. We got our water from streams and springs along the way. Our itinerary was basically following an Inca trail up from the valley…
>
> It's a fairly well known hike now. Back then, it wasn't unheard of but we didn't see any other hikers once we got on the trail. We did run into some local people who used the trail to bring products down to the markets in the valley and back up to their villages. We spent our first night in a shepherd's hut above the smaller of the two lakes…we had brought a bottle of *pisco* (a high octane Peruvian grape brandy) that was supposed to last us the whole trip. We finished it that first night….on the way up to the pass, the three of us, each with about 40-50 pounds of equipment, sleeping bags, food, etc. in our ergonomically-designed packs were pretty winded, stopping every couple of hundred yards of the ascent, but we were passed by this old Indian guy, who must have been about seventy, who trotted past us with a huge sack of potatoes over his shoulder. He grinned at us and wished us "buenas tardes" and went on his way, leaving us in the dust, feeling just a little wimpy.[8]

At the end of August Sid was in New Orleans for both the AHP and APA conventions, where on August 29th he led an AHP workshop on his current interest with "Some Dimensions of Dialogue: In Research, Teaching, Therapy and Here," described in the AHP newsletter:

> Dialogue as a central phenomenon is largely neglected in psychology. Psychology has been primarily a study of man *out* of the mode of dialogue. I have been exploring the possibilities of research and practice as dialogue, and would like to share these. We'll form a small group and experience, explore and expand the dimensions of dialogue that are needed in our personal and professional growth.

During this double convention Sid was interviewed by C. Roger Meyers, one of his professors from undergraduate years, for the Canadian Psychological Association Archives. In the interview Meyers asks Sid to pick a psychology book that "really turned you on." Sid replies:

> The irony is, not many in psychology as such. A lot of psychology is dreadful prose, and not very illuminating, but I remember as an undergraduate, I read all the forbidden literature. I read Freud, I read Moreno[9], ...Wilhelm Reich...Marx...sociology and anthropology, I read widely in English naturally,...Shakespeare, the great American and English writers, and then Jung later. Moreno I read because Mary Northway had recommended him, and then later Carl Rogers...Maslow...Martin Buber had a powerful influence on me, and Kazantzakis had a powerful influence on me...I've been rereading Buber lately because my interests are taking yet another turn. It all revolves one way or another around the theme of dialogue. I am fascinated with—what does it mean to listen, and what does it mean to speak and how does this connect with imagination, and how does that connect with the body, and what about metaphors. So I don't know where that's going to lead.
>
> Q: What's your expectation of what is going to be the bandwagon next in psychology?
>
> A: I'll tell you what I see happening, and I'm trying to have a hand in it; it's very glibly called the effort to humanize the various disciplines, including our own, and I've been very much involved—I've just created a way of reconciling the contradictions between, let's say a manipulative behavioral approach to the study of man, and the humanistic and dialogic approach, so that it's not one or the other, but a way to do research which covers the waterfront by varying the way the experimenter and the subject relate to each other, and I've been able to see what, for political and economic and philosophical reasons has been an impersonal relationship between experimenter and subject, or between doctor and patient, or therapist and patient, or teacher and pupil, there's only one of a whole slew of possibilities, and I've worked out a way experimentally to vary that through various possibilities, and see what happens to data, doctor-patient outcomes, psychotherapist-patient outcomes, teacher-pupil outcomes, and so on and experimenter-subject outcomes. I'm going to be involved in that—since I invented it, why not?

In October Sid traveled to Waltham, Massachusetts for an "Espousal Center Workshop" and then to St. Louis for the Convention of Marriage Counselors, whose theme that year was "The Art and Science of Love and Intimacy." Sid's contribution was "Marriage is For Life" (commenting in a note, "pun intended").

Marriage Is For Life

The title of my talk has nothing to do with chronological time. When I chose a title "Marriage is for Life" I meant that marriage is to enhance life, and it is not so much an answer as it is a search. I want to direct my remarks to that search, the search for life itself.

The image of the good marriage is perhaps one of its most destructive features. The ideal marriage is a snare, a trap, an image the worship of which destroys life. The ideal marriage is like the ideal body or any other ideal, useful only if it engenders the divine discontent which leads to questing and authenticity. Whose image of a way to live together will guide a relationship? This is a question relevant for a president and his electorate, a doctor and his patient, a parent and child, a researcher and his subject, or a husband and wife. Shall it be an exercise in the concealment and display of power or a commitment to dialogue? Failure of dialogue is the crisis of our time, whether it be between nation and nation, us and them, or you and I.

Sid then mentions two destructive fallacies that cause conflict in marriage:

One is the myth of the right partner. The other is the myth of the right way to act so as to ensure peace, joy, and happiness. People believe, or are led to believe, that if they just find the right partner, the right answer to the riddle of their existence will be found. Once having found the right person and the way of relating that is satisfying at this time, the partners try to do everything to prevent change.

Sid proposes a healthy marriage as a dialogue, in the sense of Martin Buber's definition of dialogue: actively listening to the other, then responding as the other person listens with full attention and in good faith:

Marriage at its best, according to the image that is making more sense to me, is a relationship within which change is generated by the very way of relating—dialogue, so that growth as well as identity and a sense of rootedness are engendered. Change is not so much a threat as it is the fruit of a good marriage, according to this image. Marriage is for growth, for life. It's a place to call home, but like all homes one must leave it in its present form and then return, and then leave it, and then return, like Odysseus, leaving Ithaca and returning.

The Homeric Odyssey myth continued its metaphoric allure for Sid, as does the concept of idolatry, taken from the Old Testament and applied to marital conflict:

I take it as true that there is no way to go through life without some pain, suffering, loneliness, and fear. We can help one another minimize the shadow side of life; none can avoid it completely. To seek to avoid pain at all costs is to make an idol out of pleasure or painlessness. To avoid solitude at all costs is to make an idol out of chronic companionship. To avoid anxiety and depression at all costs is to make an idol out of safety and elation. To have to achieve orgasm with somebody in particular is to make an idol of that person or of the genital experience. To sacrifice everything for the breathless experience of being in love is to make an idol of breathlessness.

This view of marriage brings Sid to selectively disclose his personal life, his separation from Toni after seven years of marriage and his own rather romanticized self-description:

Through some fluke, though, within a month of a decree of divorce, we decided to resume our by now somewhat scarred relationship, rather wiser and more honest with one another about who we were. This openness for those not practiced in it was pure hell. It was painful, I assure you. It was painful for me to learn that my wife had a mind, a perspective, and feelings of her own different from mine. She was not the girl I married; in fact, she never was. I married my fantasy, and so did she. She had some coping to do, discovering that I was not the saint I had once seemed. She learned I was, and still am to some extent, a scarcely bridled privateer, a pirate, and adventurer, barely domesticated to her or American conceptions of married males.

He then mentions Israel Charny's *Marital Love and Hate* and its descriptions of

the depths of misery and destructiveness which are the other side of personal growth. Charny sees the family not strictly as haven or a place for fun and games, although it can be that, or as a place for sexual delights, but as a place where that most savage of all creatures, man, can learn to share time and space nonviolently and nondestructively.

As for the effectiveness of marriage counselors—the very people he was addressing—Sid's presentation became one of those occasions wherein he criticized his audience directly to their face, with honesty if not tact:

> According to this view, marriage is not for happiness, I have concluded after 26 1/2 years [of marriage]. It's a many-splendored thing, a place to learn how to live with human beings who differ from oneself in ages, sex, values and perspectives. It's a place to learn how to hate and to control hate. It's a place to learn laughter and love and dialogue. I'm not entirely persuaded that marriage and family counseling is a profession with any particular contribution to make to the quality of life. There is so far as I now know no way for people to live alone or with others that God endorsed as *the way* that She intended. [Laughter] Why is that funny? Certainly She intended that we cohabit to conceive and then to rear children, but the exact way we should live with one another was never specified. We have to grope and search, according to this view. As near as I can see, such groping for viable, non-destructive ways proceeds best within a context of dialogue.

He then describes marriage as

> not an answer, but a search, a process, a search for life, just as dialogue is a search for truth. Yesterday's marriage or way of being married is today's trap. The way out of the trap is to resume the dialogue, not to end it, unless someone is pledged not to grow and change.

Dialogue again comes to the forefront of Sid's current thought:

> As in all realms where human beings deal with one another, there is no place in family counseling for dissembling and technical manipulation by the professional person. Marriage and family counseling to enhance or to terminate marriages proceeds best, perhaps, only, through dialogue.

When considered from a contemporary perspective, Sid's mid-seventies view of marriage—during a time of alternative living arrangements, "open marriage" and gay, black and women's liberation movements—sounds rational and downright sensible. Sid's talk received much attention in the marriage counseling arena and was published in the *Journal of Marriage and Family Counseling* and later in *Humanistic and Transpersonal Psychology: A Sourcebook*.[10]

John Vasconcellos

During 1974 Sid struggled to find new subjects of interest to explore and to research, even doubting if he had anything further to contribute to his field. I recall him once saying he wished he were simple, and at another time that he wasn't sure what he'd do next—maybe become a plumber. This was certainly a joke, but Sid had a respect for craftspersons in all fields. He also told me that he had been "crazy" for a while in recent times. When I asked for how long, he replied "For about a year."

But Sid worked through this impasse and was currently focused on a methodology of measuring the degree of self-disclosure between pairs of participants in varied societal roles. This idea was described in a letter written to John Vasconcellos, a veteran California politician whom Sid had met in 1965 while leading an encounter workshop at Big Sur's Esalen Institute. John Vasconcellos (1932-2014) was an American Democratic politician from California who for thirty years represented the district known as Silicon Valley as a member of the California Assembly before being elected to the California State Senate for eight years, making him one of California's longest serving politicians. Vasconcellos sponsored the first bill to legalize marijuana in any form in 2003.[11] His lifelong interest in psychology led to his advocacy of the self-esteem movement in California politics and in 1990 initiated and produced "Toward a State of Esteem: The Final Report of the California Task Force to Promote Self-Esteem and Personal and Social Responsibility," a sociological research report that was culturally conspicuous enough to be parodied in the Doonesbury comic strip. John was a close friend of Sid's and keenly interested in "humanizing" politics, a major challenge as applied to a field where concealment and deception was and remains an integral part of the political process. By the fall of 1974 Sid had developed an idea he called The Grid. In this letter to Vasconcellos he outlines a method of correlating self-disclosure with outcome:

November 11, 1974
Dear John,

Truly, you have made a leap ahead, with this latest glimpse of your
thinking and planning. Of course I want to take part in this movement, and I
will come to talk to your constituents when you give the word. I can't think
of anything more bold, timely, or imaginative for a "politician" to introduce
to his constituents....One reason why I am so excited by our proposals for
a humanistic alternative is that I have finally worked out a way of looking at
all relationships between professional persons and their clients, sellers and
buyers, doctors/patients, experimenters/subjects, politicians/citizens. I
developed this scheme, after much wheel-spinning, trying to reconcile the
apparently irreconcilable contradiction between the manipulative approaches
of behaviorism, and the inviting approaches of humanistic psychology. Here
is the scheme:

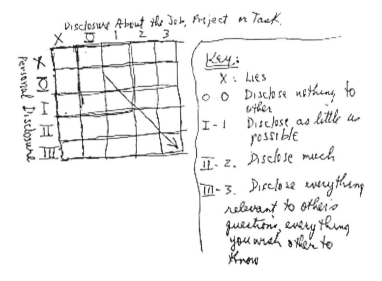

As you see, this is a "grid" with columns and rows, producing cells that
represent varying degrees of self-disclosure from a person of high power to
someone of lower power. Reading across the top, you see X, 0, 1, 2, and 3,
which stands for degrees of disclosure about the task that brought the two
together. X stands for lying, 0 stands for no disclosure, and 1, 2, and 3 stand
for degrees of disclosure about the task ranging from very little to complete
candor, complete response to all questions dealing with the task.

The rows, also labeled X, O, I, II and III, stand for varying degrees of <u>personal</u>

self-disclosure, the numbers standing for the varying degrees of disclosure.

I developed this first to look at research in psychology, In examining what researchers tell the people whom they are studying in the various experiments that psychologists do, it becomes obvious that the researchers lie, or at most, tell nothing or as little as possible to their subjects, about the experiment, and about the experimenter as a human being. The reason for such reticence or duplicity has always been to keep the subject "naive," so that the study will more nearly resemble and experiment in biology or chemistry. All psychological research, then, has gone on in cells XX, OO, or I-1, or combinations of them. In short, researchers are in dialogue, if at all, only with each other, and with those who pay for research. The people whom they study benefit not at all from such research. I have begun to get students to do experiments, not only in the conventional way, but moving across the diagonal, varying the degrees to which they disclose to the subject information about the experiment, and information about themselves. This amounts to including the subject as a collaborator, not as a guinea pig of the researcher—which I see as the humanistic alternative in psychological research.

There is some place for minimal disclosure between experimenter and subject, but psychological research must not be "locked" into that limiting model any more, as it has been for political economic and philosophical reasons for 90 years.

When psychological scientists include the subjects as collaborators in research, the possibility emerges that new images of man, new dimensions of human possibility can emerge from research, instead of mere confirmation of views of man as predictable, manipulable, controllable.

Now, I'll switch to the fields of psychotherapy, counseling, medical practice, nursing, and other "helping" professions. I'll re-do the diagram to make it clearer:

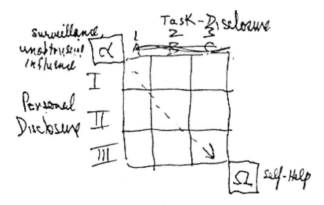

Now you see it is a 3 x 3 table, with 9 cells, and 2 additional ones at the extreme end of the diagonal, one cell marked α and the other Ω. The Roman and Arabic numerals stand for degrees of disclosure by the professional person to his client or patient—disclosure about the task, the illness, the treatment and self-disclosure by the professional person about himself as a person. Alpha (α) stands for "unobtrusive" efforts to influence or heal the patient—where the patient doesn't even know he is being "treated." Omega (Ω) stands for self-healing. Most professional work has gone on in cell I-1, where the professional person tells his patient nothing, or very little about himself, or the true nature of the treatment: "I'm Dr. Jones, and I'm going to help you feel better." My approach to psychotherapy certainly starts in I-1, but as the relationship unfolds, my patient and I move to II-2, then to III-3, and finally, to Omega, where the patient learns to help himself, and is no longer dependent on his therapist. Conventional therapies, conducted in I-1, keep the patient mystified, dependent on his guru, and encourage him to become a "true believer" in the "method" (e.g., gestalt, TA, primal, etc.).

Now let us move to teaching and pedagogy—all the manipulative approaches, emphasizing prediction and control take place in I-1. Humanistic teachers, like humanistic therapists and doctors, move across the diagonal with their pupils.

Now, finally, on to your project. Traditional politics has gone on in cell I-1, or in the first, diagram, cell X-X, where the politician lies to everyone about his personal self, and about the way in which he is going to govern. Actually, if he is in dialogue with anyone, it is with those have "bought" him. Certainly, he is not in truth with his constituents. This is where I see you as a bold new searcher, whose re-election represents a kind of confirmation. You can be candid with your electorate about your personal searching for meaning in life, and your professional, task-related search for the political conditions that make personal life and growth possible....

You wish to inaugurate politics in III-3, or at the least, II-3. A public figure is entitled to privacy and so only conventional disclosure about his personal life may be "enough"—but maybe not; perhaps entry into public life should call for exemplary transparency—to be a leader in integrity, not in duplicity and the abuse of power.

I am calling on all professional people to desist from work in cells with X, and to move beyond I-1 into II-3, or III-3 when they do research, or psychological practice of any kind. I expect that if this is done, public confidence in the professions will be warranted, and new potentialities of man will become realities. The diagram is a useful visual aid for "locating" relationships on a continuum from mystification and control, at one extreme, to full sharing in dialogue and partnership at the other.

Your political stance has done just this. Certainly all our institutions—family, school, church, military, government—are in their crisis because the spokesmen for these institutions have refused to get out of cell II-1, have refused to grant full human status to the "rank and file." It is urgent, I agree, to reverse this trend and to assume leadership through example.

Count on me to participate in this humanistic alternative in all ways, In fact, I have been doing just that anyway in my profession—trying to <u>show</u> alternate ways to do research and therapy that are in keeping with a view of man as free, human and responsible, rather than a view of man as organism, machine, or other determined being.

Education As Dialogue

Two weeks later Sid was at Stanford University for the AHP conference "Reading, Riting, and Reality: Exploring New foundations for Educational Change" on November 22nd and 23rd. Sid's talk, entitled "The Challenge of Schooling: Synthesizing, Training, and Educating," was transcribed and condensed by Tom Greening, editor of the *Journal of Humanistic Psychology*, where it was published as "Education as Dialogue."[12]

The opening paragraphs present his thesis clearly:

The crisis of our time is not shortage of food, space, and energy; it is the failure of dialogue. The learned incapacity to hear and understand what another human being is saying, and the choice to respond in dishonesty, is at the heart of our dilemma on the shrinking planet we call Earth.

There are too few places to learn dialogue. From infancy, children are exposed to those who wish to shape, influence, persuade, bribe, command, or threaten them. Too few people invite them to speak their truth. Too few listen and hear, and speak truth in return. Everywhere there is the struggle to dominate and impose one's views upon others.

Education, if it is anything, is dialogue. It is an invitation from someone, living or dead, to engage in a process which enlarges one's perspective. If education is not dialogue, then it is not education. . . .

The purpose of education is to transmute biological creatures into human beings, into persons whose stay on earth is life-giving for themselves and not destructive to the lives of other persons, other creatures, and the people of other lands, now, and in the generations that follow. Education is to help persons of distorted, uneven, provincial development become more whole, to become persons of understanding.

Sid's definition of the purpose of education was distinctly humanistic and in harmony with the natural world, including all forms of life.

December 2nd, 1974

Sid returned to Florida, and after spending Thanksgiving in Gainesville with family and friends he drove to nearby Crescent Beach to spend the weekend at the beach house our family had owned since the late sixties. Sid planned to return Sunday night and on Monday morning resume his usual routine of teaching, counseling, handball, guitar lessons, correspondence, reading, writing, and working on his disclosure grid concept.

But instead, on Monday morning, December 2nd, Sid died.

I was there, and here's how it happened. After a year away at college I had moved back to Gainesville and was living at home and working as a musician in a rock band performing in venues around the southeast. After a Saturday performance at a local club on Thanksgiving weekend, the band had agreed to meet at noon Monday to pack up the gear.

Sunday I drove to the beach house for the day. Late that afternoon before returning to Gainesville, Sid noted that his car wouldn't start. As we walked toward the car so I could assist in push-starting it, he asked to borrow money to see a movie. I handed my father a twenty dollar bill and we joked about this reversal of roles. With Sid in the driver's seat I pushed the car from behind as he engaged the clutch, and the engine started. Sid waved goodbye and drove back to Gainesville. Later in the evening he borrowed Toni's car and drove to the Center Theatre, where he saw *The Odessa File*.

Early Monday morning around 7 a.m. Sid decided to jack up his car and fix the starter. From the kitchen he called up to Toni, who was still in bed, asking if she wanted breakfast, and she remembers sleepily answering no. Sid walked outside to the front of the house where the car was parked, removed the scissors-jack from the trunk and jacked up the car. The jack stands he normally used while working under the car remained in a shed in the side yard. Sid lay on his back, slid under the car and began using a socket wrench to tighten what was a loose nut on the starter wire connector. The tightening motion of the socket wrench moved the car sideways and caused it to fall off the jack onto Sid's head, killing him instantly.

Approximately one hour passed.

Around nine a.m. Toni woke up, walked downstairs to the kitchen where I had just finished making an omelet, called out Sid's name, got no response, walked out the front door, saw his legs protruding from under the low-slung body of the car and shouted for help. I ran outside and pulled up on the front bumper of the car. Having heard of superhuman feats of strength in times of need, I assumed I could lift the car off the ground. That was not the case. Pulling up on the bumper did lift the shock absorbers high enough, however, so that Toni could pull Sid's body from beneath the car.

Or did I pull Sid's body from beneath the car as Toni pulled up on the bumper? I will never know.

Sid's eyes were tightly closed and his face frozen in a grimace of what must have been a sudden realization. The left temple of the eyeglasses was broken at the hinge but still in place. It looked like a straight shot. I knew he was dead and probably had been for a while. I ran to our wall-mounted kitchen phone, dialed 0 and told the operator to send an ambulance to our address, describing the situation. I ran back to the car where Toni had returned with a blanket to cover Sid, as she believed he was alive but seriously injured and in shock. I completely covered Sid with the colorful blanket he had brought back from Peru, but she said don't cover his face, he won't be able to breathe.

I then put my arm around my mother and we both walked back and forth in the front yard waiting for the ambulance to arrive. We eventually heard the rising sound of a siren and watched as the ambulance came into view and then sped past our house. The driver soon realized his mistake and the vehicle returned, pulling into our driveway. I brought Toni inside the house as the two medical technicians approached Sid.

A few minutes later one of them entered the living room holding a blood pressure monitor and he began attaching the cuff to Toni's upper right arm while she sat on the sofa. When Toni asked "How is he?" the medic replied "I'm afraid there's not much we can do for him."

Toni phoned Ted Landsman, who soon arrived and began to telephone others. A police detective showed up and asked me questions regarding what time we had discovered Sid, then left.

I must have been in shock because my main thought was wondering if I looked sad enough considering what had happened. I felt as if I was observing myself from a distance. Every moment felt dramatic. A hearse arrived and took Sid away. At one point during the morning I walked outside where I watched Ted Landsman rinse off an area of the driveway with a garden hose.

As the day progressed friends surrounded my mother while she sat on the sofa, their hands touching and holding her. No one paid much attention to me until a graduate student of Sid's who had just arrived suggested we go for a walk down the road, where I told him what had happened; what I'd seen; what I had done.

Sid's morning lecture class had assembled as usual and a faculty member notified the class of his passing. Sid also had a noon lunch appointment with his PSY 640 graduate students at a restaurant. Entries in his pocket calendar for following months include attending a lecture by Swami Muktananda in January (location not noted), an unspecified event in Baltimore, a presentation in February at the New Life Center in Milwaukee; a talk on Human Sexuality at a college in Mesquite, Texas, and in April, the notation London (?).

The following morning the college newspaper ran the following article at the top of the front page:

Jourard dies in freak accident
By Mindy Kiernan
Alligator Staff Writer

Nationally recognized UF psychology Prof. Sidney M. Jourard was killed Monday while trying to repair his Triumph sportscar.

The 48-year-old Jourard was working under the car when the jack slipped and the frame crushed his skull, according to Sgt. Kenny Mack of the Alachua County Sheriff's Department.

Mack said Jourard's 20-year-old son Martin discovered the body shortly after 9 a.m.

Jourard gained prominence for his books "The Transparent Self," "Healthy Personality" and "Disclosing Man to Himself."

He also has served as a consultant for various organizations including the Florida State Board of Health, the U.S. National Office of Vital Statistics, the Peace Corps and the National League for Nursing.

Jourard started teaching at UF in 1958. Prior to that time he taught at the University of Alabama Medical School, Emory University in Atlanta and the University of Buffalo.

Jourard has traveled throughout the country speaking to various groups on topics relating to mental health. Last week he spoke to the American Humanistic Psychology Association Conference in California.

UF Psychology Prof. Henry Pennypacker called Jourard "a rare sort of colleague. He actually lived an academic life of true inquiry. He followed his sense of curiosity wherever it led him.

"He was extremely close to a great number of students because he was so sensitive and concerned about their problems," Pennypacker said. "He was simply the sort of person who one looks to as a friend."

Jourard received his bachelors and masters degrees from the University of Toronto. He earned his doctorate at the University of Buffalo.

Jourard was born in Canada and did not become a United States citizen until 1951.

He is survived by his wife Antoinette and their sons Jeffrey, 23, Martin, 20, and Leonard, 18.

Funeral services have been scheduled for 10:30 a.m. Wednesday at the Williams Thomas Funeral Home Chapel.

The family requests that in place of flowers, a donation be made to the Humanistic Psychology Fund in care of Dr. W.B. Webb, Department of Psychology at UF.

According to the funeral director the attendance was one of the largest in the history of the facility. Four of Sid's siblings—Harry, Sam, Sadie and Claire—flew in from Canada and California to attend. Sid's mother Annie was in ill health at the time and her family in Toronto faced the dilemma of whether to tell her of Sid's death or conceal it. In the words of Sid's sister Sadie:

> She was in hospital and was not expected to survive the heart attack. Rightly or wrongly, Sid's death was concealed from her.
>
> She survived a second heart attack and awoke from a coma on New Year's Day, 1975, demanding to know what was going on and who was responsible for her being there. She may have suspected something was wrong about Sidney's prolonged silence (he wrote her constantly) and not believed the story that he was "lecturing abroad," but she died after a third heart attack on April 16, 1975, without being told the truth and with her two daughters holding her hands.[13]

Sid, non-religious, was buried according to Jewish law, in his natural physical state and in a wooden casket, ensuring that the body gradually united with the soil. He is interred in the B'Nai Israel cemetery east of downtown Gainesville.

A few weeks after Sid's passing a student's letter appeared in the Florida Alligator college newspaper:

He was a teacher… and a man

EDITOR: Today I've learned something—not by cramming or coercion, either. For the first time I've lost a friend… for good. Yesterday death was a vague, inevitable concept, not yet a part of my life. Now, I too feel the loss death brings.

I took Sidney Jourard's Personality Development course during my lonely confusing freshman year. And I grew as a person —not a more skillful regurgitator.

I began to see, to know myself. That course opened my eyes to so many things, lessons you can't learn from books alone.

I learned of choices, new ways of being myself, freedom to be happy… just to be. They're lessons I'll never forget, and I have Professor Jourard to thank for planting the seeds of growth in me.

He was a teacher — and he was a man—emitting a constant positive energy, a joy for living life to its fullest.

Funny, I always wanted to tell him all this, but I was afraid — his greatness intimidated me… (you know, the old "authority figure syndrome.")

…Guess I've grown again today…

And it hurts —- I'll miss him

He helped me to see I DO make a difference!

Joni Kosakoski
4NR

Sid left behind no life insurance, most likely in the belief that income from his book royalties would be a perennial source of financial security for Toni. Sid's will, a hand-written one-page document found in his file cabinet in a folder labeled My Will, had only one witness signature and was invalid. Attached to the will with a paper clip was a signed and undated blank check.

The Triumph TR3 was given to a family friend, Henry Moore, who collected sports cars and had always expressed tremendous gratitude for the counseling he had received from Sid in prior years. Henry started the car, waved goodbye and drove away. Sid had fixed the starter.

Six months passed before the placing of the gravestone, designed by Toni and a sculptor friend who both traveled to a granite quarry in Georgia where it was crafted from a large block of unpolished granite.

Grave marker, B'Nai Israel Cemetery, Gainesville, Florida

Aftermath

Everyone eventually dies. The only variables are when, where, and how. Sid's friends, family and colleagues took it for granted that he would be around for a long time. Physically Sid was in excellent health. He had overcome a longtime addiction to tobacco and gained some pounds but swam vigorously and played handball; he still drank wine and enjoyed the occasional scotch on the rocks. Sid had new projects, his relationship with Toni had mellowed, and my two brothers and I were doing well, three children who were raised in an atypical, somewhat chaotic but loving home environment. Sid and Toni's eventual move to the West Coast seemed inevitable or probable—he had mentioned living in California as early as 1958 in a letter to Abraham Maslow. With his academic reputation Sid would likely have found a position at a leading university. He was the author of a vast body of writing and self-disclosure research, had arguably invented the term "self-disclosure" and was a pioneer in the study of its variety and effects in culture and mental health.

He also had developed a wide circle of friends from varied social strata. Many of Sid's friends considered him their best friend. It was Sid's singular blend of humor, intellect and spirit that helped define him. But, to use the vernacular of the times, Sid had fucked up. Although his death was recorded as accidental, a more accurate description is death by misadventure—the outcome of a risk taken voluntarily. The cause of death was blunt trauma to the head; the brief sequence that led up to it was misadventure. Considering the various ways people die, from lengthy illness to suicide to murder, Sid's manner of passing did have its positive aspects. But all manners of death lead to the same result for the living: loss.

The trauma of losing a parent is a singular experience; losing a beloved parent through their own misadventure brings an additional layer of anxiety and confused emotions. In the weeks that followed, my mother and I began to feel it was an inevitable occurrence; we looked for and seemingly found certain events that appeared to be prescient of his demise. I can't now recall what they were but at the time we saw them everywhere.

As strange as it seems, neither of us sought counseling for the traumatic experience we had just been through. Sid was a therapist and now he was gone; in our minds how could anyone possibly compare with him? What could a therapist say to us that would be of value? These were a few of our illogical rationalizations. There was an odd arrogance in this refusal, of how anyone could help us now that he had died, a protective armor of sorts.

I didn't cry when Sid died. But as often happens, repressed pain surfaced eventually and indirectly. Twenty years after his death I began experiencing disabling anxiety attacks whenever I could not immediately locate my infant daughter as she wandered about the house. My wife, an attentive mother, had no such concerns. I began to receive counseling, seeking the cause of this anxiety. The therapist's approach was based on Albert Ellis's Rational-Emotive Behavior therapy, and it worked by applying rational thought processes to negative emotional states. And because the therapist had overcome her own life crises and was an authentic voice of reason and experience she helped me confront and then express my pain as well as a deeply suppressed and guilt-provoking anger toward my father for the cause of his death. At her suggestion I visited his grave and read aloud a letter to him I had written to express these and other emotions. I began to heal.

Legacy   14

MEMORIES OF SIDNEY's personality and presence continue to resonate with those who knew him, and through his writings his place in the history of psychology has been assured. The image of a pebble dropped into a still body of water causing ripples to expand outward is an apt metaphor for how certain aspects of Sid's thought and writings have made their way into areas of mainstream American culture.

In the final chapter of *Encountering America,* a cultural history of the humanistic psychology movement, Jessica Grogan outlines the decline of humanistic psychology's presence by the nineteen-eighties, coinciding with an "increased demand for short-term interventions, new interest in cognitive-behavioral therapies focused on isolated mental problems, and a preponderance of diagnosis-based treatments reimbursable by insurance companies."[1] Despite that trend, Grogan writes:

> This lack of recognition, though, is a poor measure of the movement's impact. The greatest testaments to humanistic psychology's enduring significance are the numerous ways in which American mental health professionals have adopted the leading concepts of prominent humanistic psychologists; the way that later movements in mainstream psychology have subtly replicated its values and reproduced its goals and the way that the American vernacular, and American ideas of self, have incorporated its language and ideas. If anything, it's the utter pervasiveness of the humanistic perspective that has made evidence of its influence so elusive.[2]

Sid's writings continue to be cited, anthologized and reprinted. His 1962 paper "Some Lethal Aspects of the Male Role" was included in 1974's *Men and Masculinity*.[3] The back cover states "'Seek achievement and suppress emotion,' the masculine role tells men. *Men and Masculinity* describes how this role is learned, how it limits men, and how men today are freeing themselves from it." This social awareness of maleness was possibly a reaction to the feminist movement; the book is divided into sections labeled Growing Up Male (with Sid's contribution), Men and Women, Men and Children, Men and Men, Men and Work, Men and Society and Men's Liberation.

The Transparent Self appeared in a work of fiction. Robert Rimmer, author of the 1966 best-seller novel *The Harrad Experiment*, was a critic of monogamy as a societal norm. Rimmer continued writing books promoting bigamy, including 1975's *The Premar Experiments* with the premise of students of the opposite sex paired off in dormitory rooms. The book begins with an epigraph from *The Transparent Self*:

> There is no university that I know of where experiments are being
> conducted in alternatives to monogamous suburbs-living family life; where
> Utopias are subjected to study and testing by people who live in them and
> people who study them. There is no department of any university that
> I know of where new ways to be a man and woman, parent and spouse,
> doctor, lawyer, governor, or even thief are being explored and evaluated.
> There is no university with a cadre of exemplary "compleat" men and
> women who can serve as models for emulation, as pioneers along new
> dimensions of human existence.[4]

The following book excerpt is from an exchange between students Samantha Brown, a statuesque black woman, and Julian Howe, a white Jewish male, paired by the school as roommates. They are in bed together as the scene unfolds. The year is 1974.

> I grabbed his copy of Sidney Jourard's book *The Transparent Self*. "Here,
> we'll take turns reading it aloud to each other. Bren said the only way we're
> going to really understand this stuff is to keep talking it over—even while
> we're making love." We read for about an hour, and while I kept Julie from
> touching my breasts and belly, and getting both of us too excited, I found
> out he really understood the book pretty good.
>
> "Jourard says we don't dare to honestly reveal the kinds of person we

really are to each other. We beat around the bush." He laughed. "So I might as well start with being honest with you. If we don't make love tonight, I'll have to jerk off. My balls are aching from the hard-on I've had from most of the last two weeks."[5]

Sid, whose taste in literature was broad, would likely have found the epigraph professionally satisfying and the couples scene an amusing combination of social commentary and pulp fiction.

Published the following year, *The Hazards of Being Male: Surviving the Myth of Masculine Privilege*[6] included this quote from *The Transparent Self*:

> When a man's self is hidden from everybody else…it seems also to become much hidden even from himself, and it permits disease and death to gnaw into his substance without his clear knowledge. Men who are unknown and/or inadequately loved fall ill, or even die, as if suddenly and without warning…If one had direct access to the person's real self, one would have had many earlier signals that the present way of life was generating illness.[7]

In 1976 *Humanism and Behaviorism: Dialogue and Growth* was published, excerpts of which are in Chapter 11, a compendium built around the symposium in Cornell that featured Sid's dialogue and interaction with behaviorist Joseph Wolpe. *Humanistic Psychology: New Frontiers,* published in 1977 gathers contributions from authors on major issues in the field, and in the Preface editor Dorothy D. Nevill states "Many of the articles in this book came from a conference held January, 1976, in memorial to Sidney M. Jourard. His work and his influence run like a golden thread throughout the entire book, binding it together." The book includes a tribute by his colleague Ted Landsman who writes:

> This book is in tribute to a man of our times who could not wait for time to change the channels of his profession but who took its future into his own hands and helped make a science of white rats into a science of tender, loving, angry, ecstatic, joyful, tearful, saddened and frightened, in other words, human, entirely human beings.
>
> Sidney Jourard was a joyous, irrepressible, mischievous, mystic of a man who was a powerful mover of hearts and of thoughts, of ideas and of truths. The body image first excited him, then the idea of a self that was open, that did not seek to hide itself from its friend, its lover, its partner, the transparent self. Then authenticity became his spoken and written

vigorous ambition to therapist and client. It became a watchword of the third force in psychology—a relentless guerrilla-type intellectual and sentimental movement that reached beyond behaviorism, that loved and left psychoanalysis, and that sang paeans to a new trinity, existentialism, phenomenology, and humanism, all of which were enriched by this surprisingly, severely self-disciplined but always forceful and forever free spirit.[8]

1978's *Humanistic Psychology: A Sourcebook*[9] included Sid's "Changing Personal Worlds: A Humanistic Approach to Psychotherapy" and "Psychology: Control or Liberation?," both from 1972, and 1974's "Marriage is For Life" along with articles by Abraham Maslow, Carl Rogers, James Bugental, Viktor Frankl, and James B. Klee, who was a colleague of Abraham Maslow in the psychology department at Brandeis from the early fifties into the early sixties. The book is dedicated to "Arthur W. Combs, Sidney Jourard, Earl C. Kelley, Abraham H. Maslow, Carl R. Rogers—Pioneers of modern humanistic psychology."

The following year, in *The Therapeutic Touch: How to Use Your Hands to Help or Heal* Dolores Kreiger writes:

> As Jourard has pointed out, when a person touches another, he or she is in fact saying, "I want to share, I want to help," and when the other allows his space to be penetrated and permits touch to occur, he is replying, "I want to share, I want to be helped."[10]

Healthy Personality Redux

In 1980 Macmillan released a fourth edition of *Healthy Personality* with new content and editing from Ted Landsman, who is listed as co-author. Included in the editing process was elimination of the consistent usage by Sidney in his writing of the word "man" when referring to all humans, an unanticipated semantic problem built from the word *mankind* and a distraction for contemporary readers. In his Preface Ted Landsman notes that the copy editor "...put a sharp pencil to many of my professional obscurities and saw to what Dr. Jourard would certainly wish for—that all sexist language was removed. Where sexist pronouns could not be avoided, we have alternated between masculine and feminine forms."[11]

The Essential Psychotherapies: Theory and Practice by the Masters, published as a mass-market paperback in 1982, is a compendium of writings by therapists illuminating their varied approaches. Described on the book cover as containing key essays by the most influential psychotherapists from Freud until today, Sidney is among the "twelve other seminal figures," and is represented through "The Psychotherapist as Exemplar" from *The Transparent Self*. The editors write:

> Sidney Jourard, a clinical psychologist, was a spokesman for the humanistic orientation in therapy. Like many in the humanistic movement, Jourard's outlook was shaped by the writings of philosophers like Martin Buber, theologians like Paul Tillich, as well as the existentialists. His most direct lineage as a therapist, though, descends through Eric Fromm and Carl Rogers.
>
> Jourard was an active advocate of openness and self-disclosure as healing in and of themselves. He saw the distance and aloofness of the therapist's role as it has been traditionally fulfilled as an impediment to authenticity. To help the patient be comfortable with his private feelings and thoughts, the therapist must unveil his own.[12]

The idea of a therapist presenting oneself as an exemplar and a model of how to live in healthy ways was a theme Sid explored in an essay for the journal *Voices*, "The Therapist as Guru," using a term popularized in the late '60s through the increasing presence in America of such spiritual "gurus" as Maharishi Mahesh Yogi, Rajneesh (Osho), Guru Maharah Ji and others. Sid saw himself as a guru, or teacher, offering the wisdom of one who has experienced growth in one form or another and who draws parallels between his growth and the potential of growth in the patient.

But it was Sid's research and insights regarding self-disclosure that continued to resonate with social scientists. In *The Human Face of Psychology: Humanistic Psychology in its Historical Social and Cultural Context*, author Helen Graham quotes Sid's comment in *The Transparent Self* regarding the seeming passivity of genuine empathy in contrast to practicing specific technique:

> Indeed it can be discerned among beginning therapists that there is often a considerable dread of such passivity because it constitutes a threat to masculine identity. Beginning therapists seem to be most fascinated by "manly" active techniques such as hypnosis, reflection, interpretation etc.—the kinds which will be difficult for them to master but which will make them feel that they are *doing something* to the patient which will get him well. These techniques, however, leave the self of the therapist hidden behind the mask of his professional role and have limited effectiveness.[13]

In the mid-eighties several of Sid's studies on body-awareness were cited in Ashley Montagu's *Touching: The Human Significance of Skin*,[14] an examination of the importance of tactile interaction.[15]

In 1994 *Sidney M. Jourard: Selected Writings* was self-published by his family. Edited by Antoinette Jourard, graduate student Michael Lowman and myself, the book presented twenty-five papers, articles, essays, and chapters from Sid's books and material previously published solely in academic journals. In the appendices are the bibliographies of *Disclosing Man to Himself* and *The Transparent Self* as well as a complete personal bibliography. Also included is a list of the Jourard Collection of Sid's personal papers, donated by Toni Jourard to the archives of the University of West Georgia in Carrollton, Georgia. The Jourard papers include correspondence, drafts of his various publications, six hundred books from Sid's personal and professional library, a collection of published papers by Sid and others, and audio of selected lectures from 1965-1974. Of particular significance is his correspondence with Abraham Maslow, O. Hobart Mowrer, David Riesman, Carl Rogers, Thomas Szasz, and other prominent figures in the social sciences.

At the end of the nineties two faculty members of the Department of Psychology at the University of West Georgia secured a publisher for *Invitations to Dialogue: The Legacy of Sidney Jourard*.[16] They write:

> In 1993, as the 20th anniversary of Sid's death approached, California State Senator John Vasconcellos (13th district) mentioned to others that he thought it would be fitting and timely to honor Sidney Jourard's legacy. This book is the result of a long process of exploring ways in which we could contribute to this effort.[17]

One contributor to the book is Thomas Moore, author of the best-selling *Care of the Soul*. In describing his fellowship during the seventies at Syracuse University in the religion department Moore recalls

> At this time Sidney Jourard's writings were important to me both academically and personally. I couldn't separate my search for a life work in psychology and religion from my personal longing to find my place in the world and to arrive at some resolution of my early quest for religious and spiritual understanding. Jourard's wisdom and clarity sustained me as I tried to keep my sights on my own issues of authenticity. In his writings, too, I found a steady and grounded therapeutic attitude in contrast to the rhapsodic style of Maslow.[18]

Counting Touches in Cafés

One of Sid's most-cited studies of human behavior is his observation of how many times in an hour couples touched each other in a public environment—in this case at cafés and restaurants. Included as "An Exploratory Study of Body-Contact" in *Disclosing Man To Himself,* Sid comments

> that we know little about the conditions under which a person will permit another to touch him, the meanings people attach to touching and being touched, the loci of acceptable touch, and little of the consequences of body-contact. It is as if the touch-taboo most of us learned in childhood has produced a scotoma of our professional vision, making us describe man in our textbooks as if he did not come closer to his fellows than a foot or so. Illustration of such differences is provided by some observations during pilot stages of the present investigation.[19]

This informal set of observations has been mentioned in such publications as *Reader's Digest* (excerpted from Life magazine), *Psychology Today,* several online sites, the textbook *Psychology* by Carole Wade & Carol Tavris, and *Touch: The Science of Hand, Heart, and Mind* by David J. Linden (2015). In a critique of methodology and significance, "Touch Revisited: Observations and Methodological Recommendations," the authors note: "The 'coffee shop' study has been cited at least 444 times, according to Google Scholar."[20]

I was listening to the radio one day in Seattle in 1994, twenty years after Sid's passing, when I heard the following commercial:

> Here's something I bet you've been waiting to hear. Did you know that if you're an American talking to a friend in a coffee shop, you'll touch each other twice in an hour? Wait, there's more. If you're Parisians in a cafe on the Champs Élysées you'll touch 110 times in an hour, and if you're Brits in a pub in London well, you won't touch at all. So, where does that lead us? Why, to Jeep Wranglers, of course! Now no one knows for sure whether owning a Jeep Wrangler makes you more of a touchy-feely person or not, however, rumor has it that the Jeep Wrangler is *so* much fun, that people just naturally seem to touch a bit more. ...

This ad is one more reason I wish Sid was alive, if only to hear his reaction to this presentation of his research.

During the writing of this book, the APA announced *2018 Guidelines for Psychological Practice with Men and Boys*. This controversial document describes aspects of the masculine role in our culture that preclude self-disclosure and encourage competition among men, with the potential for increased isolation, the sort of stoic "strong but silent" archetype described by Sidney in his correspondence with writer Will Sparks. Sid had addressed the subject fifty-four years previously in his 1964 essay "Some Lethal Aspects of the Male Role."

Overseas

Requests for information on Sid's self-disclosure research increased in the 21st century. Surprisingly or perhaps not, the majority of these requests originate in countries such as the Phillippines, India, Pakistan and Malaysia. These requests were directed to a website[21] dedicated to his work that includes online access to various academic papers, self-disclosure questionnaires and a link to download the now out-of-print *The Transparent Self.* Requests sent through the site continue to affirm a resurgent level of interest in his research in self-disclosure, the example below reflective of other requests by undergraduate students in these universities for permission to use his research methodologies.

9/10/2018

...I am Ade Putri Andayani as a psychology student of Surabaya University, East Jave, Indonesia. I want to ask for permission regarding the use of measuring instruments *Shortened Version of the Jourard Self-Disclosure Inventory* (SD-25) which I will use to fulfill my final assignment. I am currently making related research about the relationship between self-disclosure and intimacy in emerging adulthood who are dating.

I will translate these items into Indonesian to make it easier for my respondent to answer and I will make some changes to certain items to suit the people in Indonesia, if you let me ... .

Best regard,
Ade Putri Andayani

Progenitor

In his book *Self-Disclosure in Psychotherapy* Barry Farber traces the early history of self-disclosure as a therapeutic tool on the part of both patient and therapist. An epigraph by Sid begins Chapter 1, The Nature of Self-Disclosure: "No man can come to know himself except as an outcome of disclosing himself to another person."[22] Farber writes:

> Sidney Jourard, the progenitor of contemporary research in this topic, defined self-disclosure as permitting one's true self to be known to others. This is a seemingly elegant and straightforward definition, involving some degree of intentionality, but it sidesteps the intriguing question of how to define the "true self."
>
> Writing before the dawn of postmodernism or of discussions of the nature of multiple selves, Jourard did not engage in philosophical discourses of this sort. What he did suggest was that individuals need to find the courage to share deeply held thoughts and feelings with others. Implicitly, Jourard reminds us that disclosures can range from the mundane to the profound and that consistent but superficial disclosures still leave us strangers to others. He also believed that each of us is constantly confronted with an existential challenge: "Shall we permit our fellow persons to know us as we are, or shall we seek instead to remain an enigma, an uncertain quality, wishing to be seen as something we are not?" Here, of course, Jourard observes that silence is also a choice, a decision with its own implications, including the possibility that we would not just be "unknown" but "misknown," prey perhaps to others' assumptions or projections.
>
> Furthermore, Jourard conceived of self-disclosure as a circular and interactive phenomenon, moving continuously between the self and another. It is only in this manner, thought Jourard, that one could honor the maxim of "know thyself," for in revealing oneself to another one necessarily learns about oneself. In disclosing, we often become aware of thoughts, feelings and behaviors we did not know we had.[23]

Pioneering seems an accurate descriptor of Sid's work, as Farber notes:

> The contemporary study of self-disclosure can essentially be traced to the work that Jourard began over 40 years ago. As part of his own existential quest, specifically his interest in finding out what it means to be a "real self," Jourard began studying lapses in understanding between people, a

phenomenon he believed was at the root of problems in the family and in the greater society. His interest was spurred by the ideas of Fromm, Horney, and Riesman, all of whom, though employing different vocabularies, wrote about the deep sense of alienation they had observed in people and the tendency of most individuals to hide from or misrepresent themselves to others.[24]

Humanistic psychologists would approach this investigation through fine-tuning their theories through testing what "seemed" true against data generated from investigations, both subjective and experimental.

Both Abraham Maslow and Sidney Jourard had written explicitly about the dialogic process by which they hoped to arrive at a functional definition of the concept of health. In Jourard's 1958 book *Personal Adjustment: An Approach Through the Study of Healthy Personalty,* he recognized the subjective territory into which he needed to travel in order to quantify health. He also argued, however, that such subjectivity was actually at the root, historically, of mainstream psychological methods. The steps humanistic psychologists would take to define the values of health, he contended, mirrored the process mainstream psychologists had used to arrive at ostensibly objective scientific categories and operational definitions of illness.[25]

More examples of the continued presence of Sid's research in self-disclosure, the social boundaries of touching, and inspiritedness can be located and cited, but the preceding chronological examples are representative.

A Colleague's View

Sid had many friends in fields of academia in the social and biological sciences, and numerous remembrances of him were published, several expressing not only their warmth toward him as a person but also anger at Sid's utterly preventable risk-taking that led to his demise. One reminiscence appropriate for inclusion is that of the late psychologist and neurobiologist Robert L. Isaacson, an associate of Sid's in the Psychology Department of the University of Florida.

Isaacson, author of *The Limbic System,* performed research on the brain activities of small mammals, and was a President of the International Behavioral Neuroscience Society. After his years at the the University of Florida from 1968 to 1977 he moved to SUNY Binghamton in New York where he remained as a Distinguished Professor until his passing in 2015.

Despite disparate backgrounds and research interests, the two psychologists formed a strong connection. In an undated manuscript Isaacson speaks of this relationship:[26]

> Over the past several years Sid and I became very close friends, but my relationship with him was different from that of any other person because it originated in professional exchanges and slowly merged into the personal realm. For the first year or two that I was at Florida we hardly knew each other but when we began to talk we realized that in each other we had found someone to talk to—about the larger ideas of life, science and behavior. We learned from each other and despite different backgrounds, life styles, and specific research interests, our long range goals were identical. Over time we became as close friends as two men can be.
>
> We found that we could talk to each other at anytime, at any place, about almost any topic, because through quite independent pathways in life we had reached a point where we shared "ultimate goals." Furthermore, we shared a belief in how knowledge about them could be obtained, namely, by the use of the <u>experimental</u> approach to the study of behavior.
>
> Many people couldn't understand why Sid and I were so close. They felt that he and I should have been "enemies." Sidney, the great humanist, I the laboratory worker. These people seemed to think that Sid was, or should have been, against the experimental study of the brain or mechanisms of behavior. Nonsense, Sid was first and foremost an experimental psychologist. He wanted to test his ideas. He had very little patience with colleagues' ideas that were incapable of test. I remember his "blue penciling" a manuscript of a psychologist who was speculating about mental states using an introspective approach. When he started, the paper was about forty pages long. When he finished, three blue pencils later, there was less than a page that had not been deleted.
>
> Sid viewed his interactions with clients and with people he met everywhere as his laboratory. From these interactions he gained new ideas which could be refined and expanded but then put to the acid test of experimental study. At the time of his death he was just beginning a large experimental study of the effects of how much subjects and experimenters know about each other on the performance of the subjects in rather "straightforward" paper and pencil tests. He thought he knew what would happen but had to demonstrate these expectations directly. Further, he was

prepared to admit that his expectations could be wrong. The data would tell him. Some of his happiest hours were spent in analyzing data, running the electronic calculator himself, and watching patterns emerge from the data.

Living as he did, in a world of ideas <u>and</u> data, Sid saw himself as a <u>professional</u> experimental psychologist. I was pleased and flattered that Sid believed that I, too, was one.

Several times over the past several years Sid and I amazed some of our students and colleagues by becoming totally involved in professional discussions in the department's large seminar room. These discussions lasted for hours, at times, and we completely covered the long blackboard with ideas and plans for experiments. These open discussions between faculty were, and are, unknown in our department. They were lively and heated. We paced incessantly and often interrupted each other. We couldn't wait to tell the other a new idea or plan.

In discussing these sessions, afterwards, Sid felt that one of their great values was to show our students and junior faculty that professional discourse is possible between professionals with different training. Indeed, it was fun. It is the way it should be but the way it too seldom is. It was his belief that it was during these exchanges we were most effective as academic models. It was also during these exchanges that Sid acted most effectively as a rabbi: who is a teacher and also a judge of ideas.

These spontaneous discussions led us to continuing them in private. Several times we went to my apartment or to a sauna or to the beach to pursue the ideas in depth.

There is no doubt that Sid was a scholar. He was far more widely read than most of us. He read incessantly and on all topics relating to Man as he lives in his various conditions in the world. This reading, of course, was supplemented by travel and by talking to people everywhere. The point is that Sid had a basic love of knowledge <u>for its own sake.</u> He was most stimulated by ideas which had importance and scope. These ideas did not have to be directly related to his own research or his own life. They had to be exciting, wide ranging, and new. Such ideas brought him to full being, full enjoyment, full activation of all his abilities.

During these bouts of stimulation by ideas, I saw Sid expressing the traditional Jewish value of knowledge for itself. Although he was far from being orthodox in Judaism, or anything else, the traditional values of his Jewish heritage were embedded in him. These values found expression in different and novel ways but this heritage influenced his actions, nevertheless.

Sid's preferred world was one of ideas. He was most at home there, despite the fact that he loved competition and physical expression of his energies. He was a reasonably alert traveler, although the insights obtained from his trips were <u>not</u> exceptional. He was a <u>good</u> handball player but not top-flight. He was a reasonable sailor although he once hit a sea buoy head on. Give him an idea, however, and he was the best. He was unexcelled. He put all of himself into the pursuit and examination of the idea and all of its implications. His huge energy was directed toward ideas when playing handball, traveling, or sailing.

His devotion to ideas led him to perseverate. One day after he told me one of his ideas for the one hundredth time, he said, "God I <u>do</u> perseverate. I even bore myself." Those of us around him did not mind this perseveration, however, because the ideas were good ones. They were novel. They never had been thought before. They were unique. They were expressed with skill and brilliance. One thing that Sid prized very highly was the ability to express ideas clearly—in good English. He was intolerant of those who could not write clearly and doubly so for those who would not take the time to do so when they had the ability. Writing to him was important, and as it is for all good writers, writing was work for him. Sid wrote and re-wrote. He struggled and sweated. Clarity and succinctness were his goals and he welcomed help and criticism that improved his work. . . .

Research and study are also work. Much of Sid's time was spent in studying the research and ideas of others. He not only studied the work of others, but organized them. He kept their reports and article filed in a meticulous fashion so that he could retrieve what he wanted when he wanted.

His writing, teaching, and research took energy. He was fortunate in that this was a quality he had in abundance. He had the energy for all of his professional activities in addition to his diversions: sport, travel, and people. Yet, his major commitment was to ideas. He was into ideas when traveling or playing handball or sailing. The message, however, is that for the professional sheer energy and interest in not enough. Energy has to be bridled, controlled, and directed in order to make contributions to mankind. He knew and accepted the fact that to be a professional required hard work. To be really good required hard, incessant work. Sid would settle for nothing less than being the best.

Sid's closest friend was Thomas Hanna. As stated earlier, after serving as the Chair of the Philosophy Department at the University of Florida, in 1973, Hanna moved to San Francisco and became the Director of the Graduate School at the Humanistic Psychology Institute. In a previously cited reminiscence requested by Sid's eldest son Jeff, Hanna provides additional insights into Sid's persona:

> Another thing that was obvious about Sidney is that he didn't study to become a psychologist, he went to school essentially to allow himself professionally and legally to do what he was already doing. He was a very rare bird; namely, a natural, an intuitive psychologist who could not help being what he was. And it stemmed out of the same kind of enthusiasm for life. Because for God's sake you gotta live just one time and there's only one life you're gonna live so why not be enthusiastic about it rather than to regret it. And that's reasonable enough to say but very few people live as if that's the case. They live most of the time with regret, and with grudge, as if they were pushed into a situation they didn't want to be in: namely, living. And many people, in my observation are happy to get it over with—they don't rush it, because it's not polite to commit suicide, but they stay their term and then with a certain amount of ill grace, check out. That wasn't · Sidney's game.
>
> He had a different feeling about things and he was very healthy in that regard, and I think being very healthy and very enthusiastic and boyish are all tied up in the same bundle, and as part of that enthusiasm Sidney was fascinated with other human beings. To him, human beings were a barrel of monkeys. It was just fascinating. I mean normally you pick a subject as a psychologist and you study it, it has an interesting point of view and you study the variables and this and that and the other and you think it out with your left hemisphere; Sidney didn't get involved with that sort of thing, even though he frequently claimed to be a "scientist." But he always had a sort of grin when he said "As a scientist I have discovered," but Sidney was just intuitively interested in human beings and studied them with an intensity and passion that was extraordinary. Because he saw what variety there was in human behavior. And how curious were peoples differences, and trying to figure out why they were so different was something that was like a puzzle, like each person was a kind of puzzle, and he observed them. And the observation of the eccentricities of other individuals is something that was a never-ending fascination with Sidney.[27]

Today

Several indicators underscore the viability of Sid's research in contemporary culture. Postings on social media platforms are often ubiquitously and compulsively self-disclosing, or some would argue "imaginary ideal-self disclosing," as participants in Facebook post thoughts, opinions, physical complaints, and photos of where they've been, where they are and what they are about to eat. The need to connect with other people is as strong as ever, but social media postings can present a carefully-crafted surrogate of the real self that often borders on self-promotion.

The concept of "transparency" in human interaction, in politics and in business has become a marketable social concept, as the term is now viewed as an essentially positive trait. The university library where much of this book research took place displays posters with professors' descriptions of how their research is shared under the title "How I Work Open." In congruence with Sid's comment that psychological data and insights "should be given away" to those who provide the source of data, Justin Marlow, Professor at the Evans School of Public Policy and Governance at the University of Washington co-created what he describes as "the first open textbook in the field of Public Administration…done through the Rebus Community project, and the Pressbooks software. It's a set of tools that can take you from an idea to an open textbook." In answer to the question "Why do you teach openly?" he writes: "Students expect transparency; they see no reason to not have access to public information whenever they want it. It seems silly to then say 'Okay, you have to pay $400 for a textbook and we can't tell you why.' Having a textbook that squares with those values is powerful." In answering "What's your vision for an open future?" Marlow writes: "The term we're using around the Evans School is 'big transparency.' How do we think beyond transparency as compliance—doing it only because that's what the law demands? It requires rethinking large parts of what we do and how we do it."

Taking a concept such as "transparency" from Sid's research and thought and making connections to its varied applications in personal interaction up through politics and academic research is somewhat of a leap of faith, but the very popularity of the term "transparency" in today's cultural arena brings some validity to this connection.

More common is the lack of transparency, as one of the more reliable ways to make money is to psychologically manipulate consumers into purchasing goods and services, from beer and automobiles and branded clothing to "Premium,"

"Preferred" and "Platinum Level" memberships offered by businesses to generate a sense of privilege and prestige. One book that demonstrates this approach is *Covert Persuasion: Psychological Tactics and Tricks to Win the Game*. It is co-written by Kevin Hogan, a public speaker and corporate trainer with a doctorate in psychology, and James Speakman, whose company is "committed to sharing the power of persuasion with salespeople and others whose careers depend on their powers of persuasion." It would be difficult to find a more concise description of psychological manipulation than the one on the book jacket:

> When we make decisions we like to think we weigh the options carefully, look at all the possibilities, and make the best choice based on a rational examination of the facts. But in truth, much of our decision making happens on a subconscious level based on feelings we might not even be aware of. Understanding and managing those subconscious feelings is the key to the art of persuasion.
>
> By observing and predicting human behavior, we can learn to react and direct behavior in others with the right kind of words and body language. If you want to learn how to convince people to buy your product, contribute to your cause, or vote for your candidate, this book has the answers. *Covert Persuasion* synthesizes the latest research in psychology, linguistics, sales tactics, and human communication to reveal the most effective methods for consistently and effectively persuading anyone of virtually anything.
>
> *Covert Persuasion* sounds like a secret operation because it is; when you master these techniques and put them to use, no one will even notice your tactics. But that doesn't mean these techniques are sneaky or underhanded. They aren't! You aren't tricking anyone; you're simply using all your abilities to encourage them to make the choice you want them to make. It's not unfair or underhanded—it's just powerful, practical and effective.[28]

Covert Persuasion and its disingenuous rationalization of such techniques leads us to confront the so-called elephant in the room: deceit and covert persuasion are the very cornerstone of corporate marketing, consistently effective approaches when applied through advertising to gain market share. Social critic Vance Packard covered this ground in 1957 with his million-selling book *The Hidden Persuaders*. Any philosophy or value-system in conflict with such techniques will not be welcomed or supported through research grants. This could also help us understand why the basics of critical thinking are not a required course of study in our school systems.

Sid was an intellectual with a humanistic orientation and a set of humanist values that guided his thought and research throughout his life. A streak of idealism and classicism runs through Sid's values, grounded in the Greek philosophers and the so-called eternal verities—truth, beauty, justice, freedom. These values, and his ability to explore and promote them through a clear writing style has kept much of Sid's perspective on the human condition alive and viable. He was a champion for the common good of each person. I have no doubt that, for these reasons, his writings and thoughts will continue to be valued and rediscovered into the indefinite future, due to their inspiring and timeless relevance for persons seeking to better understand themselves and the human condition.

Notes

Author Notes

1. Meyers, C. Roger. (1974 September 1). *Interview of Sidney M. Jourard for Canadian Psychological Association Archive.* Unpublished transcript of audio interview. Copy in possession of author.

2. Jourard, S.M. (1971). *The Transparent Self.* (pp. 110-113). New York: Van Nostrand Reinhold.

Introduction

1. Welch, I. David (1982, November 10). Reminiscences: Abraham Maslow, Arthur W. Combs, Sidney M. Jourard. Shared as part of a panel discussion (also including Mike Arons, James B. Klee, and Fred Richards) in Horizon Seminar, 401-04/601-04: Maslow, Combs & Jourard (Anne C. Richards, Instructor), Psychology Department, West Georgia College, Carrollton, GA.

Chapter 1: Antecedents

1. The approximate month and day is based on the 6th candle of Chanukah and that date varies according to year.

2. Brown, Sadie. The Jourard Family History. Undated unpublished manuscript. Copy in possession of author.

3. ibid.

4. ibid.

Chapter 2: Differentiation

1. Brown, Sadie, (2006, August 26) email to author.

2. Brown, Sadie (1994, November 12). *Remembering Sidney.* Unpublished manuscript. Sidney Jourard Memorial, U.C. Sonoma, CA.

3. McGarvey, Pete. (1992, September 13). Proud to Call Him Friend. *Orillia Packet & Times.*

4. Jourard, Sidney. (1994). On Becoming a Therapist. In Lowman, Jourard & Jourard (Eds.) Sidney M. Jourard: Selected Writings. p.183. Marina Del Rey: Round Right Press.

5. ibid. p. 184.

6. ibid. p. 184.

7. Sam Jourard arrived in England July 9, 1943 as part of the 1st Canadian Tank Brigade.

Chapter 3: Adventurous Ways

1. Jourard, Sidney. (1975). Book Review. Contemporary Psychology, Vol 20, No. 1 p. 50-51.

2. Jourard, Sidney. (1994). On Becoming a Therapist. In Lowman, Jourard & Jourard (Eds.). *Sidney M. Jourard: Selected Writings.* p.187. Marina Del Rey: Round Right Press.

3. Jourard, Antoinette. (2003 September 26). My Life With Sid. Unpublished manuscript. Copy in possession of author.

4. Edgar Alexander Bott (1887-1974) was the first president of the Canadian Psychological Association and worked at the Institute of Child Study.

5. Jourard, Sidney. (1948) Sociometric Status and Its Relation to Attitudes, Values, Adjustment, and Degree of Acquaintance in a Group of University Residence Males. Unpublished master's thesis.   University of Buffalo, Buffalo, NY.

Chapter 4: Digging In

1. Jourard, Sidney. (1971). *The Transparent Self,* Revised Edition. New York: Van Nostrand. p. 10.

2. Carl Curt Pfieffer (1908–1988) was a physician and biochemist who researched schizophrenia and was involved with behavior experiments for the CIA between 1955 and 1964, administering LSD to inmates in the Atlanta penitentiary, exploring mind control. He was Chair of the Pharmacology Department at Emory University and considered himself a founder of what Linus Pauling named orthomolecular psychiatry

3. Jourard, Sidney M. (1968). *Disclosing Man To Himself.* New York: Van Nostrand. p. 94.

4. Jourard, Sidney. (1958, May). A Study of Self-Disclosure. *Scientific American,* p. 77-82.

5. Maslow, Abraham. (1970). *Motivation and Personality.* New York: Harper & Row. p. 288.

6. Watson, John B. (1930) *Behaviorism.* Chicago: University of Chicago Press.

7. Matson, Floyd (1966) *The Broken Image.* New York: Doubleday.

8. Maslow, Abraham. (1968). *Toward a Psychology of Being.* 2nd edition. New York: Van Nostrand p. 29.

9. ibid. p. 30-31.

10. Maslow, Abraham. (1970). *Motivation and Personality.* New York: Harper & Row.

11. Anderson, Richard J. (1980). *The Department of Psychology, University of Florida: A Fifty-Year History, 1930—1980.* Gainesville: University of Florida. p. 48.

Chapter 5: Potential For Growth

1. The Journal of Consulting Psychology (5), the Journal of Abnormal and Social Psychology (3), British Journal of Psychology, The Journal of Clinical Psychology.

2. Jourard, Sidney. (1958). *Personal Adjustment: An Approach Through the Study of Healthy Personality.* New York: MacMillan. pp. vii-viii.

3. ibid. p. 429.

4. Prepared for meeting of the Subcommittee on the Quantification of Wellness of the United States Department of Health and Human Services National Committee on Vital and Health Statistics, Washington, DC, November 18, 1958.

5. Matson, Floyd W. (1978). Humanistic Theory: The Third Revolution in Psychology. In Welch, Tate, Richards (Eds.), *Humanistic Psychology: A Source Book.* p. 25. Amherst: Prometheus Books .

6. Jourard, Sidney. (1964). *The Transparent Self.* Princeton: Van Nostrand. p. 69.

7. ibid p. 69

8. O. Hobart Mowrer (1907-1982), a past president of the APA (1954), was an American psychologist known for his research in behavior therapy and the founding of integrity groups.

9. Jourard, S.M. (1963). Some observations by a psychologist of the Peace Corps' "Outward Bound" training program at Camp Crozier, Puerto Rico. Washington, D.C.: Peace Corps

10. Phillip, Norman L. (1964) Review of Personal Adjustment, 2nd edition. *Contemporary Psychology*, 9, 488-489.

11. Jourard, S.M. (1964). How do people learn? *Canadian Nurse*, 60 (4), 347-350.

12. Fein, Ellen, & Schneider, Sherry. (1995). *The Rules: Time-tested Secrets for Capturing the Heart of Mr. Right*. New York: Grand Central Publishing.

Chapter 6: Europe

1. *The Divided Self* (1960), *The Self and Others* (1961) and 1964's *Sanity, Madness and the Family*, co-written with Aaron Esterson

2. Laing, Adrian. (2006). *R.D. Laing: A Life*. Phoenix Mill: Sutton Publishing. p. 92.

3. May, Rollo;, Angel, Ernest; Ellenberger, Henri. (Eds.). (1958). *Existence*. New York: Basic Books, p.48.

4. Kazantzakis, Nikos (1952). *Zorba the Greek*. p. 35. New York: Simon & Schuster.

5. Maslow, A.H. (1968). *Toward a Psychology of Being*, Second Edition. pp. 16-17. New York: Van Nostrand .

6. Jourard, S.M. (1967). Meeting of East and West. Contemporary Psychology, Vol.12, No.3, p. 171-2.

7. Laing, Adrian. (2006). *R.D. Laing: A Life*. Phoenix Mill: Sutton Publishing. p.62.

8. Jourard, Sidney M. (1968). *Disclosing Man To Himself*. pp. 167-169. New York: Van Nostrand.

9. Kazantzakis, Nikos. (1952). *Zorba the Greek*. p. 35. New York: Simon and Schuster.

10. John Heaton e-mail to author. 12-29-2016.

11. Jourard, S.M. (1966). An exploratory study of body-accessibility. *British Journal of Social and Clinical Psychology*, 5 (3), 221-231. This study was cited in several books and articles, including Montagu, Ashley. (1971). *Touching: The Human Significance of the Skin*. New York: Harper & Row.

Chapter 7: New Directions

1. Laing, R.D., & Cooper, David. (1971). *Reason and Violence: a Decade of Sartre's Philosophy 1950 -1960* New York: Pantheon Books.

2. Jourard, S.M. (1968) *Disclosing Man to Himself*. p. 116. New York: Van Nostrand.

3. ibid. p. 118.

4. Becker, Carol. S. (1992). *Living and Relating: An Introduction to Phenomenology*. p. 13. Newbury Park: Sage Publications.

5. Lowman, Michael; Jourard, Antoinette, & Jourard, Marty, (Eds). (1994). *Sidney M. Jourard: Selected Writings*. pp. 149-156. Marina Del Rey: Round Right Press.

6. See Ch. 8 footnote 5 in *Encountering America* by Jessica Grogan (2013).

7. (1965) AAHP (American Association of Humanistic Psychology) Newsletter November (2), 3.

8. Jourard, S. M.(1965). Human Uses of Behavioral Research. Big Sur Records, Esalen Institute, Esalen, CA.

9. Hanna, Thomas (1986 September). Thomas Hanna to Jeff Jourard Re: Sidney Jourard. Transcription of audio recording. Novato, California.

10. Jourard, S.M. (1966). An Odyssey Within. *Personal Growth*, 18 (6), 13-20.

11. Jourard, S.M. (1966). You Can Do Whatever You Wish Here. pp. 110-111. *Voices*: Spring.

12. Jourard, S.M. (1968) *Disclosing Man to Himself*. p. 5. New York: Van Nostrand.

13. ibid. p.5.

14. ibid.

15. Jourard, Sidney M.(1965). Human Uses of Behavioral Research. Big Sur Records, Esalen Institute, Esalen, CA.

16. Buber, Martin. (1987). *I and Thou*. New York: Collier Books

17. Jourard, S.M. (1968). *Disclosing Man to Himself*. pp. 103-104. New York: Van Nostrand.

18. Independent Florida Alligator (1968 February 19). p. 5.

Chapter 8: Demystify, Enlighten, Transcend

1. Eysenck, H.J. (1973). Reason With Compassion. *The Humanist Alternative: Some Definitions of* Humanism. Buffalo: Prometheus Books. pp. 89-92.

2. Maslow, Abraham H. (1970). *Motivation and Personality*, Second Edition. New York: Harper & Row, p. 288.

3. *Phoenix: Newsletter of the American Association for Humanistic Psychology*. December 1963. p.4.

4. Jourard, Sidney M. (1967) (Ed.) *TO BE OR NOT TO BE...Existential-Psychological Perspectives on the Self*. Gainesville: University of Florida Monographs Social Sciences No. 34.

5. McLaughlin, Frank. (1971 December) Conversation: Two Humanists. *Media & Methods*. p. 28.

6. AHP Newsletter January 1975. pp. 5-7.

7. Jourard, Sidney. (1973 August) audio interview by Ernest Kramer [Tape recording]. Montreal.

8. Jourard, Sidney. (1968). *Disclosing Man to Himself*. pp. 77-79. New York: Van Nostrand.

9. Bergantino, Len (2012). What Sid Jourard and Timothy Leary Were Like In Person. *AHP Perspective* June-July. pp. 10-11.

10. Jourard, S.M. (1976). Changing Personal Worlds: A Humanistic Perspective. In A. Wandersman, P.J. Poppen, & D.F. Ricks (Eds.). *Humanism and Behaviorism: Dialogue and Growth*. pp. 49. New York: Pergamon Press.

11. Jourard, Sidney (1968). Growing Awareness and the Awareness of Growth. In *Ways of Growth: Approaches to Expanding Awareness*. New York: The Viking Press.

12. Jourard, Sidney. (1969). Sex In Marriage. In *Readings in Humanistic Psychology*. New York: The Free Press.

13. Shneidman, Edwin S.(Ed.). (1969). *On The Nature of Suicide*. p.132. San Francisco: Jossey-Bass.

14. Jourard, S.M. (1969). The therapist as guru. *Voices*, 5 (2), 49-51.

15. Hanna, Thomas. (1986). *Remembrance of Sidney Jourard*. Transcript of audio tape. Novato, California.

16. Jourard, Sidney M. (1974) *Healthy Personality: An Approach From the View of Humanistic Psychology*. New York: McMillan. pp. 194-196.

Chapter 9: International

1. The chapter is Jourard, S.M. (1969). The effects of experimenters' self-disclosure on subjects' behavior. In C.D.Spielberger (Ed.), *Current Topics in Clinical and Community Psychology*. (1) pp. 109-150. New York: Academic Press.

2. Richards, Anne. E-mail to author 9-13-2018.

3. Jourard, S.M. (1972). One of the Names of God is "Life Itself." In Adams, Paul. (Ed.), *Humane Social Psychiatry: a book of readings in honor of Robert Ollendorff in celebration of his sixtieth birthday.* Gainesville: Tree of Life Press.

4. *AHP Newsletter* Vol.7 No. 2 November 1970.

5. *AHP Newsletter* Vol.7 No. 5 February 1971.

6. Ida Pauline Rolf (1896-1979) was the inventor of Structural Integration or "Rolfing," a form of manual physical therapy that addresses the entire body in relation to gravity.

Chapter 10: The Transparent Self

1. Grogan, Jessica.(2013) *Encountering America.* p. 256. New York: Harper Perennial.

2. Fisher, Dena. (1970, January 28). [letter to Sidney Jourard.]

3. Jourard, S.M. (1971). *The Transparent Self.* pp. 49-50. New York: D.Van Nostrand.

4. ibid.

5. Appropriately, the image is from a theater poster for Franz Kafka's The Trial by Roman Cieslwicz

6. Booknotes. (1973) *Journal of Pastoral Care* Vol. 27. (1) p. 66.

7. Jourard, Sidney. (1973 August) audio interview by Ernest Kramer [Tape recording]. Montreal. https://www.worldcat.org/title/interview-with-dr-sidney-jourard/oclc/10164241

8. Jourard, Sidney (1971) Self-Disclosure: An Experimental Analysis of the Transparent Self. Book flap. New York: Wiley-Interscience.

9. Booknotes. (1973) *Journal of Pastoral Care* Vol. 27 (1) p. 66.

10. Himelstein, Philip. (1972). Book review: Openness in the Laboratory. *Contemporary Psychology.* Vol.17, No. 4, pp. 218-219.

11. ibid.

12. Jourard, Sidney (1971). Prophets as Psychotherapists, and Psychotherapists as Prophets. Voices. Fall p. 11-16. Also in Lowman, Michael, Jourard, Antoinette, & Jourard, Marty, (Eds.). (1994). *Sidney Jourard: Selected Writings.* pp. 157-166. Marina Del Rey: Round Right Press.

13. ibid. pp. 164-5.

Chapter 11: In, Out and About

1. (1972 Feb). *AHP Newsletter.* p.12.

2. Jourard, S.M. (1971/72). Psychology: Control or Liberation? *Journal of Interpersonal Development.* 2, (2) 65-72. Reprinted in Welch, I.D., Tate, G.A., & Richards, F. (Eds.). (1978). *Humanistic Psychology: A Sourcebook* (pp. 343-350). Buffalo, NY: Prometheus.

3. ibid.

4. Jourard, S.M. (1976). Changing Personal Worlds: A Humanistic Perspective. In A. Wandersman, P.J. Poppen, & D.F. Ricks (Eds.), *Humanism and Behaviorism: Dialogue and Growth* (pp. 35-53). New York: Pergamon Press. Reprinted as Jourard, S.M. (1978). Changing Personal Worlds: A Humanistic Approach to Psychotherapy. Reprinted in Welch, I.D., Tate, G.A., & Richards, F. (Eds.) (1978) *Humanistic Psychology: A Sourcebook* (pp. 153-164). Buffalo, NY: Prometheus.

5. ibid. p. 42.

6. ibid p. 43.

7. Kazantzakis, Nikos. (1952) *Zorba the Greek.* p. 302. New York: Simon & Schuster.

8. Hanna, Thomas (1986 September) *Reminiscence of Sidney Jourard.* [Transcribed audio tape]. Novato, CA. Carl Rogers outlived Sid by thirteen years.

Chapter 12: A Modern Odyssey

1. Mearns, David (2018 November 11) email to author.

2. Jourard, Sidney (1973 May 15) Commentary on The Transparent Self. transcribed audio interview. 3rd Annual Philosophy Symposium. Cal State Fullerton, Fullerton, CA.

3. A Conversation with Dr. Sidney M. Jourard, transcription of Crisis Telephone Service conference call, August 1973, from University of West Georgia Ingram Library Sidney M. Jourard Special Collections.

4. Jourard, Sidney (1969) The Invitation to Die. In Shneidman, Edwin S. (Ed.) *On The Nature of Suicide.* (pp. 129-141.) San Francisco: Jossey-Bass,

5. McLaughlin, Frank. "Two Humanists." *Media & Methods* Vol. 8, No. 4 December 1971. p. 29.

6. *Contemporary Psychology.* 1972, Vol. 17, No. 7 p. 373-4.

7. Jourard, Sidney. (1971) Prophets As Psychotherapists, And Psychotherapists As Prophets. *Voices*, Fall 1971 p. 13.

8. ibid p. 14.

Chapter 13: Adventure and Misadventure

1. Jourard, Sidney M. (1974). *La Transparence de Soi*. Ottawa: Les Éditions Saint-Yves.

2. The Acknowledgments page in Self Disclosure: An Experimental Analysis of the Transparent Self (1971) for permission to reprint materials include: *Journal of Abnormal and Social Psychology, Merrill-Palmer Quarterly of Behavior and Development, Journal of Humanistic Psychology, Journal of Applied Psychology, Academic Press, Journal of Social Psychology, Psychological Reports, Perceptual and Motor Skills, Journal of Counseling Psychology, University of Florida Press, Duke University: Law and Contemporary Problems, Journal of Personality and Social Psychology*.

3. Ernest Becker's 1973 book *The Denial of Death* explores this theme, and was awarded the 1974 Pulitzer Prize in Non-Fiction.

4. Olson, Robert G. (1962). *An Introduction to Existentialism*. p.19. New York: Dover Publications.

5. Watson, J. B. (1913). Psychology as the behaviorist views it. *Psychological Review, 20*(2), 158–177.

6. Jourard, Sidney. (1968) *Disclosing Man To Himself* pp. 103-104.

7. George R. Bach (1914-1986) was a clinical psychologist and the founder of the Institute of Group Psychotherapy in Los Angeles.

8. Anthony Oliver Smith email to author 12-19-18

9. Jacob Levy Moreno was a founder of group psychotherapy.

10. Jourard, S.M. (1975). Marriage is for life. *Journal of Marriage and Family Counseling,* 1(3),199-208. Reprinted in Welch, I.D., Tate, G.A. & Richards, F. (Eds.) (1978). *Humanistic Psychology: A Sourcebook* (pp. 197-205). New York: Prometheus.

11. https://leginfo.legislature.ca.gov/faces/billNavClient.xhtml?bill_id=200320040SB420

12. Jourard, S.M. (1978). Education as Dialogue. *Journal of Humanistic Psychology*. 18(1), 47-52.

13. Sadie Jourard Brown (1914-2014) was the family historian and this excerpt is from her unpublished manuscript The Jourard Family History (January 1990)

Chapter 14: Legacy

1. Grogan, Jessica (2013). *Encountering America: Humanistic Psychology, Sixties Culture & the Shaping of the Modern Self.* p. 308. New York: Harper Perennial.

2. ibid. p. 309-10. Grogan references Richard Farson's comments; Farson was a psychologist who co-founded the Western Behavioral Sciences Institute in 1958 and worked with Maslow and Carl Rogers at that facility.

3. Pleck, Joseph H. & Sawyer, Jack (Eds.). (1974). *Men and Masculinity.* pp. 21-29. Englewood Cliffs, NJ: Prentice-Hall.

4. Rimmer, Robert. (1975). *The Premar Experiments.* p. 13. New York: Crown Publishers.

5. ibid p. 77.

6. Goldberg, Herb. (1976). *The Hazards of Being Male: Surviving the Myth of Masculine Privilege.* p.172. New York: Signet.

7. Jourard, S.M. (1971). *Transparent Self.* p.40.

8. Nevill, D. D. (Ed.).(1977). *Humanistic Psychology: New Frontiers.* p. 225. New York: Gardner Press, Inc.

9. Welch, D. I., Tate, G. A., & Richards, Fred. (Eds.). (1978) *Humanistic Psychology: A Sourcebook.* Buffalo: Prometheus Books.

10. Kreiger, Dolores. (1979). *The Therapeutic Touch.* p.82. New York: Prentice Hall.

11. Jourard, Sidney M., & Landsman, Ted. (1980). *Healthy Personality: An Approach from the Viewpoint of Humanistic Psychology,* Fourth Edition. p. vi. New York: Macmillan.

12. Goleman, Daniel, & Speeth, Kathleen Riordan (Eds.). (1982). *The Essential Psychotherapies: Theory and Practice of the Masters.* p. 301 New York: Mentor.

13. Jourard, S.M. *The Transparent Self* (1971). p. 38.

14. Montagu, Ashley. (1986). *Touching: The Human Significance of Skin,* Third Edition. New York: Harper & Row.

15. Jourard, S.M.(1966). An Exploratory Study of Body-Accessibility. *British Journal of Social and Clinical Psychology,* 5, pp. 221-231; Jourard, S.M. & Rubin, J.E. (1968). Self Disclosure and Touching: A Study of Two Mode of Interpersonal Encounter and Their Interaction. *Journal of Humanistic Psychology* 8, pp. 39-48.

16. Richards, Anne C., & Schumrum, Tiparat. (Eds.). (1999). *Invitations to Dialogue: The Legacy of Sidney Jourard*. Dubuque: Kendall/Hunt.

17. ibid, p. x.

18. ibid pp. 259-260

19. Jourard, S.M. (1968) *Disclosing Man to Himself*. p. 137.

20. Dutton, J., Johnson A., & Hickson, M. (2017). Touch Revisited: Observations and Methodological Recommendations. *Journal of Mass Communication and Journalism* 7: 348.

21. www.sidneyjourard.com

22. Jourard, Sidney. *The Transparent Self*. (1971). p 6.

23. Farber, Barry A. (2006). *Self-Disclosure in Psychotherapy*. p. 4. New York: The Guilford Press.

24. ibid. p 10

25. Grogan, Jessica. *Encountering America*. p. 100.

26. Isaacson, Robert L. (2009) *Sidney M. Jourard—My Friend, My Colleague*. Unpublished manuscript. Copy in possession of author.

27. Hanna, Thomas. (1986 September). *Thomas Hanna to Jeff Jourard Re: Sidney Jourard*. Unpublished transcription of audio recording. Novato, California. Copy in possession of the author.

28. Hogan, Kevin & Speakman, James. (2006). *Covert Persuasion: Psychological Tactics and Tricks to Win the Game*. Hoboken: Wiley.

Quotation on back cover taken from talk presented at the AHP conference "Reading, Riting, and Reality," Stanford University, November, 1974. Adapted and condensed by Tom Greening (Editor of the *Journal of Humanistic Psychology*) in Jourard, S.M. 1978. Education as Dialogue. *Journal of Humanistic Psychology*, 18 (1), 47-52.

Chronological Bibliography
of the Professional Publications
of Sidney M. Jourard

1952

Jourard, S.M. (1952). A study of ego strength by means of the Rorschach test and the interruption of tasks experiment. (Doctoral Dissertation, University of Buffalo, 1953) *Dissertation Abstracts,* 13(3),435. Publ. #5120. MIC A53-737.

1953

Secord, P.F., & Jourard, S.M. (1953). The appraisal of body cathexis: Body cathexis and the self. *Journal of Consulting Psychology,* 17 (5), 343-347.

1954

Jourard, S.M. (1954). Ego strength and the recall of tasks. *Journal of Abnormal and Social Psychology* 49 (1), 51-58.

Jourard, S.M. (1954). Moral indignation: A correlate of denied dislike of parents' traits. *Journal of Consulting Psychology,*18(1), 59-60.

Jourard, S.M. and Secord, P.F. (1954). Body size and body-cathexis. *Journal of Consulting Psychology,* 18 (3), 184.

1955

Jourard, S.M. & Remy, R.M. (1955). Perceived parental attitudes, the self, and security. *Journal of Consulting Psychology,* 19 (5),364-366.

Jourard, S.M. & Secord, P.F.(1955a). Body-cathexis and the ideal female figure. *Journal of Abnormal and Social Psychology,* 50 (2), 243-246.

Jourard, S.M. & Secord, P.F. (1955b). Body-cathexis and personality. *British Journal of Psychology,* 46 (2), 130-138.

1956

Secord, P.F. & Jourard, S.M. (1956). Mother-concepts and judgments of young women's faces. *Journal of Abnormal and Social Psychology*, 52 (2), 246-250.

1957

Jourard, S.M. (1957). Identification, parent cathexis and self-esteem. *Journal of Consulting Psychology*, 21 (5), 375-380.

Jourard, S.M. & Remy, R.M. (1957). Individual variance score: An index of the degree of differentiation of the self and the body image. *Journal of Clinical Psychology*, 13 (1), 62-63.

1958

Jourard, S.M. (1958). *Personal Adjustment: An approach through the study of healthy personality.* New York: Macmillan.

Jourard, S.M. (1958). A study of self-disclosure. *Scientific American*, 1958 (5),77-82.

Jourard, S.M. & Lasakow, P. (1958). Some factors in self-disclosure. *Journal of Abnormal and Social Psychology*, 56 (1), 91-98.

1959

Jourard, S.M. (1959). Healthy personality and self-disclosure. *Mental Hygiene*, 43 (4), 499-507.

Jourard, S.M. (1959). How well do you know your patients? *The American Journal of Nursing*, 59 (11), 1568-1571.

Jourard, S.M. (1959). I-Thou relationship versus manipulation in counseling and psychotherapy. *Journal of Individual Psychology*, 15 (2),174-179.

Jourard, S.M. (1959). Self-disclosure and other-cathexis. *Journal of Abnormal and Social Psychology*, 59 (3), 428-431.

1960

Jourard, S.M. (1960). The bedside manner. *The American Journal of Nursing*, 60 (1), 63-66.

Jourard, S.M. & Landsman, M.J. (1960). Cognition, cathexis, and the "dyadic effect" in men's self-disclosing behavior. *Merrill-Palmer Quarterly of Behavior and Development*, 6 (3), 178-186.

1961

Jourard, S.M. (1961). Age trends in self-disclosure. *Merrill-Palmer Quarterly of Behavior and Development*, 7 (3), 191-198.

Jourard, S.M. (1961). On the problem of reinforcement by the psychotherapist of healthy behavior in the patient. In F.I. Shaw (Ed.). *Behavioristic approaches to counseling and psychotherapy* (pp. 8-19). Tuscaloosa, AL: University of Alabama Press.

Jourard, S.M. (1961). The phenomenon of resistance in the psychotherapist. *Counseling Center Discussion Papers*, 7 (13), 1-12. Chicago, IL: University of Chicago.

Jourard, S.M. (1961). Religious denomination and self-disclosure. *Psychological Reports*, 8 (3), 446.

Jourard, S.M. (1961). Roles that sicken and transactions that heal. *Canadian Nurse*, 57 (7), 628-634.

Jourard, S.M. (1961). Self-disclosure and Rorschach productivity. *Perceptual and Motor Skills*, 13 (2), 232.

Jourard, S.M. (1961). Self-disclosure patterns in British and American college females. *Journal of Social Psychology*, 54 (2), 315-320.

Jourard, S.M. (1961). Self-disclosure scores and grades in nursing college. *Journal of Applied Psychology*, 45 (4),244-247.

Jourard, S.M. (1961). Sex in marriage. *Journal of Humanistic Psychology*, 1 (2),23-29.

Jourard, S.M. (1961). Some implications of self-disclosure research for counseling and psychotherapy. *Counseling Center Discussion Papers* 7 (14), 1-15. Chicago, IL: University of Chicago.

Jourard, S.M. (1961). To whom can a nurse give personalized care? *The American Journal of Nursing*, 61 (3), 86-88.

1962

Jourard, S.M. (1962, May). Cool, beat and timid? Contribution to discussion "What is the purpose of the university and how is this reflected at the University of Florida?" *Comment*. A communication of the Episcopal Center at the University of Florida, p. 2.

Jourard, S.M. (1962). Integrating mental health into the curriculum. *Canadian Nurse*, 58 (4), 307-313.

Jourard, S.M. (1962). Some lethal aspects of the male role. *Journal of Existential Psychiatry*, II (7), 333-344. Reprinted in I. H. Pleck & I. Sawyer (Eds.). (1974). *Men and masculinity* (pp. 21-29).Englewood Cliffs, NI: Prentice-Hall.

Guertin, W.H. & Jourard, S.M. (1962). Characteristics of real-self-ideal-self discrepancy scores revealed by factor analysis. *Journal of Consulting Psychology*, 26 (3), 241-245.

1963

Jourard, S.M. (1963). Inward look, spirit, and healthy personality. *Review of Existential Psychology and Psychiatry*, J (I), 83-90.

Jourard, S.M. (1963). *Personal adjustment. An approach through the study of healthy personality.* (2nd ed.) New York: Macmillan.

Jourard, S.M. (1963). The role of spirit and 'inspiriting' in human wellness. *Journal of Existential Psychiatry*, III (11),293-306.

Jourard, S.M. & Richman, P. (1963). Factors in the self-disclosure inputs of college students. *Merrill-Palmer Quarterly of Behavior and Development*, 9 (2), 141-148.

Powell, W.I. & Jourard, S.M. (1963). Some objective evidence of immaturity in underachieving college students. *Journal of Counseling Psychology*, 10 (3), 276-282. .

1964

Jourard, S.M. (1964). How do people learn? *Canadian Nurse*, 60 (4),347-350.

Jourard, S.M. (1964). Let's look at the teacher. *Canadian Nurse*, 60 (5),471-474.

Jourard, S.M. (1964). Personal contact in teaching. *Canadian Nurse*, 60 (6),556-559.

Jourard, S.M. (1964). *The Transparent Self. Self-disclosure and well-being.* New York: Van Nostrand Reinhold.

1965

Jourard, S.M. (1965). The servo theory. *Canadian Nurse*, 61 (1),40-42.

1966

Jourard, S.M. (1966). An exploratory study of body-accessibility.*British Journal of Social and Clinical Psychology*, 5 (3), 221-231.

Jourard, S.M. (1966). The "awareness of potentialities" syndrome. *Journal of Humanistic Psychology*, 6 (2): 139-140.

Jourard, S.M. (1966). Some psychological aspects of privacy. *Law and Contemporary Problems*, J1 (2), 307-318.

Jourard, S.M. (1966). Toward a psychology of transcendent behavior. In H.A. Otto (Ed.), *Explorations in human potentialities* (pp. 349-377). Springfield, IL: Charles C. Thomas.

Jourard, S.M. (1966). You can do whatever you wish here. *Voices*, 2 (I), 110-111.

Jourard, S.M. & Overlade, D.C. (Eds.). (1966). *Reconciliation: A theory of man transcending*. (From the work of Franklin I. Shaw, Dec.). Princeton, NJ: D. Van Nostrand.

1967

Jourard, S.M. (1967). Automation, stupefaction and education. In R.R. Leeper (Ed.), *Humanizing education: The person in the process* (pp. 42-52). Washington, DC: Association for Supervision and Curriculum Development, NEA.

Jourard, S.M. (1967). Experimenter-subject dialogue: A paradigm for a humanistic science of psychology. In I.F.T. Bugental (Ed.), *Challenges of Humanistic Psychology* (pp.109-116). New York: McGraw-Hill. Reprinted in A.G. Miller (Ed.). (1972). *The Social Psychology of Psychological Research* (pp. 14-24). London: The Free Press.

Jourard, S.M. (1967). Fascination: A phenomenological perspective on independent learning. In G.T. Gleason (Ed.), *The Theory and Nature of Independent Learning* (pp. 79-101). Scranton, PA: International Textbook Company.

Jourard, S.M. (1967). The human challenge of automation. *Humanitas*, 111(1),45-56.

Jourard, S.M. (1967, November 9). Out of touch: The body taboo. *New Society*, pp. 660-662.

Jourard, S.M. (1967, May 25). Privacy, the psychological need. *New Society*, pp. 757-758.

Jourard, S.M. (1967). The psychotherapist as existential guide. New York: International Center for Integrative Studies.

Jourard, S.M. (1967). Psychotherapy as invitation. *Existential Psychiatry*, 6 (21),19-34.

Jourard, S.M. (Ed.). (1967). *To be or not to be... Existential-psychological perspectives on the self*. University of Florida Monographs, Social Sciences, #34. Gainesville, FL: University of Florida Press.

Jourard, S.M. (1967). To be or not to be transparent. In S.M. Jourard (Ed.). *To be or not to be... Existential-psychological perspectives on the self*. University of Florida Monographs, Social Sciences, #34 (pp. 27-36). Gainesville, FL: University of

Florida Press.

Jourard, S.M. (1967). *Two papers by Sidney M Jourard: To be or not to be TRANSPARENT* and *THE EXPERIENCE OF FREEDOM*. Big Sur, CA: Esalen Institute.

1968

Jourard, S.M. (1968). *Disclosing Man to Himself*: Princeton, NJ: D. Van Nostrand. Jou National Concerns Conference. *Conference Proceedings. Principal Addresses. Summary Report* (pp. 29-38). Muncie, IN: Ball State University.

Jourard, S.M. (1968). Growing awareness and the awareness of growth. In H.A. Otto & I. Mann (Eds.), *Ways of growth. Approaches to expanding awareness* (pp. 1-14). New York: The Viking Press.

Jourard, S.M. & Kormann, L.A. (1968). Getting to know the experimenter and its effect on psychological test performance. *Journal of Humanistic Psychology*, 8 (2), 155-159.

Jourard, S.M. & Rubin, J.E. (1968). Self-disclosure and touching: A study of two modes of interpersonal encounter and their inter-relation. *Journal of Humanistic Psychology*, 8 (1), 39-48).

1969

Jourard, S.M. (1969). The effects of experimenters' self-disclosure on subjects' behavior. In C.D.Spielberger (Ed.), *Current topics in clinical and community psychology*. Vol.1 pp. 109-150. New York: Academic Press.

Jourard, S.M. (1969). The Invitation to Die. In E.S. Schneidman (Ed). *On the Nature of Suicide* (pp. 129-141). San Francisco, CA: Jossey-Bass.

Jourard, S.M. (1969). The therapist as guru. *Voices*, 5 (2),49-51.

1970

Jourard, S.M. (1970). The beginnings of self-disclosure. *Voices*, 6 (1), 42-51.

Jourard, S.M. (1970). Human revolution: Confronting the realities of "them" and "us." In M. Scobey & G. Graham (Eds.). *To Nurture Humaneness: Commitment for the 70's* (pp.52-62). Washington, DC: Association for Supervision and Curriculum Development, NEA.

Jourard, S.M. (1970). Living and dying. Suicide: An invitation to die. *American Journal of Nursing*, 70 (2),269,273-275.

Jourard, S.M. (1970). On personal growth. Presented at the work conference March 19-20, 1970. *Minnesota League for Nursing Bulletin*, 18 (4),3-9.

Jourard, S.M. (1970). Reinventing marriage: The perspective of a psychologist. In H.A. Otto (Ed.). *The family in Search of a Future: Alternate Models for Moderns* (pp.43-49). New York: Appleton-Century-Crofts.

Jourard, S.M. & Friedman, R. (1970). Experimenter-subject "distance" and self-disclosure. *Journal of Personality and Social Psychology*, 15 (3), 278-282.

Jourard, S.M. & Jaffe, P .E. (1970). Influence of an interviewer's disclosure on the self-disclosing behavior of interviewees. *Journal of Counseling Psychology*, 17 (3),252-257.

Jourard, S.M. & Resnick, J. L. (1970). Some effects of self-disclosure among college women. *Journal of Humanistic Psychology*, 10 (1), 84-93.

Breed, G. & Jourard, S.M. (1970). *Research in Self-disclosure. An annotated bibliography.* Sine Loco: Sine Nomine.

1971

Jourard, S.M. (1971). On Kemp's article, "Existential Counseling." *Counseling Psychologist*, 2 (3), 41.

Jourard, S.M. (1971). Prophets as psychotherapists and psychotherapists as prophets. *Voices*, 7 (3), 11-16.

Jourard, S.M. (1971). *Self-disclosure. An Experimental Analysis of the Transparent Self.* New York: Wiley.

Jourard, S.M. (1971). *The Transparent Self* (Rev. ed.) New York: Van Nostrand Reinhold.

Jourard, S.M. (1971). A Way to Encounter. In L. Blank, G.B. Gottsegan, & M.G. Gottsegan (Eds.), *Confrontation: Encounters in Self and Interpersonal Awareness* (pp. 107 to 119). New York: Macmillan.

Jourard, S.M. with Whitman, A. (1971). The fear that cheats us of love. *Redbook*, 137(6), 82-83, 154, 157-58, 160.

Bloch, E.L, Goodstein, L.D., Jourard, S.M. & Jaffe, P. E. (1971). Comment on "Influence of an interviewer's disclosure on the self-disclosing behavior of interviewees." *Journal of Counseling Psychology*, 18 (6), 595-600.

McLaughlin, F. (Ed.) with Jourard, S. & Combs, A.W. (1971). Conversation: Two Humanists. *Media & Methods*, 8 (4), 24-29.

1972

Jourard, S.M. (1972). A Humanistic Revolution in Psychology. In A.G. Miller (Ed.), *The Social Psychology of Psychological Research* (pp. 6-13). New York: Free Press.

Jourard, S.M. (1971/72). Psychology: Control or Liberation? *Journal of Interpersonal Development.* 2, (2) 65-72. Reprinted in ID. Welch, G.A. Tate, & F. Richards (Eds.)(1978) *Humanistic Psychology: A Sourcebook* (pp. 343-350). Buffalo, NY: Prometheus.

Jourard, S.M. (1972). Some dimensions of the loving experience. In H.A. Otto (Ed.), *Love Today: A New Exploration* (pp. 42-48). New York: Association Press.

Jourard, S.M. (1972). Some Notes on the Experience of Commitment. *Humanitas,* 8 (1), 5-8.

Jourard, S.M. (1972). Some Reflections on a Quiet Revolution. *Professional Psychology,* 3(4),380-381.

Jourard, S.M. (1972). The Transcending Therapist. *Voices,* 8 (3),66-69.

1973

Jourard, S.M. (1973). An Odyssey Within. *Personal Growth,* 18 (6), 13-20.

Jourard, S.M. (1973). A Future for Psychotherapy. *Voices,* 9 (3),68-69.

1974

Jourard. S.M. (1974). *Healthy Personality. An Approach from the Viewpoint of Humanistic Psychology.* New York: Macmillan.

1975

Jourard, S.M. (1975). Marriage is for life. *Journal of Marriage and Family Counseling,* 1(3),199-208. Reprinted in I.D. Welch, G.A. Tate & F. Richards (Eds.) (1978). *Humanistic Psychology: A Sourcebook* (pp. 197-205). New York: Prometheus.

Jourard, S.M. (1975, January). On Being Persuaded Who You Are. *AHP Perspective,* pp.5-7.

1976

Jourard, S.M. (1976). A brief survey of thirty cases of alcoholism [Microform]: AA evaluation of the collaboration in the management of thirty cases of alcoholism by the Florida Probation and Parole Commission and the Florida Alcoholic

Rehabilitation Program, Avon Park, FL. Glen Rock, NJ: Microfilming Corp. of America. (NIMH   Project O.M. 550)

Jourard, S.M. (1976). Changing Personal Worlds: A Humanistic Perspective. In A. Wandersman, P.J. Poppen, & D.F. Ricks (Eds.), *Humanism and Behaviorism: Dialogue and Growth* (pp. 35-53). New York: Pergamon Press. Reprinted as Jourard, S.M. (1978). Changing Personal Worlds: A Humanistic Approach to Psychotherapy. In ID. Welch, G.A. Tate, & F. Richards (Eds). *Humanistic Psychology: A Sourcebook* (pp. 153-164). Buffalo, NY: Prometheus.

Jourard, S.M. (1976). Existential Quest. In A. Wandersman, P.J. Poppen & D.F. Ricks (Eds.), *Humanism and Behaviorism: Dialogue and Growth* (pp. 83-95). New York: Pergamon Press.

Jourard, S.M. (1976). Some Ways of Unembodiment and Re-embodiment. *Somatics*, 1 (1), 3-7.

Barrell, J.J. & Jourard, S.M. (1976). Being Honest with Persons we Like. *Journal of Individual Psychology*, 32 (2), 185-193.

1978

Jourard, S.M. (1978). Astrological Sun Signs and Self-disclosure. *Journal of Humanistic Psychology* 18 (1),53-56.

Jourard, S.M. (1978). Education as Dialogue. *Journal of Humanistic Psychology*, 18(1), 47-52.

1980

Jourard, S.M. & Landsman, T. (1980). *Healthy Personality. An Approach from the Viewpoint of Humanistic Psychology.* (4th ed.) New York: Macmillan.

1994

Jourard, S.M. (1994). The Laugh that Heals, a Case Study. In M. Lowman, A. Jourard & M. Jourard (Eds.), *Sidney M Jourard: Selected Writings* (pp. 99-124) Marina del Rey, CA: Round Right Press.

Jourard, S.M. (1994). The Mystic Dimension of Self. In M. Lowman, A. Jourard & M. Jourard (Eds.), *Sidney M Jourard. Selected Writings* (pp. 149-156). Marina del Rey, CA: Round Right Press.

Jourard, S.M. (1994). On Becoming a Psychotherapist. In M. Lowman, A. Jourard & M. Jourard (Eds.), *Sidney M Jourard: Selected Writings* (pp. 183-187). Marina del Rey, CA: Round Right Press.

Translated Works

Jourard, S.M. (1971). Japanese edition of *The Transparent Self* Tokyo: Litton Educational Publishing through Charles E. Tuttle.

Jourard, S.M. (1973). Briefeiner Versuchs-person an einen Versuchsleiter. *Gruppendynamik. Forschung und Praxis.* Heft 1, 4. Jahrg., 27-30.

Jourard, S.M. (1974). *La Transparence de Soi.* Saint-Foy, Quebec: Saint-Ives.

Jourard, S.M. (1974). Japanese edition of *Healthy Personality.* Tokyo: Sangyo Nohritsu Tanki Daigaku through Charles E. Tuttle.

Jourard, S.M. (1975) *Zelfkennis als Kracht.* Dutch translation of *Disclosing Man to Himself.* Rotterdam: Lemniscaat

Jourard, S.M. (1982, April). Ehe furs leben-ehe zum leben. *Familien-dynamik* 2, 171-182.

Jourard, S.M. & Landsman, T. (1987). *La Personalidad Saludable: El Punto de la Psicologia Humanistic* (J.S. Palacios, Trans.; Revision tecnica, D. Mercado). Mexico: Trillas.

Jourard, S.M. (1987). *Ying yung hsin li hsueh/Ho-lan-te yuan chu; Hsieh Kuang-chin pien i.* Tai-pei: Huei kuan tu shu kung ssu.

Publications Dedicated to Sidney M. Jourard

Lowman, M., Jourard, A., Jourard, M. (1994). *Sidney M Jourard. Selected Writings.* Marina del Rey, CA: Round Right Press.

Morris, K.T. & Cinnamon, K.M. (Eds.) (1976). *Controversial Issues in Human Relations Training Groups.* Springfield, IL: Charles C. Thomas.

Nevill, D.D. (Ed.). (1977). *Humanistic Psychology. New Frontiers.* New York: Gardner Press.

Richards, Anne C., & Schumrum, Tiparat, eds. (1999) *Invitations to Dialogue:The Legacy of Sidney Jourard.* Dubuque: Kendall/Hunt,

Van Horn (now Lowman), M. (1975). *The Phoenix: Babblings of a Man going San.* San Francisco: Shields Publishing.

Vasconcellos, J. (1979). *A Liberating Vision. Politics for Growing Humans.* San Luis

Obispo, CA: Impact Publishers.

Welch, I.D., Tate, G.A., & Richards, F. (1978). *Humanistic Psychology: A Sourcebook.* Buffalo, NY: Prometheus.

Whitman, A, (1972, April). The Invitation to Live. *Reader's Digest,* pp. 83-87.

Acknowledgments

For their contributions to the book I gratefully acknowledge the assistance of Anne and Fred Richards for advice, encouragement and editing, Jeff Jourard for editorial suggestions, Amedeo Giorgi, John Heaton, and David Mearns for their written reminiscences, Maria Holdorf for initial research, Blynne Olivieri, head of the Ingram Library Special Collections at the University of West Georgia for access to the Sidney Jourard collection, and the University of Akron Psychology Archives for providing the exchange of letters between Sidney Jourard and Abraham Maslow.

About the Author

Marty Jourard was born in Atlanta and grew up in north Florida. After moving to Los Angeles in 1976, he played keyboard and sax for The Motels from 1979 to 1986, which earned him two gold albums and two Top Ten singles. He rejoined the group in 2010 and continues to record and tour. He has written three other books: Start Your Own Band (1997), The Marty Method (2004) and Music Everywhere: The Rock and Roll Roots of a Southern Town (2016), which won a Florida Book Award for Nonfiction. He lives in Seattle where he continues to write and play and teach music.

Author and subject circa 1970

Index

Note: Page numbers in *italics* denote photographs.

marriage to Antoinette, 27, 30
maternal ancestry of, 2
paternal ancestry of, 1–2
people as viewed by, x
personal interests of, 79–81
personal life of, 162–163, 198
photographs of, *10, 18, 27, 95, 106, 134, 141–142, 148, 188*
physical characteristics of, 126–127
remembrances of, 222–226
tributes to, 215–216
values of, 229
yearbook photograph of, 27
Jourard family
antecedents of, 1–5
dinnertime with, 9
education of, 11
history of, 1
home environment of, 9
household of, 8
photograph of, *10*
surname origins of, 1–2
Journal of Abnormal and Social Psychology, 35–36, 49
Journal of Clinical Psychology, 35
Journal of Consulting Psychology, 35
Journal of Counseling Psychology, 137
Journal of Humanistic Psychology, 72, 113, 126, 137, 204
Journal of Individual Psychology, 69
Journal of Marriage and Family Counseling, 200
Journal of Pastoral Care, 149–150
Journal of Personality and Social Psychology, 137
Joyce, James, 36
Joyous Cosmology: Adventures in the Chemistry of Consciousness, The, 105
Judaism, xi
Jung, Carl, 36, 67, 154, 196

K

Kazantzakis, Nikos, 36, 98–100, 102, 154
Kehz, Sarah, 1
Kennelly, Tom, 29
Khajuraho, 143
Kierkegaard, Søren, 35, 67, 92–93

Kiernan, Mindy, 207
King, Martin Luther Jr., 105
Kingsland, Kevin, 139
Klee, James B., 216
Kodak camera factory, 4, 5
Kosakoski, Joni, 209
Kreiger, Dolores, 216
Krishnamurti, 140

L

Laing, Ronald, 89, 91–92, 94, 96, 106, 111, 154, 187
Landsman, Ted, ix, 138, 206, 215–216
Langhorne, Curtis, 37
Lasakow, Paul, 49
Law and Contemporary Problems, 113
Leary, Timothy, 70, 92, 112
Legacy, 213–229
Letters
Abraham Maslow, 54–63
donation of, 218
John Vasconcellos, 200–204
Mr. Hardy, 102–104
O. Hobart Mowrer, 74–79
Warren E. Preece, 151–152
Will Sparks, 49–52
Liberal party, 10
Life Bound, 152
Limbic System, The, 222
Linden, David J., 219
Lithuania, 1
London, 91
London, Jack, 67
Love, 147
Lowman, Michael, 218
LSD, 37–43, 91, 96–98, 108, 113, 136
Lynch, Stan, 138
Lyrical Existentialists, The, 111

M

Magnificence, 66, 100, 133
Maisiagala, 1
Malcolm X, 105
Manliness, 89

O

Odyssey, 112, 165, 198
Ohsawa, George, 139
Old Testament, 138–139, 153, 198
"On Being Persuaded Who You Are," 126
On the Nature of Suicide, 133
Ontario News-Packet, 9
Open-mindedness, 37
Operant conditioning, 89–90
Organized religion, 172
Orgastic potency, 68
Orwell, George, 154
Osidge Elementary, 94

P

Packard, Vance, 228
Party To Be Remembered, A, 24
Pastoral counseling, 109
Pavlov, Ivan, 192
Peace Corps, 81
Peak experiences, 124
Pennypacker, Henry, 161
Personal adjustment, 67–69
Personal Adjustment: An Approach Through the Study of Healthy Personality, 17, 42–43, 51–52, 62, 65–66, 68, 81–82, 87, 154
    revising of, 165–166, 189–190
Personal growth theories, 68
Personal life, 162–163, 198
Personality
    "adjustment," 33
    Freud's view of, 33
    healthy, 66–70, 120, 154
    natural interest in, 16
    unhealthy, 66–67
    Watson's view of, 53
Personality adjustments and maladjustments, 151–152
Personality Theory, 106
Peru, 195–197
Pfeiffer, Carl Curt, 38
Phenomenology, 107, 119–120, 126, 192–193
"Phenomenon of Resistance in the Psychotherapist, The," 72

Philadelphia Association, 94
Phoenix, 124
Physical contact, 101–102
Physical health, 68
Plato, 112
Popular periodical writings, 45
Post-traumatic stress disorder, 160
Preece, Warren E., 151
Premar Experiments, The, 214
Price, Richard, 108
Productive orientation, 68
Prophets, 152–154, 174, 186–187
"Prophets as Psychotherapists, and Psychotherapists as Prophets," 152
PSY 300, 154
Psychedelic drugs, 37–43, 91, 96–98, 105, 113
Psychoanalysis
    experience and, 120
    humanistic psychology versus, 70–71, 85, 192
    principles of, 71
Psychological manipulation, 228
Psychology
    behaviorist approaches to, 176, 192
    as college undergraduate major, 157
    controversies in, 28
    early interests in, 11–12
    experimental methodology in, 27
    future of, 196
    "HEP," 191–193
    research studies in, 27–28
    subjectivity of, 176
    as University of Toronto major, 15
Psychology, 219
"Psychology: Control or Liberation?", 216
Psychology as a Human Science: A Phenomenologically Based Approach, 177–179, 181
Psychology Today, 219
"Psychotherapeutic Dialogue and Personal Growth, The" workshop, 175
"Psychotherapist as Exemplar, The," 217
Psychotherapists
    as prophets, 186–187
    prophets and, 152–154

Psychotherapy, 12
  healthy personality promoted by, 68
  lecture on, 109–110
  personal growth theories used in, 68
  writings about, 184–186
"Psychotherapy As A Secular Calling," 186
Psychotherapy East and West, 105
Psychotherapy practice
  changes in approach, 72
  client-therapist relationship in, 129–131
  description of, 128–129
  questions about, 133
  Rogerian training in, 44–45, 128
PTSD. *See* Post-traumatic stress disorder
Puerto Rico, 81, 101
Purkey, William, x

Q

Quinn, Anthony, 99

R

Rajneesh (Osho), 217
"Ramona," 7
Rank, Otto, 67, 68, 171
Rational-emotive behavior therapy, 184, 211
Reader's Digest, 219
Readings, 35
Readings in Humanistic Psychology, 133
REBT. *See* Rational-emotive behavior therapy
Reconciliation: A Theory of Man Transcending, 113
Reich, Wilhelm, 68, 187, 196
Reitz, J. Wayne, 102
Religion, x, 172
Remembrances, 222–226
Repression, 34
Research Fellowship grant application, 30–32
Research studies
  legacy of, 227–229
  in psychology, 27–28, 65
  with Secord, 35
  in self-disclosure, 137–138, 159, 189, 217, 220
  subjects in, 160
  topics of, 35, 105

Richards, Fred, 138
Rimmer, Robert, 214
Rogers, Carl, ix, xiii, 17, 44, 54, 68, 71, 128, 216
Rolfing, 139
Royce, Joseph R., 180–181
Rubinoff, Annie (Jourard)
  in Czarist Russia, 8
  death of, 208
  description of, 2, 4, 8
  household of, 8
  photograph of, *4, 10*
Rubinoff, Bertha, 2
Rubinoff, Fannie, 2
Rubinoff, Israel, 2
Rubinoff, Rachmael, 2, 4
Rules, The, 90
Russia, 1–2
Russian Revolution, 8
Russo-Japanese War, 2

S

Sabbaticals, 89, 91–92, 100, 107, 163, 165–168, 177
San Diego, 166–168
Sartre, Jean-Paul, 35, 67, 92–93, 106, 192
Satie, Erik, 146
Satir, Virginia, xiii
Schizophrenia, 94, 114
Science and Human Behavior, 117
Scientific American, 49–50, 65
Secord, Paul, 35
Self realization, 68
Self-actualization, 124
Self-alienation, xiv
Self-awareness, 158
Self-disclosure
  description of, xiii, 12, 141, 175, 189, 210
  history of, 221–222
  legacy of, 227
  measurement of, 200
  outcome and, 200–201
  research in, 137–138, 159, 189, 217, 220
  on social media, 227
  writings about, 49, 61, 84, 86, 133, 137, 145, 149

Writings. *See also specific papers*
  on body-awareness, 218
  commercial mainstream, 36
  critiques of, 45–49
  Disclosing Man to Himself, 118–121, 154,
    192–193, 218–219
  Encyclopedia Britannica, 151–152
  fictional characters in, 24–25
  *Healthy Personality: An Approach from the
    Viewpoint of Humanistic Psychology,* 17,
    166, 189–191, 216
  *Humanism and Behaviorism: Dialogue and
    Growth,* 160, 215
  Humanistic Psychology: New Frontiers, 215
  legacy of, 214–218
  literary approach to, 146
  manuscripts, 45–49
  on marriage, 133, 197–200
  A Party To Be Remembered, 24
  *Personal Adjustment: An Approach Through
    the Study of Healthy Personality,* 17,
    42–43, 51–52, 65–66, 68, 81–82, 87
  popular periodicals, 45
  precision in, 36
  presentation of, 69–70
  revising of, 34
  on self-disclosure, 49, 61, 84, 86, 133, 137,
    145, 149
  *Self-Disclosure: An Experimental Analysis of
    the Transparent Self,* 149–150
  short stories, 19–24
  Sidney M. Jourard: Selected Writings, 218
  on suicide, 133
  textbook, 45
  Transparent Self, The, xiii, 35, 69, 79,
    81–82, 84–87, 91, 118, 134, 136–137,
    145–150, 214
Wundt, Wilhelm, 192

Y

Yoga, 105, 139–143, 171
Yogi, Maharishi Mahesh, 134, 217
York Memorial Collegiate, 7, 11
You Are All Sanpaku, 139

Z

Zaddik, xi
Zen, 94–95, 139
Zorba the Greek, 93, 98–100, 154, 162
Zurar, Michael, 1
Zurar, Riva, 1
Zurar, Simeon, xvi, *1,* 2